Early praise for *Real-Time Phoenix*

Real-Time Phoenix is hands down the best book to showcase the power of Phoenix and Elixir. The example application is exciting to build and explore. Steve is the perfect guide while sharing his hard won knowledge to help you make informed decisions about your next project.

➤ **Amos King**
Founder, Binary Noggin and Elixir Outlaws

In *Real-Time Phoenix*, Steve covers what you need to know to build a real-time web application. What sets it apart however is a truly practical approach that goes beyond simply covering Phoenix Channels, and explains building systems with the BEAM virtual machine, testing, deployments, and figuring out all kinds of performance issues or other problems you'll inevitably encounter. This isn't just a getting started book, but a way to get compressed experience without having to make all the mistakes on your own.

➤ **Fred Hebert**
Senior Platform Developer, Postmates

Real-Time Phoenix tackles one of the killer features of Phoenix head on. Starting with a WebSocket, Steve clearly and convincingly explains why Phoenix Channels is the right technology for real-time applications. At the conclusion of the book, you'll have the tools you need to build your own real-time applications using Phoenix Channels. If you need real-time interactions in your app—and who doesn't?—do yourself a favor and get Real-Time Phoenix.

➤ **Ben Marx**
Principal Software Engineer, Co-Author of "Adopting Elixir"

You're not going to find a more comprehensive guide on the real-time features of Phoenix and how to use them. This book doesn't shy away from the practical aspects of a real web application, from managing clients and setting up data pipelines, to various strategies for updating the UI and handling your service in production.

➤ **Johanna Larsson**
  Software Engineer, Castle

Real-Time Phoenix is my new go-to guide for bringing real-time features to customers.

➤ **Grant Powell**
  Senior Software Engineer, SalesLoft

As someone who is new to Phoenix, *Real-Time Phoenix* does a superb job of explaining the tools the framework provides that can supercharge your web application. Topics of Channels, PubSub, and Tracker will show new and experienced developers how to leverage WebSockets to power soft real-time features in easy ways. I cannot recommend this book enough for anyone who is interested in Phoenix.

➤ **John Oxford**
  Senior Software Engineer, PowerSecure

Real-Time Phoenix

Build Highly Scalable Systems with Channels

Stephen Bussey

The Pragmatic Bookshelf

Raleigh, North Carolina

Many of the designations used by manufacturers and sellers to distinguish their products are claimed as trademarks. Where those designations appear in this book, and The Pragmatic Programmers, LLC was aware of a trademark claim, the designations have been printed in initial capital letters or in all capitals. The Pragmatic Starter Kit, The Pragmatic Programmer, Pragmatic Programming, Pragmatic Bookshelf, PragProg and the linking *g* device are trademarks of The Pragmatic Programmers, LLC.

Every precaution was taken in the preparation of this book. However, the publisher assumes no responsibility for errors or omissions, or for damages that may result from the use of information (including program listings) contained herein.

Our Pragmatic books, screencasts, and audio books can help you and your team create better software and have more fun. Visit us at *https://pragprog.com*.

The team that produced this book includes:

Publisher: Andy Hunt
VP of Operations: Janet Furlow
Executive Editor: Dave Rankin
Series Editor: Bruce A. Tate
Development Editor: Jacquelyn Carter
Copy Editor: Sean Dennis
Indexing: Potomac Indexing, LLC
Layout: Gilson Graphics

For sales, volume licensing, and support, please contact *support@pragprog.com*.

For international rights, please contact *rights@pragprog.com*.

Copyright © 2020 The Pragmatic Programmers, LLC.

All rights reserved. No part of this publication may be reproduced, stored in a retrieval system, or transmitted, in any form, or by any means, electronic, mechanical, photocopying, recording, or otherwise, without the prior consent of the publisher.

ISBN-13: 978-1-68050-719-5
Book version: P1.0—March 2020

Contents

Part II — Building a Real-Time Application

Part III — Bringing Real-Time Applications to Production

Part IV — Exploring Front-End Technologies

Acknowledgments

Authors have said it before, and I'll repeat it here: writing a book is a long effort that requires the input of many people. Because of the people on this page, the final version of this book is far beyond what I could have produced when I first started.

The staff at The Pragmatic Bookshelf have been amazing to work with. Thanks to Jackie Carter, my editor, for your guidance, wisdom, and teachings throughout this process. Learning how to be a good author was one of my goals, and you helped teach me the ways. Thanks to Bruce Tate, the Elixir series editor, for helping me out of several ruts that I fell into along the way, and for seeing the original vision of this book.

There were many technical reviewers on this book. These people provided guidance at several points throughout this book. This book certainly benefited from their suggestions and reviews. A large thanks to each of you: Amos King, Ben Olive, Chris Keathley, Dan Dresselhaus, Grant Powell, Gábor László Hajba, Johanna Larsson, John Oxford, Ray Gesualdo, Stefan Turalski, and Ulisses H. F. de Almeida. Others have also provided suggestions along the way. If you submitted errata or alerted me to other issues regarding this book, thank you.

I would not have written a book about Phoenix or Elixir without these projects' authors. Thanks to the maintainers of these libraries for your tireless work and quality code. I give a special call-out to Chris McCord, who went above and beyond to patiently explain the solution to various problems I ran into when I was learning about Channels.

Thanks to the people in my life who have fueled my curiosity. I would not be in the position to write this book without the help of my peers and managers at SalesLoft. Thanks to Brian Culler, Rob Forman, and Scott Mitchell for supporting me along the way. Thanks to Dr. Carol Wellington of Shippensburg

University. You have always pushed me to achieve more than I think I can, which I appreciate immensely.

Finally, and most importantly, I give special thanks to my fiancée Jess. It takes a lot of emotional capital to write a book, and you have supported and assisted me throughout this entire journey more than anyone else.

Introduction

I remember working on the first production-facing Elixir application I wrote—it was a real-time application to drive an innovative new feature for our platform. Excitement, curiosity, and a good bit of nervousness led me through that project. It was a trial by fire as the application would receive more requests per minute than any other part of our platform. It still stands today without much involvement needed over the past years.

I have gotten to work on many other real-time applications since that first project. The lessons I learned were sometimes hard to come by—a critical piece of the application would fail, applications would overuse resources like CPU and RAM, or I would code something in a nonoptimal way. However, I was able to leverage the strong foundations of Elixir and Phoenix to solve any problem that appeared. This book aims to collect the experience that I have gained working with Elixir and Phoenix Channels over the last several years and distill it into the parts that matter most.

Elixir has changed the way that I think about, design, and code applications. The creators, community, and libraries empower me to think about code with a fresh perspective. My time with Elixir has been filled with enthusiasm, to say the least. Throughout this book, I hope to share that enthusiasm with you.

Who Should Read This Book?

Do you work on modern web applications? Do you want to build applications that are different than the traditional web model of request-in response-out? Have you started working on Elixir or Phoenix projects and want to dive deeper into the ecosystem?

If any of these questions ring a bell for you, then you will probably have a good experience with this book. If not, you will still find an interesting approach to modern applications in these pages.

This book is targeted at intermediate to advanced developers. There will be Elixir code snippets throughout each chapter, but you will be guided through each of them in order to have working examples locally. This book will not teach you Elixir—there are other books out there that are suited for that task. However, you will quickly catch on if you have a small amount of existing Elixir or Phoenix knowledge. You will walk away with a deep understanding of the real-time Phoenix stack.

About This Book

The three parts of this book build on each other to teach you about WebSockets, Phoenix Channels, and real-time application design. Part I focuses on the most important part of the real-time stack in Elixir—Phoenix Channels, WebSockets, and GenStage. We'll cover a lot of ground in these chapters, and you will gain the foundations necessary to build real-time applications.

You will leverage the foundations from Part I when we work on a real-time application in Part II. You will add real-time features to an e-commerce application that serves many users simultaneously. You will also get to work with some of the more advanced features of Phoenix, such as Phoenix Tracker.

Part III finishes the book with guidance on running real-time applications in production. The battle is only beginning when you write an application. You have to then keep it healthy and happy in production.

About the Code

Elixir is required for this book, although setup is a bit outside of this book's focus. I recommend using a version manager like asdf[1] in order to configure both Erlang and Elixir. Make sure to use a recent version of both—I used OTP 22 and Elixir 1.9 for all examples. You will also need to have Phoenix installed for the samples in this book. You can follow the HexDocs Installation guide[2] in order to get Phoenix set up.

Elixir snippets in this book are not formatted according to the Mix formatter, due to book formatting needs. You can use mix format to make sure all snippets that you copy or hand-type are formatted properly.

Part II uses an application that comes already started for you. This helps keep the focus of the book on real-time features rather than the other parts of the application. You will need to download the base for the project in Part

---

1.   https://github.com/asdf-vm/asdf
2.   https://hexdocs.pm/phoenix/installation.html

II before you can start it. There will be instructions on how to get the project set up when it's time to do so.

Online Resources

The examples and source code shown in this book can be found under the source code link on the Pragmatic Bookshelf website.[3] You will also find the sample application for Part II there.

Please report any errors or suggestions using the errata link that is available on the Pragmatic Bookshelf website.[4]

If you like this book and it serves you well, I hope that you will let others know about it—your reviews really do help. Tweets and posts are a great way to help spread the word. You can find me on Twitter at @yoooodaaaa, or you can tweet @pragprog directly.

Stephen Bussey
August 2019

---

3. https://pragprog.com/book/sbsockets/real-time-phoenix
4. https://pragprog.com/book/sbsockets/real-time-phoenix

## CHAPTER 1

Real-Time is Now

Users have higher demands than ever before. It's no longer good enough to have fast requests that complete in 100 ms or less. Today's software users expect the data on their screen to reflect *now*, even before they ask for it. You will win your users' trust by giving them a seamless application experience powered by real-time features.

Building a system that provides this real-time data flow and feedback was previously a challenging endeavor that involved trade-offs in either application development, maintenance, or run time. These trade-offs can now be reduced due to modern advances in real-time application development. This means that developing a real-time application is now in the hands of everyday developers—you and me.

Elixir has emerged as a language that can more easily solve the challenges of building and running a real-time application. Advancements in web standards have enabled new communication layers for interacting with a system in real-time. This contributes to *now* being the perfect time for you to learn how to write real-time applications.

In this chapter, we'll look at what a real-time system means to us throughout this book. We'll see several aspects of how an application can be scalable and understand the tension that exists between the different types of scalability. We'll see how Elixir can help enable the creation of real-time systems in a way that maximizes all aspects of scalability.

The Case for Real-Time Systems

Today's software users have high demands, and for good reason. There are often many different applications that do the same thing; the application that works the most like the user expects and that minimizes the amount of frustration experienced will be able to win the user's attention. Real-time features are a way to ensure that what users know to be true is reflected in their view of an application, improving the usability and minimizing frustration. Historically, real-time systems have been difficult to achieve, reserved only for development teams with large budgets and experience. Now, due to modern advancements, real-time systems are accessible to *every* programmer.

Users expect applications to reflect the correct state of the world. Imagine an online shopping cart for a fashion store. You browsed around and finally found the perfect item, but there's only a few left in your size. You were able to successfully navigate through the checkout process and have entered your payment information. Just as you checkout, you get a message that your item is sold out! Your expectations of a simple checkout experience are dashed, and you are understandably frustrated that you entered your billing information, only to not actually buy the item you want.

In the second part of this book, we're going to build a real-time solution to this particular problem that will delight our customers in the checkout process by letting them know that their item is sold out—before they complete the entire checkout flow.

It's often not enough to reflect what was true when a page was loaded. In the case of the above e-commerce application, the item could have been in-stock when the checkout page loaded and then became out-of-stock while you entered your billing information. Applications need to be able to reflect the most up-to-date information without requiring a user to take action. A chat application, for example, will insert new chats in your window without you needing to press a "fetch new chats" button. The real-time aspect of a chat system allows it to be more useful and enjoyable for the people that use it.

Real-time systems have always been important, but it has been costly and difficult to build them, meaning that real-time features either didn't work properly or that they were never added. The hacks used to achieve real-time communication in older applications, such as using an infinitely loading IFrame, were brittle and would often break across browsers. This meant that an application would need to support several different real-time solutions in order to work properly, which added to the cost of development. Advancements in technology such as WebSockets and Elixir make it easy for everyone to add scalable real-time features to their applications. No longer is this critical user-experience tool reserved for large corporations.

We'll next go into a more technical evaluation of what real-time is. We'll look at the layers present in order to understand the various components that make up our real-time system.

The Layers of a Real-Time System

Real-time applications consist of clients, a real-time communication layer, and back-end servers working together to achieve business objectives. The cooperation and proper function of each layer is important in developing a successful application. For example, a bug in the client could prevent proper connection to the server, which reduces the ability to operate instantly. A defect on the server could delay or prevent messages being sent to a connected client. Before we look at the layers of a real-time system, let's define "real-time."

There are different levels of guarantee in a real-time system. Hardware systems that have strict time guarantees are considered to be "hard" real-time. For example, an airplane's control system needs to always respond within strict time limits. This book will look at "soft" real-time applications, also known as near real-time. Soft real-time applications can have several seconds of delay when updating the user's view, with a goal of minimizing the amount of time the update takes. A soft real-time application should update to the correct state without user intervention.

The applications in this book are web-based—they utilize a network to receive requests from and respond to a client. It is possible for real-time applications to be run in a browser or to leverage a mobile client for user interaction. In fact, any device capable of networking, such as a stand-alone piece of hardware, could be used as a client for these applications.

Now that our terminology is defined, let's look at the layers of a real-time system. You can see the layers in the following figure.

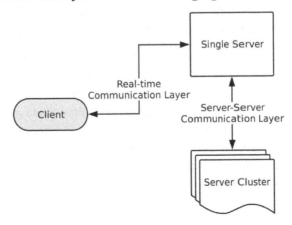

Clients connect to a server via a two-way communication layer. Each server utilizes a server-to-server communication layer to ensure that real-time messages are delivered across a cluster to the appropriate user. Let's take a closer look at each layer.

On the Client

Clients are the entry point to our application from the perspective of users. They are the frontline of an application and exist to display data and controls to the user, send user requests to the server, and process incoming messages from the server in order to update the interface. Clients can exist in any language that supports networking. It's most common in the web ecosystem to use JavaScript to power clients. However, applications written in other languages, such as Java and Swift, can be used to connect to the same real-time server.

One of the most important functions of a client, in the context of real-time applications, is to maintain a connection to the server at all times. Without the proper real-time communication layer, the application won't function as expected. This can prove challenging because many users may be accessing the application from less-than-ideal networks such as a mobile phone or weak Wi-Fi connection. We'll see examples of testing how our application behaves in these conditions in Chapter 8, Break Your Application with Acceptance Tests, on page 141.

Communication Layer

The communication layer facilitates data exchange between a server and a client. The communication layer affects how the user experiences the application—if data is not sent instantly, then the application will feel slow. The communication layer needs to be reliable—any disconnection could prevent data from being exchanged. In order to reduce latency, the connection between a client and the server is often persistent. A persistent connection is one that lasts for many requests or even for as long as the client wants to stay connected.

Significant improvements in web communication have occurred over the last few years. The HTTP/1 protocol has been improved upon with HTTP/2. New techniques and technologies such as server-sent events and WebSockets have offered new ways to implement real-time communication layers. Improvements in the communication layer have enabled a wave of modern applications that satisfy real-time needs of users. This book will focus on WebSockets as a general solution for the communication layer. We'll see what a WebSocket is and why it's excellent for this task in the next chapter.

It's important that server and client application code is not tied to a particular communication technology. Of course, there will always be code that uses the communication layer, but it can be separated from application behavior so that improvements over time can be added to an existing application. If clients and servers are tightly coupled to a communication layer, it may be very difficult to implement a new communication layer in the future. This reduces the maintainability of an application.

On the Server

In a real-time application, a client connects to a single server using the application's communication layer. The server will keep the connection open for an extended period of time, often as long as the client wants. This is different than a traditional web request, which uses a short-lived connection. Real-time applications are similar to traditional web applications in fundamental ways—ultimately the server receives a request from a client and processes it. One major difference between traditional web requests and real-time requests is statefulness.

HTTP web requests are stateless, meaning that the server doesn't maintain state between requests. A client making HTTP requests must send state, such as cookies, with each request. A real-time server can associate state, such as user or application data, with a specific connection. This allows real-time systems to avoid setting up the world with each request, which means that your application will do less work and respond to requests faster.

A client connects to a single server, but an application has many clients issuing requests. It is important for resilience and performance to have multiple servers capable of serving requests. In a stateless web-request world, it is possible for each server to exist in near-isolation so that one request doesn't affect another directly. In a real-time application, it is often desirable and even required to have servers that can talk to each other. For example, real-time chat servers would communicate with each other about who is connected and who needs to receive a particular message.

Applications that maintain state and behavior across multiple instances are called distributed systems. Distributed systems can bring many benefits, especially in performance, but they also come with many challenges. Today, most systems are distributed. You get to decide whether to build them yourself or let the infrastructure do the work, but the best developers will need to understand the trade-offs either way.

We'll spend the most time in this book focusing on the server side of our real-time application. Every layer is important in the proper functioning of our application, but the server has the highest potential for encountering scalability problems due to the complexity of dealing with many independent clients.

Types of Scalability

Applications may be small or large depending on the needs of the project. Throughout this book, we'll be looking at how to develop systems that can scale to a large number of users while still maintaining the properties of scalability. Scalable does not just mean performance, although it's an understandable definition to use. We have to consider multiple types of scalability such as performance, maintenance, and cost in order to be successful with our applications over long periods of time. Let's take a look at the different types of scalability.

Scalability of Performance

Performance is the most common consideration of scalability. As our application gains more users, more data, and more features, we want it to be fast and responsive. An application that has successfully scaled performance-wise will have similar, or at least acceptably slower, response times with 1000 client connections as it does with 50,000 client connections. Later in this chapter, we'll cover why Elixir's virtual machine, the BEAM, is well-suited to scale to many users.

There are many aspects of performance that will affect our real-time application. As with standard web applications, the data store will be a very likely culprit of performance problems as an application grows. There are performance considerations that affect real-time applications but may not affect non-real-time applications. For example, you will need to share information about a large number of real-time connections between the servers of your application, which is something you wouldn't need to do in a non-real-time application.

We'll see common performance pitfalls and solutions in Chapter 6, Avoid Performance Pitfalls, on page 91.

Scalability of Maintenance

Maintenance scalability is a deeply important concern to the developers of an application. Maintenance occurs when we add new features, debug issues, or ensure uptime of an application over time. Poor maintainability means that developers have to spend more time—often in frustration—when adding features or diagnosing existing problems in an application.

Maintenance is a hard concern to optimize because we can often be blind to things that will be problematic in the future. We may leverage a new technique or tool that we anticipate will make changes easier in the future, but the exact opposite could happen! Our perception of what is maintainable could also change over time; new developers on a project may not have as much experience with a technology, which makes maintenance more challenging for them. This begs the question of how we can stay ahead of maintenance and ensure that development on our application is easy in the future.

Leveraging programming best practices and clear boundaries in our application is a time-tested way to ensure future maintenance. Luckily for us, Elixir gives us the ability to write our systems with very clear layers and boundaries. Layers can nominally increase the amount of computation in our application, but well-designed layers give us many maintenance benefits by making it easier for us to make changes.

Throughout this book, we'll see examples of how to design real-time applications that are easy to understand and change in the future. We'll build a larger project that satisfies real-world business needs in Part II, Building a Real-Time Application, on page 119. We'll also be leveraging the power of a framework that doesn't tie itself to a particular communication layer. This clear boundary between application and communication layers will start us off on a good footing for writing maintainable applications.

Scalability of Cost

Cost is something that is easy to take for granted. As developers, we are often separated from the financial cost of our applications. However, we are able to control several different components that contribute to the cost of our application. We are able to conserve, or spend, server resources such as CPU, memory, and bandwidth. We will also experience costs associated with future development time that we want to minimize.

Elixir, and more specifically Erlang/OTP applications, can have relatively low costs compared to other languages. There are examples of large Erlang applications, such as WhatsApp, running with millions of users, but with a small number of servers and a small team of engineers. These types of success stories are rare, of course, and depend on the type of application being developed, but the technology has been vetted and proven to be successful at keeping costs low in large applications.

Tension of Scalability

The different types of scalability exist in tension with each other. This can end up causing our applications to reduce one type of scalability when we increase another. It would be ideal if we could maximize every type of scalability perfectly, although the reality is that this is very difficult to do. You might know the old rule of thumb: "fast, reliable, cheap—pick two." This is certainly true for many systems that we develop, although we're often able to keep this in control by caring about it when we start developing an application. Let's look at how the different types of scalability can hold each other in tension.

Performance vs. Cost

You can often increase application performance by paying for additional server resources—throwing hardware at the problem. This technique is used to improve performance without addressing the root cause that is causing the performance problem. Spending money on a performance problem may indeed be the right choice if a problem has been heavily evaluated by the development team and determined to be costly in development hours to fix. It may also be early in an application's existence and new feature development is prioritized over performance.

An example of acceptably reducing cost while also reducing potential performance is to scale the number of servers down during periods of application inactivity. You can be successful in reducing cost this way, as long as the application is able to properly serve requests.

Performance vs. Maintenance

Writing high-performance code can also mean writing complex and harder-to-maintain code. One way to increase application performance is to reduce or remove boundaries in code. For example, tightly coupling a communication layer to the server implementation could allow for a more-optimized solution that directly processes incoming requests. However, boundaries exist for the purpose of creating more understandable and maintainable code. By removing the layers, we could potentially reduce the ability to maintain the code in the future.

Most applications should focus on maximizing maintenance ability as this allows new features to be easily added over time. However, there may come a point when performance needs become greater than the need to add new features.

Maintenance vs. Cost

Maintenance involves people, and people are expensive. By reducing the difficulty of maintenance, you can save development hours in the future and reduce cost. You can also minimize cost by not fixing technical debt over time, which could reduce immediate costs but potentially increase maintenance costs.

Maintenance and cost are often very important to technical managers or non-technical stakeholders in an organization. As developers, we must consider their perspective to help ensure the long-term success of our projects.

All of the various components of scalability affect each other. The real world is full of trade-offs and decisions that may be outside of your control. Understand the concerns of scalability with key stakeholders in order to inform decisions you make on a project.

Achieving Real-Time in Elixir

Elixir is a functional programming language that enables scalable application development. Elixir is a low-ceremony language—it places an emphasis on expressive syntax that conveys the meaning of code quickly. These properties help to reduce the complexity of code and, by proxy, help to improve maintenance scalability over time.

Elixir builds on top of Erlang/OTP to provide an excellent foundation for soft real-time applications. Elixir leverages lightweight virtual machine processes, often implemented as GenServers, that allow for encapsulation and modeling of the various components of a real-time system. It's possible to scale Elixir applications to multiple cores without any special constructs, just as it is simple to connect servers together to form a cluster. This means that Elixir applications can scale up vertically on a single large machine or horizontally to many machines in order to meet the needs of different usage profiles.

Any system that we write, especially a real-time system where time matters, should have reliable isolation of data and isolated error handling. A classic example to consider, very relevant to the Erlang ecosystem due to its history in telecom, is a phone system. When two people are talking on the phone, we expect that their conversation is private (data isolation) and also that their call will not end before they hang up. Two people talking on the phone should not be able to cause a crash of any other users, even if their call encounters a bug (error isolation). Data isolation and error isolation are handled for us, nearly freely, by using separate OTP processes for different elements of our real-time system.

Elixir is a fantastic choice for development of real-time systems due to its usage of Erlang/OTP and functional design, but it is possible to experience issues in an Elixir application when using a software design that doesn't take advantage of Elixir's strengths. We'll focus on clean OTP design throughout this book in order to promote best practices and, ultimately, success with our application.

Building Real-Time Systems

In this book, you're going to learn how to build real-time systems, but first we're going to walk through the foundations of real-time communication. When you understand the foundations that real-time systems in Elixir are built on, you will be able to build and debug applications more easily.

Elixir is a great choice for developing real-time systems, but it is just a language. We will leverage several different Elixir libraries for building our real-time systems—the most important one is Phoenix. Phoenix[1] is a web framework written in Elixir that drives productive web application development. One component of Phoenix that we will use for building real-time systems is Phoenix Channels. You'll start learning about Channels in Chapter 3, First Steps with Phoenix Channels, on page 27.

Elixir and Phoenix have different libraries that will help you build real-time systems. You'll learn about GenStage in Chapter 6, Avoid Performance Pitfalls, on page 91 and Phoenix Tracker in Chapter 10, Track Connected Carts with Presence, on page 191. By the end of this book, all of the different libraries will have come together and you will have built a real-time e-commerce application.

Wrapping Up

Real-time applications help you to win your users' trust by creating an experience that always reflects the current state of their data. This seamless experience has become table stakes in modern applications. Real-time applications consist of clients, a real-time communication layer, and back-end servers working together to achieve business objectives. Any client capable of an internet connection can connect to a real-time server, which allows you to write a single application that can be utilized by many different types of clients.

You must plan for scalability when building a real-time application. There are multiple types of scalability that are important to consider: performance,

---

1. https://phoenixframework.org/

maintenance, and cost. These different aspects of scalability are always in tension with each other. They influence the different decisions you make in how you write and run applications.

Elixir is a not-so-secret weapon for developing real-time applications, and using it creates a setting for success. It allows us to maximize the different aspects of scalability for an application while reducing trade-offs. This isn't necessarily unique to Elixir, but it has allowed it to become positioned as a forerunner in the real-time application space.

In the next chapter, we're going to look at the real-time communication layer. We'll see how WebSockets are an excellent general purpose communication layer that can efficiently satisfy a variety of real-time needs. We will dissect a WebSocket connection using developer tools in order to understand the protocol more deeply. This will prepare us to move into building real-time applications.

Part I

Powering Real-Time Applications with Phoenix

In this first part, we will learn the fundamentals of real-time applications powered by Phoenix Channels. We'll be diving deep in order to fully understand the different challenges we may face in real applications and how to solve those challenges before they become large issues.

## CHAPTER 2

Connect a Simple WebSocket

Real-time systems are all about getting data from the server to the user, or vice versa, as quickly and efficiently as possible. A critical piece of a real-time system is the communication layer that sits between the server and the user. The user may be on a browser, a mobile app, or even another server. This means that we want to pick a communication layer that can work well in a variety of different circumstances, from high-latency mobile connections to very fast connections.

In this book, we'll use WebSockets as our communication layer; they form the backbone of real-time web applications today. This may change as technology evolves over time, but it's the best solution in the current technology landscape. We'll start building real-time applications in the next chapter, but first we're going to break down how WebSockets work. Understanding Web-Sockets is crucial in order to build and deliver real-time applications to users. We'll use a "Hello, World!"-style Phoenix application to see the communication of a WebSocket. Once this application is running, we'll look at the different components of a WebSocket to understand how they work.

You can build a real-time system without understanding all the different layers, such as WebSockets, but lacking this knowledge may hurt you in the long run. I remember shipping my first real-time Phoenix application where I didn't fully understand all the layers involved. My WebSockets weren't able to connect! I researched and realized that I needed to understand more about WebSockets in order to get them working with my production load balancer and to reduce my application's memory usage. Learning more about the different layers allowed me to ensure each was working properly.

Let's look at what a WebSocket is and then move into our "Hello WebSocket" application.

Why WebSockets?

It used to be difficult to write real-time systems due to technology limitations at the communication layer. Developers of real-time systems had to make trade-offs between performance, cost, and maintenance; the complicated techniques used often pushed browsers to the limit of their capabilities. Those techniques were highly dependent on the particular web browser used. This meant that a client would be working correctly in one browser but not work in another.

The RFC for the WebSocket protocol emerged with the HTML5 spec in 2011 to solve the challenges of real-time web communication. It took a bit of time for WebSockets to gain support, but they are now supported natively by all major browsers and can be considered mature for application development. We'll be using WebSockets as the primary communication layer in this book because of these strengths:

- WebSockets allow for efficient two-way data communication over a single TCP connection. This helps to minimize message bandwidth and avoids the overhead of creating frequent connections.

- WebSockets have strong support in Elixir with the cowboy web server.[1] They map very well to the Erlang process model which helps to create robust performance-focused applications.

- WebSockets originate with an HTTP request, which means that many standard web technologies such as load balancers and proxies can be used with them.

- WebSockets are able to stay at the edge of our Elixir application. We can change out our communication layer in the future if a better technology becomes available.

WebSockets are powerful. This is evident by the popular and successful applications built using them. Facebook Messenger[2] uses WebSockets to send and receive real-time chats from user clients, allowing Messenger chats to feel snappy. Yahoo Finance[3] uses WebSockets to power their real-time stock ticker across global financial markets. Multiplayer games such as Slither[4] are very popular (not to mention fun!) and are powered completely via WebSockets.

---

1. https://github.com/ninenines/cowboy
2. https://messenger.com
3. https://finance.yahoo.com
4. https://slither.io

I first dug into the nuts and bolts of WebSockets while developing systems at SalesLoft,[5] an enterprise software as a service (SaaS) company. We use WebSockets to power many important features for our business users, such as real-time notifications and live website information. We send hundreds of millions of events over WebSockets each day.

Enough talk, though, it's time for some action! We'll use a small local Elixir application that exposes a WebSocket in order to see how to connect a WebSocket and how data can be sent over it. You will use this technique to inspect and debug our applications later in the book.

Connecting our First WebSocket

To get up and running quickly, we're going to leverage Phoenix's[6] initial project scaffold. This is a good time to go back to Introduction, on page xi in order to make sure that Elixir and Phoenix are set up properly on your system.

We will use mix phx.new to create our first example. You will be prompted to "fetch and install dependencies" during this process. Enter Y in order for the project to be started without manual steps.

```
$ mix phx.new hello_sockets --no-ecto
* creating hello_sockets/config/config.exs
...
Fetch and install dependencies? [Yn] Y
...
```

We'll need to perform one more step to get the sample WebSocket to load. Let's remove the comment on the socket line:

```
hello_sockets/assets/js/app.js
// Import local files
//
// Local files can be imported directly using relative paths, for example:
import socket from "./socket"
```

Run mix phx.server in the hello_sockets folder to start the server. If you get an error when starting the server, double check that you are in the right folder and that you do not already have a program running on port 4000.

Once started, you will see the program running on port 4000:

---

5.   https://salesloft.com

6.   https://phoenixframework.org/

```
$ mix phx.server
Compiling 12 files (.ex)
Generated hello_sockets app
[info] Running HelloSocketsWeb.Endpoint with cowboy 2.6.3 at 0.0.0.0:4000
[info] Access HelloSocketsWeb.Endpoint at http://localhost:4000

Webpack is watching the files…
...
```

We'll use this basic WebSocket application in this chapter to observe how a WebSocket connects and transmits data. It is important to poke around and understand WebSockets so you can debug them more effectively in the future. As you're developing an application, you will spend a fair amount of time looking at what data is being sent to and from the WebSocket.

WebSocket Protocol

WebSockets follow a formal protocol that is implemented by browsers and servers. We will make use of several parts of the WebSocket protocol, but we will not use the entire protocol. In this section, we'll focus on the most basic parts of the protocol. You'll learn how to establish a connection, keep the connection alive, send and receive data, and keep the WebSocket secure.

Using the WebSocket RFC

The RFC for the WebSocket Protocol[a] doesn't make for the most entertaining, or lightest, reading. However, the RFC is highly valuable if you find yourself doing deep debugging into a WebSocket implementation. In this chapter, we'll use Chrome DevTools to inspect how a WebSocket works, but you may benefit from advanced features listed in the RFC.

The RFC can be especially useful if you have extremely tight technical requirements that are not met by the standard WebSocket implementation. However, the standard implementation provided by Phoenix will work for nearly everyone.

---

a.   https://tools.ietf.org/html/rfc6455

We'll use Google Chrome's[7] DevTools to walk through the next example. Any browser with the ability to inspect a WebSocket could be used, although each browser's DevTools vary in look and functionality. WebSockets are supported by all major browsers,[8] which means that you and your users will be able to use WebSockets from any modern device.

---

7.   https://www.google.com/chrome/
8.   https://caniuse.com/#feat=websockets

Establishing the Connection

Load the HelloSockets webpage by visiting http://localhost:4000. You will see the default generated Phoenix start screen. What we want to see is hiding from us, and we'll use the DevTools to view it. You can open the DevTools via right-click > Inspect on the webpage. You'll see a variety of tabs, but we want to select the "Network" tab. Once there, reload the webpage in order to capture the connected WebSocket.

Chrome Network Tab Missing Connections

Chrome only shows requests since DevTools was opened. This can lead to a lot of hair-pulling when you're troubleshooting a problem. Reload the webpage if you can't locate your WebSocket connection. Turning it off and on again always works, right?

Select the "WS" tab in order to only show WebSocket connections. Look for the connection labeled websocket?token=undefined&vsn=2.0.0. You may see another connected WebSocket because Phoenix comes with a developer code reloader that operates over a WebSocket, but you can ignore that one. Once you click into the connection, you will see something like this:

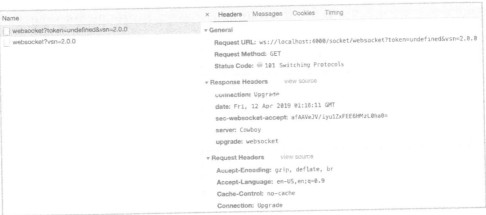

In this image, you can see a few things that reveal how a WebSocket connects. The first is that there are request headers, response headers, and an HTTP method (GET).

A WebSocket starts its life as a normal web request that becomes "upgraded" to a WebSocket. We can see this if we use cURL on the WebSocket endpoint. You'll need several required headers to make this work. The easiest way to generate the cURL request is to right-click the request labeled websocket?token=undefined&vsn=2.0.0 under the "name" column and then select the "copy as cURL" option. This will copy a cURL request to a ws protocol URL. Next,

paste the cURL request into your favorite editor and replace ws:// with http://.
Run this request in your terminal with the -i flag added. You'll end up with a
request that looks like this:

```
# cURL command abbreviated, paste your copied command
# Include all of the headers that came with the copied command
$ curl -i 'http://localhost:4000/socket/websocket?vsn=2.0.0' -H...
HTTP/1.1 101 Switching Protocols
connection: Upgrade
date: Fri, 12 Apr 2019 01:29:18 GMT
sec-websocket-accept: afAAVeJV/iyu1ZxFEE6HMzL0ha0=
server: Cowboy
upgrade: websocket
```

Our web request has received a 101 HTTP response from the server, which
indicates that the connection protocol changes from HTTP to a WebSocket.
WebSockets operate over a TCP socket using a special data protocol, with the
initial HTTP request ensuring that the connection is compatible with browsers
and server proxies. The same TCP socket that the HTTP connection request
went over becomes the data TCP socket after the upgrade—this allows Web-
Sockets to only use a single socket per connection. WebSockets were designed
for allowing browsers to connect to a TCP socket through HTTP, but it is
completely acceptable to use them in non-browser environments such as a
server or mobile client.

The following figure is a flow diagram of the WebSocket connection process.

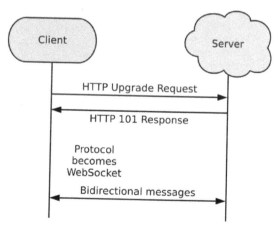

To summarize, a WebSocket connection follows this request flow:

1. Initiate a GET HTTP(S) connection request to the WebSocket endpoint.
2. Receive a 101 or error from the server.
3. Upgrade the protocol to WebSocket if 101 is received.
4. Send/receive frames over the WebSocket connection.

A connection cannot be upgraded with cURL, so we'll move back to DevTools for seeing the data exchange.

Sending and Receiving Data

When you opened the DevTools, you may have noticed a "Messages" tab. This tab shows all messages that are sent to or received from the server. The DevTools for our app looks like this:

You can ignore the error message for now; the important thing to note is that a WebSocket is capable of sending messages (green background) and receiving messages (white background). This two-way data transmission can happen in both directions simultaneously. A connection which is capable of two-way data transmission is called a full-duplex connection.

WebSockets transmit data through a data framing protocol.[9] We can't see it with the DevTools, but it's worth knowing this provides security benefits and allows WebSocket connections to work properly through different networking layers. These traits allow us to more confidently ship WebSocket-powered applications into production.

The WebSocket protocol contains extensions that provide additional functionality. Extensions are requested by the client using the Sec-WebSocket-Extensions request header. The server can optionally use any of the proposed extensions and return the list of active extensions to the client in a response header named Sec-WebSocket-Extensions. WebSocket data frames are not compressed by default, but can be compressed by using the permessage-deflate extension. This feature allows bandwidth to be reduced at the cost of processing power, which is a benefit for some applications.

Staying Alive, Keep-alive

We have a WebSocket connection that is sending and receiving data, now we have to ensure that the connection stays alive. A disconnected WebSocket is unable to send or receive data. There are things we could do to provide some

---

9.   https://tools.ietf.org/html/rfc6455#section-5

guarantees if a WebSocket disconnects, but we want to base our application on a solid foundation.

The WebSocket protocol specifies Ping and Pong frames[10] which can be used to verify that a connection is still alive. These are optional, though, and you'll soon see that Phoenix doesn't use them. Instead, clients send heartbeat-data messages to the Phoenix Server they're connected to every 30 seconds. The Phoenix WebSocket process will close a connection if it doesn't receive a ping within a timeout period, with 60 seconds the default. With Phoenix, it is possible to use a WebSocket ping control frame to keep the WebSocket connection alive, but the official Phoenix client doesn't use it.

A predictable heartbeat for the connection turns out to be very useful. A connection can be dead but not closed properly; this causes the connection to stay active on the server. A connection that is active but without a client on the other side wouldn't be sending a heartbeat, so it closes gracefully after a short period of time.

It is useful that the client manages the heartbeat rather than the server. If the server is in charge of sending pings to a client, then the server is aware of the connectivity problem but cannot establish a new connection to the client. If a connectivity problem is detected by the client via its ping request, the client can quickly attempt to reconnect and establish the connection again.

Security

Security is very important in the WebSocket protocol. Connections need to be secure from malicious actors looking to intercept data. They also need to be kept secure from proxies that may cache data incorrectly. One of the benefits of picking a well-established technology like WebSockets is that a lot of these security concerns are handled for us. However, there are a few things that we must do in order to have secure WebSocket applications.

Our HelloSocket example violates one of the most important rules of WebSocket connections: always use wss:// URIs to ensure a secure connection. We use ws:// in our example because it doesn't involve signing a local certificate for SSL, but you should always use wss protocol in production to ensure security. If you are using https to access your webpage, then you are required to use the wss protocol by the browser.

WebSocket connections can come from any webpage or other types of clients. The connection request sends a variety of headers to the server when it

---

10. https://tools.ietf.org/html/rfc6455#section-5.5.2

initiates (you can see these in the WebSocket "Network" tab). The Origin header of every connection request should be checked to ensure that it is coming from a known location. It is possible that this header was spoofed by a non-browser client, but browser security increases when we check the Origin header. Phoenix provides out-of-the-box support for checking the Origin header. We'll use it when we configure our real-time project later in this book.

WebSockets do not follow the same rules as standard web requests when it comes to cross-origin resource sharing (CORS)—the WebSocket connection request doesn't use CORS protections at all. Cookies are sent to the server, even if the page initiating the request is on a different domain than what the cookies specify. These cookies aren't readable by the initiating page, but they would allow access to the server when access should be denied. There are strategies that can help solve this problem, such as origin checking or cross-site request forgery (CSRF) tokens.

As a way to prevent CSRF attacks, Phoenix has historically disallowed cookie access when establishing a WebSocket connection. Phoenix now supports access to the session when a CSRF token is provided to the WebSocket connection. We'll cover different authentication solutions in Chapter 4, Restrict Socket and Channel Access, on page 53.

Long Polling, a Real-Time Alternative

WebSocket is not the only real-time communication technology that can be used in your applications. You may have restrictions in your application's environment that prevent using a WebSocket, such as having very inconsistent client connectivity due to your application's user profile. There may even be a newly emerged technology since this book was published that provides even better two-way web communication. It is important for the maintenance of our application that we do not design it solely around WebSocket usage. Remember, we have a WebSocket-*powered* application, not a WebSocket application.

A less efficient but still viable real-time communication layer is HTTP long polling. Phoenix ships with long polling support out-of-the-box, which means that we can add it very easily to our server when necessary. We can even run WebSockets in tandem with HTTP long polling. Let's look at how long polling works, where it is useful, and where it can fall short.

What is Long Polling?

HTTP long polling[11] is a technique that uses standard HTTP in order to asynchronously send data to a client. This fits the requirement of a real-time communication layer that can send (long poll response) and receive (client request) data from a client. Long polling is the most frequently used predecessor to WebSockets, predating it by several years. This means that the technique is very stable, despite its disadvantages.

Long polling uses a request flow as follows:

1. The client initiates an HTTP request to the server.

2. The server doesn't respond to the request, instead leaving it open. The server will respond when it has new data or too much time elapses.

3. The server sends a complete response to the client. At this point the client is aware of the real-time data from the server.

4. The client loops this flow as long as the real-time communication is desired.

The key component of the long polling flow is that the client's connection to the server remains open until new data is received. This allows data to be immediately pushed to the connected client when it's available. Long polling is a viable technique for real-time communication, but there are challenges with it that make WebSockets a clearly better choice for our applications.

Should You Use Long Polling?

Long polling is an interesting technique because it is based solely on top of HTTP, compared to WebSockets which uses HTTP only for a small part of its flow. But, long polling does have some limitations. Here are some, but not all, of the challenges that you may face when using long polling. There is a more exhaustive list of issues maintained by the IETF,[12] which is a must read if you're going to use long polling in production.

1. Request headers are processed on every long poll request. This can, potentially, dramatically increase the number of transmitted bytes which need to be processed by the server. This isn't optimal for performance.

2. Message latency can be high when a poor network is being used. Dropped packets and slower data transit times can make latency much higher

---

11. https://tools.ietf.org/html/rfc6202#section-2
12. https://tools.ietf.org/html/rfc6202#section-2.2

because multiple connections have to complete in order to reestablish the long polling connection. This can affect how real-time the application feels.

Both of these problems can affect performance and scalability of our application, which would be bad if the system becomes heavily used. WebSockets are not prone to these performance issues because the data transmission protocol is much lighter than full HTTP requests, requiring less data overhead and network round trips.

There are times that long polling can be useful, however. Long polling connections can be load-balanced across multiple servers easily, because the connections are being established often. WebSockets can be tricky to load balance if the connections have a long life; longer connections provide fewer opportunities to change which server a client is connected to. Another benefit of long polling is that it can transparently take advantage of protocol advancements, such as future versions of HTTP. Google, a well-known innovator of internet protocols, leverages a custom form of long polling to power certain real-time applications.

Phoenix ships with both a WebSocket and a long polling communication layer out-of-the-box. A client can change from WebSocket to long polling if something goes wrong, such as poor network connectivity. There are other real-time communication techniques that Phoenix does not ship with natively. Server-sent events,[13] for example, provides one-way data flow from the server to a client. The benefit and flexibility of the WebSocket protocol, especially when combined with Phoenix, enables you to write dependable and performant real-time software.

WebSockets and Phoenix Channels

WebSockets map very well to the Erlang/OTP actor model and are leveraged by one of the stars of Phoenix: Channels. WebSockets are the primary communication layer for Channels. This provides Channels with a solid foundation on which to build real-time applications. We'll be using Phoenix Channels with WebSockets throughout this book.

Maybe you're worried that WebSockets will cause high resource usage in your application. Don't worry! Phoenix and Elixir make it easy to have tens of thousands of connections on a single server. Each connected Channel and WebSocket in your application has independent memory management and

---

13. https://hex.pm/packages/sse

garbage collection because of OTP processes. An advantage of this process-based architecture is that WebSocket connections which are not being used often can be stored in a hibernated state, which consumes very little memory. This is great for scalability.

As we'll see in the next chapter, Channels use several levels of processes which provide fault tolerance and reduced memory usage across our application. This is very important for scaling our real-time application because it prevents application bottlenecks (points in code that slow down our system) from forming. You'll see tips throughout this book on how to avoid performance problems by following proper programming and deployment practices.

We will dive much deeper into Phoenix Channels in the next chapter. We'll look at how Channels are modeled into distinct layers using OTP processes, and how that provides us with a fault-tolerant and high-performance system.

Wrapping Up

The WebSocket protocol provides a strong real-time communication layer for our real-time applications. WebSockets start as normal HTTP requests before being upgraded to TCP sockets for data exchange. This allows WebSockets to work well with current web technologies and also lets them leverage faster data transport by using a single connection with minimal protocol overhead for each message. There are many successful and large products in production using WebSockets. This gives us more confidence in the stability and state of this technology.

WebSockets are a solid foundation for real-time systems and are what we'll predominately work with throughout the examples in this book. Many of the concepts presented in this chapter will reappear in future chapters in different ways. In particular, the concepts of data exchange and security will be appearing often as they are critical for the development of real-world applications.

In the next chapter we'll take our first steps with Phoenix Channels. We will learn the foundations of Channels in order to develop our real-time application toolkit, which we'll use to create a real-world application in later chapters.

## CHAPTER 3

First Steps with Phoenix Channels

Real-time applications exist at the intersection of a communication layer and business logic that satisfies the needs of users. We covered the communication layer in the previous chapter, but we haven't yet walked through how to build real applications with business logic.

In this chapter, we'll look at a popular and well-designed framework that allows development of real-time applications: Phoenix. Phoenix Channels are the most powerful real-time abstraction that currently exists in the Elixir community, and we will be exploring their basics in order to develop a real-time foundational toolkit. After an introduction to the different components of Channels, we will see specific examples of how they can be used and how we can structure our application around them.

Channels will be at the core of our real-time application. We'll see them in every chapter throughout the rest of this book, due to how greatly they enable simple and flexible real-time application design. When you understand all the details of Channels, you can make applications that deliver exceptional real-time user experiences.

It will take some time to fully understand all of the ins and outs of how to use Channels. We'll start our journey by looking at what a Channel allows us to do and going over the different components that comprise Channels. We'll send and receive real-time messages powered by an Elixir server, before moving on to the client side with JavaScript examples. We'll see more advanced concepts in the next chapter before writing a real-world application in part II.

What are Phoenix Channels?

Phoenix[1] is a web framework written in Elixir that drives productive web application development. One of the components of Phoenix is Channels, a way to effectively write bidirectional real-time web applications. They allow us to write our application code without worrying about details such as "how is the connection set up and maintained?" or "how can I scale the number of connections easily?" We don't have to use Channels in order to write our real-time applications, but Channels prevent us from needing to reinvent the wheel for each application we write. Plus, Channels are fairly generic, which makes them applicable to any type of real-time application.

Channels work, at a high level, by allowing clients to connect to the web server and subscribe to various topics. The client then sends and receives messages over its subscribed topics. A client subscribes to as many topics as desired on a single connection, which reduces the number of expensive connections. Later in this book, you'll see a way to break up Channel connections so you can take advantage of reduced connections while still having a properly working application. Once a client is connected to a Channel, it sends data to the server or receives data from the server through the Channel. The flow, from a client's perspective, works in this simple way:

In addition to the client perspective, we must also think about Channels from the perspective of the server. Channels are built using strong OTP application design. Every layer that makes up Channels is represented by separated OTP processes that allow for fault tolerance and simpler application design. You will benefit from this foundation without needing to worry too heavily about it. Even though OTP concepts are seen in nearly every Elixir application we write, the details of Channels' OTP design are largely hidden from our immediate view. This allows even Elixir beginners to use Channels to write performant and maintainable applications.

One of the benefits of Channels is that they are transport agnostic. In the last chapter we covered the real-time communication layer, with a focus on WebSockets, where you learned that our application is powered by a real-time layer but isn't defined by it. This means that, in an ideal world, we should

---

1.   https://phoenixframework.org/

have a way to easily switch out the real-time layer without changing application logic. A transport-agnostic tool, like Channels, makes this a possibility because Channels draw clear seams across different parts of the system.

The power of Channels will become unlocked when we understand a bit more about their structure and how they fit into an application's design. But we have to start somewhere a bit simpler first by looking at the different layers of Channels and how they fit together to provide us with a stable real-time foundation.

Understanding Channel Structure

Frameworks often add several layers between the user and the business logic. Don't worry if you feel a bit intimidated when you first look at Channels and see the different layers being used. You'll understand each layer and its purpose as you progress through this chapter and book. This will help you to leverage Phoenix with a great amount of confidence.

Let's look at a high-level diagram to understand the different processes and connections that exist in Channels:

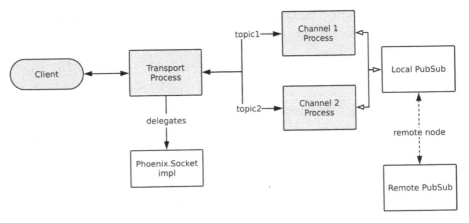

A client connects to the server via transport mechanism such as a WebSocket, by connecting directly to an OTP process that manages the connection. This process delegates certain operations, such as whether to accept or reject the connection request, to our application code that implements the Phoenix.Socket behaviour.

The module that uses Phoenix.Socket has the ability to route topics that the client requests to a provided Phoenix.Channel implementation module. The Channel module starts up a separate process for each different topic that the user connects to. Channels, like transport processes, are never shared between different connections.

Phoenix.PubSub is used to route messages to and from Channels. You can see in the diagram that a distinction is made between local and remote PubSub processes. Messages are broadcast through the PubSub process and are sent to both the local node and remote nodes. For now, just know that PubSub allows a cluster of nodes to work with Channels. We'll explore each of these components in more detail and see how they are used in our application.

Sockets

Sockets form the backbone of real-time communication in Phoenix. A Socket is a module that implements the Phoenix.Socket.Transport behaviour, but we'll be using a specific implementation called Phoenix.Socket. You'll most likely be using Phoenix.Socket in your application because it implements both WebSockets and long polling in a way that follows best practices. (If you ever need a custom transport layer, which is rare, then you do have the ability to implement your own Socket.Transport.)

We only have to implement a few functions in order to create a functional Socket implementation. The callbacks connect/3 and id/1 provide the template for our application's Socket. Let's add to our HelloSockets example from Connecting our First WebSocket, on page 17.

```
hello_sockets/lib/hello_sockets_web/channels/user_socket.ex
use Phoenix.Socket

## Channels
channel "ping", HelloSocketsWeb.PingChannel
```

The channel macro will allow us to define a topic that routes to a given Channel implementation. In this case we'll route to a PingChannel which we'll create in the next section. Remove any other channel routes listed in this file.

You will notice that the connect/3 and id/1 functions are left to their default generated values.

```
hello_sockets/lib/hello_sockets_web/channels/user_socket.ex
def connect(_params, socket, _connect_info) do
  {:ok, socket}
end

def id(_socket), do: nil
```

The defaults allow us to have a functioning Socket implementation. We'll see how to use connect/3 to implement authentication in Chapter 4, Restrict Socket and Channel Access, on page 53. id/1 is a function for identifying the currently connected client; this might be via their user identifier or some other piece of information that is specific to them. This is useful when we want to track the socket or if we want to disconnect a particular user.

Channels

Channels are the real-time entry points to our application's logic and where most of an application's request handling code lives. A Channel has several different responsibilities to enable real-time applications:

- Accept or reject a request to join.
- Handle messages from the client.
- Handle messages from the PubSub.
- Push messages to the client.

The distinction between Channels and Sockets may not be obvious at a glance. A Socket's responsibilities involve connection handling and routing of requests to the correct Channel. A Channel's responsibilities involve handling requests from a client and sending data to a client. In this way, a Channel is similar to a Controller in the MVC (Model-View-Controller) design pattern.

It has become popular in recent years to use the mantra "skinny controllers" to indicate that we don't want business logic in our controllers. This same mantra can be applied to Channels; we should strive to keep application logic in our application's core and not have it implemented in our Channels. The exception to this is that logic needed for real-time communication customization is best implemented at the Channel level, as we'll see in Customize Channel Behavior, on page 74.

Implement Our First Channel

Let's implement our PingChannel. This implementation won't have any application logic and is fully self-contained.

hello_sockets/lib/hello_sockets_web/channels/ping_channel.ex
```elixir
defmodule HelloSocketsWeb.PingChannel do
  use Phoenix.Channel

  def join(_topic, _payload, socket) do
    {:ok, socket}
  end
end
```

use is a special keyword in Elixir that invokes the _using_ macro. In the case of Phoenix.Channel, it includes the bulk of the code to make the Channel functional.

We allow any connection to this Channel to succeed by not implementing any join logic. This is acceptable for topics that we want to be fully public. It is *not* acceptable to have an empty join function if we want our Channel to be private and only accessible to certain types of clients. In this case, we need to use authentication—we'll see an example of this in the next chapter.

```
hello_sockets/lib/hello_sockets_web/channels/ping_channel.ex
def handle_in("ping", _payload, socket) do
  {:reply, {:ok, %{ping: "pong"}}, socket}
end
```

handle_in/3 receives an event, payload, and the state of the current Socket. We only allow the ping event to be processed; any other event will be an error. We are able to do several things when we receive a message:

- Reply to the message by returning {:reply, {:ok, map()}, Phoenix.Socket}. The payload must be a map.

- Do not reply to the message by returning {:noreply, Phoenix.Socket}.

- Disconnect the Channel by returning {:stop, reason, Phoenix.Socket}.

We'll be using all the available return types later in this chapter.

We implemented PingChannel and configured our Socket route to send the ping topic to our Channel. We're going to use a CLI application to test that our Channel works. wscat is an npm package that permits connecting to, sending data to, and receiving data from a WebSocket. It can be a little cumbersome to use but has the advantage of being easy to setup. Use npm install -g wscat in order to get started. Copy the input that is on the > lines below.

```
$ wscat -c 'ws://localhost:4000/socket/websocket?vsn=2.0.0'
connected (press CTRL+C to quit)
> ["1","1","ping","phx_join",{}]
< ["1","1","ping","phx_reply",{"response":{},"status":"ok"}]

> ["1","2","ping","ping",{}]
< ["1","2","ping","phx_reply",{"response":{"ping":"pong"},"status":"ok"}]
```

If you encounter any errors like "unmatched topic" when you run this example, make sure that your UserSocket module has only the ping Channel route listed.

We will cover the message structure later in this chapter. The important thing to note for now is that we first use the special message "phx_join" to connect to the ping Channel using our WebSocket connection. We receive an ok response after the join. We then send the ping Channel a "ping" message with an empty payload. It successfully responds with a pong message. You can press CTRL + C to disconnect the wscat session.

Handle Channel Errors

A major difference between a traditional web Controller and a Channel is that the Channel is long-lived. In a perfect world, a Channel will live for the entire life of the connection without being interrupted. But we don't live in a perfect world, and disconnections are going to occur in our application. They may occur because of a bug in our application causing a crash or because the client's internet connection is not stable. Let's cause a crash in our PingChannel to observe what happens.

```
$ wscat -c 'ws://localhost:4000/socket/websocket?vsn=2.0.0'
connected (press CTRL+C to quit)
> ["1","1","ping","phx_join",{}]
< ["1","1","ping","phx_reply",{"response":{},"status":"ok"}]

> ["1","2","ping","ping",{}]
< ["1","2","ping","phx_reply",{"response":{"ping":"pong"},"status":"ok"}]

> ["1","2","ping","ping2",{}]
< ["1","1","ping","phx_error",{}]

# Our previously working message will not work until we rejoin the topic
> ["1","2","ping","ping",{}]
< [null,"2","ping","phx_reply",{"response":{"reason":"unmatched topic"},
    "status":"error"}]

> ["1","1","ping","phx_join",{}]
< ["1","1","ping","phx_reply",{"response":{},"status":"ok"}]

> ["1","2","ping","ping",{}]
< ["1","2","ping","phx_reply",{"response":{"ping":"pong"},"status":"ok"}]
```

We start our session by using a normal ping message and we receive a successful response. We send a "ping2" event, which we did not write a match for in our handle_in function, so the Channel fails to match the event and crashes. If you look at the Elixir server, you will see a "no function clause" error.

We get a different error once we send the correct ping message again. This time the topic is unmatched, which means that we did not have a connected Channel for the topic "ping". The message then begins to work again once we reconnect using "phx_join".

Our connection to the server stayed alive throughout this entire process. If we had multiple Channels, all of the other Channels would also stay alive. This reinforces the important part of the Channel structure that OTP enables: fault tolerance. An error that happens in a single Channel should not affect any other Channels and should not affect the Socket. An error that happens in the Socket, however, will affect all Channels that exist under the Socket because they are dependent on the Socket working correctly. We can simulate a failure in the Socket by sending a message it does not expect:

```
$ wscat -c 'ws://localhost:4000/socket/websocket?vsn=2.0.0'
connected (press CTRL+C to quit)
> crash
disconnected (code: 1011)
```

It is up to the client to respond to the "phx_error" response by ensuring that it rejoins the Channel and responds to the connection drop by reconnecting. The official JavaScript client handles all of this for you so you don't need to worry about the orchestration of the connection. Any non-official clients will need to handle this properly, however, or they could end up being connected to the Socket but not connected to a Channel.

Topics

Topics are string identifiers used for connecting to the correct Channel when the "phx_join" message is received by the Socket. They are defined in the Socket module as we saw with our UserSocket example previously.

hello_sockets/lib/hello_sockets_web/channels/user_socket.ex
```
channel "ping", HelloSocketsWeb.PingChannel
```

A topic can be any string, but it is best practice to use a "topic:subtopic" format for the topic name. This convention allows us to have a single Socket module with different types of Channels associated to it. This is because channel/3 can accept a wildcard splat operator as the final part of the string.

Let's change our topic definitions to use a wildcard operator and then observe the effects of it:

hello_sockets/lib/hello_sockets_web/channels/user_socket.ex
```
channel "ping", HelloSocketsWeb.PingChannel
channel "ping:*", HelloSocketsWeb.PingChannel
```

We can then connect to a "ping:wild" Channels and send messages to it.

```
$ wscat -c 'ws://localhost:4000/socket/websocket?vsn=2.0.0'
connected (press CTRL+C to quit)
> ["1","1","ping:wild","phx_join",{}]
< ["1","1","ping:wild","phx_reply",{"response":{},"status":"ok"}]

> ["1","1","ping:wild","ping",{}]
< ["1","1","ping:wild","phx_reply",
    {"response":{"ping":"pong"},"status":"ok"}]
```

It's possible to use the topic of "*" to allow any topic to route to the Channel. Any routing is allowed as long as the * character is at the end of the topic string. Try adding a character after "*" in our example above to see what happens by changing "ping:*" to "ping:*a". Luckily for us, Phoenix has protections in place that cause an error at compile time:

```
$ mix phx.server
Erlang/OTP 20 [erts-9.3.3.3]

Compiling 1 file (.ex)

== Compilation error in file lib/hello_sockets_web/channels/user_socket.ex ==
** (ArgumentError) channels using splat patterns must end with *
```

It is useful to note that topic routes must end with a wildcard, but they could contain multiple pieces of dynamic data. This is due to limitations in pattern matching when the wildcard isn't at the end.

Let's walk through an example of using a wildcard route with multiple pieces of data. Our goal is to have a topic that allows "wild:a:b" where b is an integer that is double the value of a. Add the following Channel definition below the existing definitions in the UserSocket.

hello_sockets/lib/hello_sockets_web/channels/user_socket.ex
```
channel "wild:*", HelloSocketsWeb.WildcardChannel
```

We first define a new topic definition that routes any topic starting with "wild:" to a new Channel.

hello_sockets/lib/hello_sockets_web/channels/wildcard_channel.ex
```
defmodule HelloSocketsWeb.WildcardChannel do
  use Phoenix.Channel

  def join("wild:" <> numbers, _payload, socket) do
    if numbers_correct?(numbers) do
      {:ok, socket}
    else
      {:error, %{}}
    end
  end

  def handle_in("ping", _payload, socket) do
    {:reply, {:ok, %{ping: "pong"}}, socket}
  end
end
```

We have defined a Channel that looks very similar to our PingChannel but with a conditional in the join/3 function that checks if the provided numbers are correct.

```
hello_sockets/lib/hello_sockets_web/channels/wildcard_channel.ex
defp numbers_correct?(numbers) do
  numbers
  |> String.split(":")
  |> Enum.map(&String.to_integer/1)
  |> case do
    [a, b] when b == a * 2 -> true
    _ -> false
  end
end
```

In order to check that the topic is correct, we take the provided numbers string and separate it into sections separated by a colon. Pattern matching allows us to have a very strict definition of what is allowed; we require that there are exactly two numbers and that the second number is twice the value of the first. Let's try it out.

```
$ wscat -c 'ws://localhost:4000/socket/websocket?vsn=2.0.0'
connected (press CTRL+C to quit)
> ["1","1","wild:1:2","phx_join",{}]
< ["1","1","wild:1:2","phx_reply",{"response":{},"status":"ok"}]

> ["1","2","wild:1:2","ping",{}]
< ["1","2","wild:1:2","phx_reply",{"response":{"ping":"pong"},"status":"ok"}]

> ["1","3","wild:1:3","phx_join",{}]
< ["3","3","wild:1:3","phx_reply",{"response":{},"status":"error"}]

> ["1","4","wild:20:40","phx_join",{}]
< ["4","4","wild:20:40","phx_reply",{"response":{},"status":"ok"}]

> ["1","5","wild:2:4:6","phx_join",{}]
< ["5","5","wild:2:4:6","phx_reply",{"response":{},"status":"error"}]
```

We can see that any numbers matching our allowed format will join the topic, but other numbers will not be able to. It's possible to crash this code by passing in non-integer characters, but this still will not allow a connection to occur.

Dynamic topic names are very useful. I have implemented them to give stable identifiers to private Channels based on multiple pieces of data. For example, the format "notifications:t-1:u-2" could be used to identify a notifications topic for user 2 on team 1. This allows notifications to be pushed from any part of the system that is capable of providing a user and team ID. It also prevents different users from receiving each other's private notifications.

Selecting a Topic Name

A carefully selected topic name is important for the scalability and behavior of an application. For instance, a public Channel providing inventory updates to an e-commerce storefront could be implemented in a variety of ways:

- "inventory" - This topic does not delineate between different SKUs
- "inventory:*" - This topic delineates between different item SKUs with a wildcard

If an overly broad topic is selected, such as "inventory", then an inventory change to a SKU is broadcast to every connected client, even if they are not viewing the item. A narrower topic such as "inventory:*" would lead to more connected topics (1 per viewed item), but means that outgoing data could be held back from clients that aren't viewing a particular SKU.

In this example, you would select a solution based on your business needs and tolerances. The single inventory topic would involve simpler code to implement, but it would use more bandwidth. It would also expose every inventory update in a way that allows adversaries to quickly index the store. The wildcard topic provides more performance optimization possibilities at the cost of more connected topics and additional client code. It would still be possible to watch for all inventory updates, but this would be significantly more work.

The battle between scalability of performance and maintenance is a constant one; the best solution is often dependent on decisions specific to a business. Now that you understand the structure of Channels, we'll move into how data is delivered to and from the client.

PubSub

Phoenix.PubSub (publisher/subscriber) powers topic subscription and message broadcasting in our real-time application. Channels use PubSub internally, so we will rarely interact with it directly. However, it's useful to understand PubSub because we'll need to configure it properly for our application to ensure performance and communication availability.

PubSub is linked between a local node and all connected remote nodes. This allows PubSub to broadcast messages across the entire cluster. Remote message broadcasting is important when we have a situation where a client is connected to node A of our cluster, but a message originates on node B of our cluster. PubSub handles this for us out-of-the-box, but we do need to make sure that the nodes have a way to talk to each other. PubSub ships with a pg2[2] adapter out-of-the-box. There is also a Redis PubSub adapter[3] that allows for using PubSub without having nodes clustered together. We'll see an example of this in Chapter 11, Deploy Your Application to Production, on page 221.

---

2. https://erlang.org/doc/man/pg2.html
3. https://github.com/phoenixframework/phoenix_pubsub_redis

PubSub is used when we call the HelloSocketsWeb.Endpoint.broadcast/3 function. Let's see an example of this and how it can be used to push messages from our application to our Channel. We can do this without changing our application by issuing commands directly in iex. We'll start our server using iex for many examples throughout the book, because it allows us to test our application and see results quickly.

```
$ iex -S mix phx.server
Erlang/OTP 20 [erts-9.3.3.3]

[info] Running HelloSocketsWeb.Endpoint with cowboy 2.6.3 at 0.0.0.0:4000
[info] Access HelloSocketsWeb.Endpoint at http://localhost:4000
Interactive Elixir (1.6.6) - press Ctrl+C to exit
Webpack is watching the files...
```

We start our Phoenix server inside of iex by using the -S switch.

```
$ wscat -c 'ws://localhost:4000/socket/websocket?vsn=2.0.0'
connected (press CTRL+C to quit)
> ["1","1","ping","phx_join",{}]
< ["1","1","ping","phx_reply",{"response":{},"status":"ok"}]
```

We connect to the "ping" Channel so that our message has a destination.

```
iex(1)> HelloSocketsWeb.Endpoint.broadcast("ping", "test", %{data: "test"})
:ok
iex(2)> HelloSocketsWeb.Endpoint.broadcast("other", "x", %{})
:ok
```

We use the broadcast/3 function on our HelloSocketsWeb.Endpoint module. It's important to use the Endpoint that the Socket is configured in, as the PubSub is set up for that specific Endpoint. We dispatch a message to our connected Channel and also to a Channel that we're not connected to.

```
< [null,null,"ping","test",{"data":"test"}]
```

We see our message pushed from the server to our client, and we do not see the message that was sent to the other topic. We'll see in Use Channels in a Cluster, on page 71 how to connect our nodes together locally in order to see that PubSub broadcasts across a cluster. Next, we'll look at how to implement a very important part of our real-time system: sending and receiving messages from a client.

Send and Receive Messages

A real-time system that can't send and receive messages is probably not going to be very useful. We utilize Channel request handlers in order to process

Read Phoenix Source Code

Reading library source code is one of the best ways to understand how a feature works. Phoenix has taken care to be approachable by writing code that follows best practices, such as clear function names, consistent module naming, consistent folder structure, and inline function documentation.

You can get started by visiting the Phoenix repository on Github. Take a look at how Phoenix.Socket routes topics by finding the channel and _before_compile_ macros in lib/phoenix/socket.ex.[a] It relies on Elixir's pattern-matching capabilities, which means that the limitations of pattern matching apply when the topic is converted from a string to pattern-match functions. This causes the inability to have multiple wildcard characters in a pattern match. It is for this reason that the wildcard topic routes have to end with an asterisk.

The topic routing code is both powerful and simple. There are other excellent techniques like this all throughout the Phoenix codebase. Reading them is a great way to learn and grow your Elixir skills.

---

a.   https://github.com/phoenixframework/phoenix/blob/master/lib/phoenix/socket.ex

messages from a client or to send data to the client. This allows us to write handlers which are very similar to an action in a traditional MVC controller.

Before jumping right into sending messages, let's look at the message protocol used to represent every client and server message, to get an idea of what is actually being sent to a client.

Phoenix Message Structure

Phoenix Channels use a simple message protocol to represent all messages to and from a client. The contents of the Message allow clients to keep track of the request and reply flow, which is important because multiple asynchronous requests can be issued to a single Channel. In the following figure you can see the different fields in Phoenix.Message:

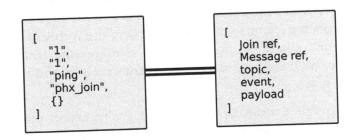

Let's break down each of these fields and their use in the Channel flow:

- Join Ref—A unique string that matches what the client provided when it connected to the Channel. This helps prevent duplicate Channel subscriptions from the client. In practice, this is a number that is incremented each time a Channel is joined.

- Message Ref—A unique string provided by the client on every message. This allows a reply to be sent in response to a client message. In practice, this is a number which is incremented each time a client sends a message.

- Topic—The topic of the Channel.

- Event—A string identifying the message. The Channel implementation can use pattern matching to handle different events easily.

- Payload—A JSON encoded map (string) that contains the data contents of the message. The Channel implementation can use pattern matching on the decoded map to handle different cases for an event.

Some pieces of the message format are optional and can be null depending on the situation. For example, we saw that the ref strings were both null when we used broadcast to send a message to our client. This happens because the information is owned by the client, so the server cannot provide it when pushing data that isn't in reply to an original message.

The official Phoenix Channel clients send a join ref and message ref with every message. The Channel sends the same topic, join ref, and message ref to a client when a successful reply is generated. This allows the client to associate the incoming message to a message that had been sent to the server, causing it to be recognized as a reply. Let's look at how a client issues requests and responses using the Phoenix.Message format.

Receiving Messages from a Client

Receiving requests from a client and being able to send a response is critical to all applications. This lets our users interact with our real-time application without us needing to write additional entry points, such as controller actions. For example, when a client sends a message over the WebSocket connection that powers their Channels, we can avoid also creating traditional HTTP controller code. We'll see how to handle a client's request and then send various response types.

When a client sends a message to a Channel, the transport process receives the message and delegates it to the Socket's handle_in/2 callback. The Socket sends the decoded Message struct to the correct Channel process and handles any errors such as a mismatched topic. The Phoenix.Channel.Server process handles the sent message by delegating to the associated Channel implementation's handle_in/3 callback. This happens transparently to us, meaning that we only need to be concerned with the client sending a message and our Channel's handle_in/3 callback processing the message.

A benefit to this flow being heavily process-based is that the Socket will not block while waiting for the Channel to process the message. This allows us to have many Channels on a single Socket while still maintaining the high performance of our system.

Using Pattern Matching to Craft Powerful Functions

Let's look at a few examples of how we can write our handle_in/3 function to use pattern matching and different return values. We'll modify our PingChannel to respond differently to a ping message if the payload contains certain values. Place this code above the existing handle_in/3 function.

hello_sockets/lib/hello_sockets_web/channels/ping_channel.ex
```
def handle_in("ping", %{"ack_phrase" => ack_phrase}, socket) do
  {:reply, {:ok, %{ping: ack_phrase}}, socket}
end
```

We are leveraging pattern matching on the payload to handle the situation of an "ack_phrase" being provided as a parameter. We will use that phrase if it is present, rather than pong. In order for this to work, the code must be inserted *above* our previous handle_in/3 function, because we pattern matched on any value of the payload previously. Our new function will never execute if it is defined below the old one.

You'll notice that the payload uses strings and not atoms. Atoms are not garbage collected by the BEAM, so Phoenix does not provide user-submitted data as atoms. You can use either atoms or string when creating a response payload.

Let's test our function using wscat.

```
$ wscat -c 'ws://localhost:4000/socket/websocket?vsn=2.0.0'
connected (press CTRL+C to quit)
> ["1","1","ping","phx_join",{}]
< ["1","1","ping","phx_reply",{"response":{},"status":"ok"}]

> ["1","2","ping","ping",{"ack_phrase":"hooray!"}]
< ["1","2","ping","phx_reply",{"response":{"ping":"hooray!"},"status":"ok"}]

> ["1","2","ping","ping",{}]
< ["1","2","ping","phx_reply",{"response":{"ping":"pong"},"status":"ok"}]
```

We can see that providing an ack_phrase parameter works properly for us! Let's use pattern matching on the event name this time.

```
hello_sockets/lib/hello_sockets_web/channels/ping_channel.ex
def handle_in("ping:" <> phrase, _payload, socket) do
  {:reply, {:ok, %{ping: phrase}}, socket}
end
```

```
$ wscat -c 'ws://localhost:4000/socket/websocket?vsn=2.0.0'
connected (press CTRL+C to quit)
> ["1","1","ping","phx_join",{}]
< ["1","1","ping","phx_reply",{"response":{},"status":"ok"}]
> ["1","2","ping","ping:hooray!",{}]
< ["1","2","ping","phx_reply",{"response":{"ping":"hooray!"},"status":"ok"}]
```

This time we are sending an event named "ping:hooray!" and using pattern matching to separate "hooray!" from the rest of the event name. We are then using that value for our acknowledgment phrase rather than pong.

The payload of the message is more flexible than the event name when designing the message handling of a system. It can be used to provide complex payloads (any JSON is valid) with values of types other than string. The event name, on the other hand, must always be a string and cannot represent complex data structures.

Other Response Types

There are other ways that we can handle an incoming event rather than replying to the client. Let's look at two different ways to respond: doing nothing or stopping the Channel.

```
hello_sockets/lib/hello_sockets_web/channels/ping_channel.ex
def handle_in("pong", _payload, socket) do
  # We only handle ping
  {:noreply, socket}
end

def handle_in("ding", _payload, socket) do
  {:stop, :shutdown, {:ok, %{msg: "shutting down"}}, socket}
end
```

Our :noreply response is the simplest here, as we simply do nothing and don't inform the client of a response. The :shutdown message is slightly more complex because we must provide an exit reason and an optional response. We are providing an :ok and map tuple as our response, but we can omit this argument for an equally correct response. The exit reason uses standard GenServer.terminate/2 reasons.[4] You most likely want to use :normal or :shutdown with this feature as it properly closes the Channel with a phx_close event.

Let's test our handle_in function now. Type the following code into your terminal. Remember to enter the lines that start with > in order to send a message to the server.

```
$ wscat -c 'ws://localhost:4000/socket/websocket?vsn=2.0.0'
connected (press CTRL+C to quit)
> ["1","1","ping","phx_join",{}]
< ["1","1","ping","phx_reply",{"response":{},"status":"ok"}]

> ["1","2","ping","pong",{}]

> ["1","2","ping","ding",{}]
< ["1","2","ping","phx_reply",{"response":
    {"msg":"shutting down"},"status":"ok"}]
< ["1","1","ping","phx_close",{}]
```

You've seen how to handle messages sent from the client to the Channel. Next, we're going to switch gears and look at how to send messages from the server to a client.

Pushing Messages to a Client

We have seen an example of how PubSub is used to broadcast from our Endpoint module. We were able to push a message to our connected topic without writing any Channel handler code. This is the default behavior of Channels: any message sent to their topic is broadcast directly to the connected client. We can customize this behavior, however, by intercepting any outgoing messages and deciding how to handle them.

Let's intercept an outgoing ping request and add some additional metadata to the request. We're going to start with a broken implementation to highlight a very common problem when adding a handle_out/3 function.

```
hello_sockets/lib/hello_sockets_web/channels/ping_channel.ex
def handle_out("request_ping", payload, socket) do
  push(socket, "send_ping", Map.put(payload, "from_node", Node.self()))
  {:noreply, socket}
end
```

We are going to handle the "request_ping" event by appending the current Node information and then pushing the augmented data to the client. We're also going to change the event name to show that it doesn't matter if we push the same data that came into our function. When we run this, however, we see a warning.

---

4. https://hexdocs.pm/elixir/GenServer.html#c:terminate/2

```
$ iex -S mix phx.server
Erlang/OTP 20 [erts-9.3.3.3]

Compiling 2 files (.ex)
lib/hello_sockets_web/channels/ping_channel.ex:44: [warning] An intercept
for event "request_ping" has not yet been defined in Elixir.HelloSockets
Web.PingChannel.handle_out/3. Add "request_ping" to your list of intercepted
events with intercept/1[info] Running HelloSocketsWeb.Endpoint with
cowboy 2.6.3 at 0.0.0.0:4000 (http)
[info] Access HelloSocketsWeb.Endpoint at http://localhost:4000
```

Our server is able to start but our broadcast event will *not* be augmented as
we want it to be. This is because we have not told our Channel that it needs
to intercept and handle this particular event. We encounter a helpful warning,
but it would be easy to miss it. Make sure to check for warnings each time
you start your server! Let's fix this by adding our intercept. You can add the
following line of code anywhere in the module's body, but it usually goes below
the use Phoenix.Channel line.

hello_sockets/lib/hello_sockets_web/channels/ping_channel.ex
```
intercept ["request_ping"]
```

This code must go above our handle_out/3 function, preferably at the top of our
source file, or you will still see the warning. We can now see that our event
is intercepted and augmented when we broadcast it using iex.

In the next example, run the broadcast function after you've joined the Channel
with wscat.

```
$ iex -S mix phx.server
iex(1)> HelloSocketsWeb.Endpoint.broadcast("ping", "request_ping", %{})
:ok

$ wscat -c 'ws://localhost:4000/socket/websocket?vsn=2.0.0'
connected (press CTRL+C to quit)
> ["1","1","ping","phx_join",{}]
< ["1","1","ping","phx_reply",{"response":{},"status":"ok"}]
< [null,null,"ping","send_ping",{"from_node":"nonode@nohost"}]
```

It is best practice to not write an intercepted event if you do not need to customize the payload, because each pushed message will be encoded by itself,
up to once per subscribed Channel, instead of a single push to all subscribed
Channels. This will decrease performance in a system with a lot of subscribers.

So far we've been using wscat to interact with our Channels. This is great for
our testing but is not useful for our users. We'll improve this by connecting
a JavaScript client to our server in the next section.

> ### Intercepting Events for Metrics
>
> While it is best practice to not intercept events that are not changed, because of the decreased performance, it can be useful for tasks such as collecting metrics about every push. You would still incur the interception penalty discussed in this section, but the benefit of metrics outweighs that.
>
> In PushEx,[a] an implementation of Channels for pushing data to clients, I use interception to capture a delivery metric for every message to every client. Capturing messages at this level allows me to keep track of the number of milliseconds that a message stays in the system for each connected client. The system must keep this metric low to ensure that users are getting their data as quickly as possible.
>
> ---
>
> a.   https://hex.pm/packages/push_ex

Channel Clients

Any networked device can be used to connect to Channels. Languages that have a WebSocket or HTTP client (for long polling) are easiest to get started with. There are official and unofficial clients that work out-of-the-box with Channels, and these clients can certainly make the task easier for us. A list of client libraries[5] is maintained in the Phoenix Channel documentation. It's a good idea to look at this list if you are getting started with a project in a language other than JavaScript, since writing a client from scratch is a decently large endeavor.

In this section, we'll be looking at the official Phoenix Channel client. We'll use JavaScript in our browsers to interact with our Channels. We'll be able to send and receive messages from the server while handling different errors that may occur. We'll see how the JavaScript client reacts when it disconnects so we can ensure our applications are always available to users.

Official JavaScript Client

The official client, worked on by the Phoenix core team, is written in JavaScript. This can be used for web applications, web extensions, React Native applications, or in any JavaScript interpreter that supports WebSocket or long polling. We'll be using this client for the major project later in the book.

Any Channel client has a few key responsibilities that should be followed, in order for all behavior to work as expected:

---

5.   https://hexdocs.pm/phoenix/channels.html#client-libraries

- Connect to the server and maintain the connection by using a heartbeat.
- Join the requested topics.
- Push messages to a topic and optionally handle responses.
- Receive messages from a topic.
- Handle disconnection and other errors gracefully; try to maintain a connection whenever possible.

We'll cover how the JavaScript client satisfies each of these responsibilities. The JavaScript client has a clean API which will feel very familiar if you have used promise-based libraries. We will cover a small, but critical, part of the client API in this chapter—covering the whole library would not be beneficial at this point. You can read the official documentation[6] to see all available functions and options.

Sending Messages with the JavaScript Client

Let's connect to the PingChannel that we built earlier in the chapter. We'll push a "ping" event and receive a reply from the server, which we will process in the web page.

hello_sockets/assets/js/app.js
```
// Import local files
//
// Local files can be imported directly using relative paths, for example:
import socket from "./socket"
```

You may have already done this step if you worked the examples in the previous chapters. We must add an import line to use our JavaScript socket file. Ensure that your socket.js file looks like the following code snippet—you may have to delete some of the boilerplate JavaScript that Phoenix initializes in a new project.

hello_sockets/assets/js/socket.js
```
import { Socket } from "phoenix"

const socket = new Socket("/socket", {})

socket.connect()

export default socket
```

We initialize our Socket with the URL that is present in our Endpoint module. It is "/socket" in this case, but it could be different based on how the Socket is configured on the server. We then connect the Socket and export it for use in other JavaScript files. The export is optional, as we will be working exclusively in socket.js for these examples.

---

6. https://hexdocs.pm/phoenix/js/index.html

```
hello_sockets/assets/js/socket.js
const channel = socket.channel("ping")

channel.join()
  .receive("ok", (resp) => { console.log("Joined ping", resp) })
  .receive("error", (resp) => { console.log("Unable to join ping", resp) })
```

Connecting to our Channel requires specifying the topic that we want to connect to. We invoke socket.channel once per topic we want to connect to. The JavaScript client will prevent us from connecting to the same topic multiple times on one Socket connection, which prevents us from being in a situation where we receive duplicate messages.

Start the application server using iex -S mix phx.server and then open the web page at http://localhost:4000. You will see a message in your developer console that indicates we joined the ping topic. Let's send a message and receive a reply back. We're using iex to start the server, so that we can broadcast messages. Add the following code to the bottom of socket.js:

```
hello_sockets/assets/js/socket.js
console.log("send ping")
channel.push("ping")
  .receive("ok", (resp) => console.log("receive", resp.ping))
```

We are sending a "ping" event with an empty payload (we have omitted a second argument). This is sent to the server with a unique message reference that allows for a reply to be received. We receive and process the reply by receiving "ok" from the client.

You can now refresh the page (it may have auto-refreshed due to development live reload) and see in the developer console that we are sending a ping and receiving a pong reply from the server. You may notice something odd though:

```
> send ping
> Joined ping {}
> receive pong
```

We are logging that the ping is sent before our joined reply comes in. This highlights an important aspect of the JavaScript client: if the client hasn't connected to the Channel yet, the message will be buffered in memory and sent as soon as the Channel is connected. It is stored in a short-lived (5-second) buffer so that it doesn't immediately fail. This behavior is useful if our Channel ever becomes disconnected due to a client network problem, because several seconds of reconnection are available before the message is handled as an error.

If you only want to send a message when the topic is connected, it is possible to do so. In that case you would move the push function inside of the join "ok" handler callback.

Sometimes messages are not handled correctly by the server. For instance, it could be under heavy load or we could have a coding bug in our Channel handlers. For this reason, it's a best practice to have error and timeout handlers whenever a message is sent to our Channel.

```
hello_sockets/assets/js/socket.js
console.log("send pong")
channel.push("pong")
  .receive("ok", (resp) => console.log("won't happen"))
  .receive("error", (resp) => console.error("won't happen yet"))
  .receive("timeout", (resp) => console.error("pong message timeout", resp))
```

Our PingChannel handles "pong" messages with a :noreply return value, which means that there is no reply to receive from the Channel and our "ok" handler will never run. After 10 seconds (this is configurable), we receive a "timeout" event from the client. You will see this when you refresh the page.

Let's add a new PingChannel handle_in/3 callback for when a payload is sent to the Channel. We'll use this to have the server respond with an error or a response containing the payload.

```
hello_sockets/lib/hello_sockets_web/channels/ping_channel.ex
def handle_in("param_ping", %{"error" => true}, socket) do
  {:reply, {:error, %{reason: "You asked for this!"}}, socket}
end

def handle_in("param_ping", payload, socket) do
  {:reply, {:ok, payload}, socket}
end
```

If our received payload contains an error: true pair, then we will respond with an error message back to the client. Otherwise the sent payload will be returned to the client.

```
hello_sockets/assets/js/socket.js
channel.push("param_ping", { error: true })
  .receive("error", (resp) => console.error("param_ping error:", resp))
channel.push("param_ping", { error: false, arr: [1, 2] })
  .receive("ok", (resp) => console.log("param_ping ok:", resp))
```

A payload is sent as the second parameter to push. This payload can be any JSON compatible object. Errors are handled via the "error" event similarly to the "ok" event.

Start your server with mix phx.server and load http://localhost:4000. You will see our caught error in the developer console as well as a successful response log which contains our sent payload.

These functions and handlers form the foundation of sending messages and handling replies with the JavaScript client. Next we'll see how to receive messages sent from the server that are not in reply to a client message.

Receiving Messages with the JavaScript Client

A Channel can send messages to a connected client at any time, not just in response to an incoming message. We coded this earlier in our PingChannel with handle_out/3. We'll leverage this message to request that the connected client sends us a ping.

```
hello_sockets/assets/js/socket.js
channel.on("send_ping", (payload) => {
  console.log("ping requested", payload)
  channel.push("ping")
    .receive("ok", (resp) => console.log("ping:", resp.ping))
})
```

The on callback of our client channel is used to register incoming message subscriptions. The first argument is the string name of the event that we want to handle; this requires us to know the exact event name for incoming messages. For this reason, it is a good idea to not use dynamic event names. You can instead place dynamic information in the message payload.

```
$ iex -S mix phx.server
iex(1)> HelloSocketsWeb.Endpoint.broadcast("ping", "request_ping", %{})
:ok
```

As we did earlier, we are using the broadcast/3 function to request a ping from our Channel. This will cause a message to be pushed to all connected clients on the "ping" topic. Our handle_out function changes the original request_ping payload into a different message. You can see the final result in the developer console.

```
> ping requested {from_node: "nonode@nohost"}
> ping: pong
```

Try loading multiple instances of the web page and broadcasting again. You will see that every connected client receives the broadcast. This makes broadcasting a very powerful way to send data to all connected clients. Replies, on the other hand, will only be sent to the client that sent the message.

JavaScript Client Fault Tolerance and Error Handling

It's a fact of software that errors and disconnections will occur. We can best prepare our application for these inevitable problems by handling caught errors ourselves and by ensuring that our client handles unexpected errors.

One of the great features of the Phoenix JavaScript client is that it tries very hard to stay connected. When the underlying connection becomes disconnected, the client will automatically attempt reconnection until it's successful. Reconnection is fairly aggressive, which is often exactly what we want, although we can customize it to be more or less aggressive based on our application's needs.

Let's see an example of Socket reconnection by forcing a connection error. Open the "Network" tab on our web page and view the "WebSocket" tab to see our WebSocket connection; you may need to refresh in order to see the old connection. We're going to stop our web server to force a connection problem. You can stop the server by using ctrl + c -> a in the iex session. You will immediately see connection attempts in the "Network" tab of our web page. The developer console will also begin logging errors stating the connection could not be established.

You will see that the connection becomes established within 10 seconds once you start the server again.

```
> // The server is stopped
> WS connection to 'ws://localhost:4000/socket/websocket?vsn=2.0.0' failed
> WS connection to 'ws://localhost:4000/socket/websocket?vsn=2.0.0' failed
> WS connection to 'ws://localhost:4000/socket/websocket?vsn=2.0.0' failed
> // The server is started
> Joined ping {}
```

In addition to Socket reconnection, the underlying Channel subscriptions try to maximize time spent connected. We saw in the previous example that the ping Channel became reconnected when the Socket did. The Channel may become disconnected for other reasons as well, such as when an application error occurs.

We're going to trigger an application error by sending a message to our PingChannel that it doesn't know how to handle. This is not considered a caught exception and our Channel crashes due to it.

hello_sockets/assets/js/socket.js
```
channel.push("invalid")
  .receive("ok", (resp) => console.log("won't happen"))
  .receive("error", (resp) => console.error("won't happen"))
  .receive("timeout", (resp) => console.error("invalid event timeout"))
```

When you refresh the page, you will not see an error message in the developer console. You will, however, see an error in the Elixir server shell. Our PingChannel crashed when it encountered the unknown event, causing the Process to die. The JavaScript client knows the Channel crashed, because it's sent a "phx_error" event, and immediately attempts to reconnect. It's able to establish the Channel again because our problem only occurs when we sent an incorrect message.

Our "error" callback does *not* execute despite the error occurring. This is because the error callback only runs for caught application errors and not for this unexpected error. We will instead see a timeout occur because our message is considered to not have received a reply.

We are now equipped to write JavaScript clients to connect to our real-time application. The real-time capabilities of Channels combined with the stability and simple interface of the JavaScript client gives us a solid foundation for our real-world project in part II.

Wrapping Up

Phoenix Channels are a very powerful abstraction that allows development of real-time applications in Elixir. Channels allow us to write applications that succeed across several scalability considerations: performance, maintenance, and cost. Elixir and OTP are perfectly suited for modeling real-time systems, and the Transport-Channel-PubSub layering of Phoenix Channels allows us to take advantage of a strongly designed OTP foundation.

Channels allow our applications to receive and send messages to users with soft real-time constraints. Our Channel code leverages handle_in and handle_out callback functions to process our user's messages and interact with our application core. The Phoenix Message structure allows our applications to handle message replies and prevent duplicate Channel subscriptions. This simple but powerful design means we can build our applications with more confidence.

The official Phoenix JavaScript client makes connecting to Channels with both WebSockets and long polling simple. The hard work of staying connected to the server is handled for us in a way that allows us to focus on application development rather than real-time communication layer development.

We'll be moving into more advanced Channel concepts next. These concepts will help elevate our knowledge from the basics of Channels into something that will allow us to start building complex application flows with ease. We'll be learning how to secure our Channels so that users do not receive messages intended for other users, all while maintaining the simplicity of Channels and seeing several patterns for how to customize the behavior of Channels.

## CHAPTER 4

Restrict Socket and Channel Access

In the last chapter, we explored the basics of real-time applications powered by Channels, which let you build simple real-time applications. However, there's still more you need to know to build full-featured applications. In this chapter, we're going to cover adding access restriction to Sockets and Channels.

We'll start this chapter by examining how to restrict access to Channels and Sockets, to ensure that data is provided only to the right users. We'll use a Phoenix.Token to pass authentication information from the server to the view, and then will use that to add Channel access restriction to the JavaScript client. You'll learn when to use a single Socket or multiple Sockets in your applications, based on the restriction needs of your system.

Let's jump into what access restriction is and why it's crucial to add to your applications.

Why Restrict Access?

It has been a common occurrence to hear about data leaks from improperly secured data or endpoints. This type of security issue can hit any application, including ones based on Phoenix Channels. Luckily, there is a built-in mechanism to close these security vulnerabilities.

There are two different types of access restriction that we'll focus on. The first type of restriction, authentication, prevents non-users from accessing your application. If someone malicious is able to discover your Socket connection URL and then successfully connect, they may be able to access more of your system. The second type of restriction, authorization, prevents users from accessing each other's data. If your application exposed information about a particular user, even non-sensitive information, you would want only that specific user to see it.

We can use authentication and authorization to solve the problem of access restriction. When you want to prevent non-users from connecting to your application, you add authentication to the Socket. When you want to restrict access to user data, you add authorization to the Channel and topic. We'll use Socket authentication in part II when we add an administrator portal, and we'll use Channel authorization when allowing a shopper to join a "cart:{userId}" Channel. The combination of restricting access to both Sockets and Channels gives you the most restrictive and secure application.

Phoenix provides two different entry points where you can add access restriction. Socket authentication is handled in the Socket.connect/3 function and Channel authorization is handled in the Channel.join/3 function. Let's look at each and consider when we might want to use one over the other. You'll use both types of restriction to fully secure your real-time application.

Add Authentication to Sockets

You can use Socket authentication when you want to restrict a client's access to a real-time connection. This is useful in situations where you don't want certain clients to access your application. For example, you would add authentication code to a Socket when user login is required to access the application, because the default Socket does not know that your application requires login. When you add authentication checks at the very edge of your application, in the Socket, you're able to avoid writing code that checks if there is a logged in user lower in the system. This improves your system's maintainability because your user session check exists in a single location.

Phoenix calls a Socket module's connect/3 callback when a new client connects. We add our authentication code at this point and either accept or reject access to the connection. A Socket's connect/3 callback function returns the tuple {:ok, socket} when the connection is allowed, or :error when the connection is rejected.

The connect/3 callback is also used to store data for the life of the connection. You can store any data you want in the Socket.assigns state. In our example of user login, we would store the authenticated user's ID. This allows us to know which user the connection is for in our Channel code without reauthenticating the user. The Channel authorization examples in the next section will use Socket state.

You can add Socket authentication to your application by using a securely signed token.

Securing a Socket with Signed Tokens

WebSockets lack CORS (cross-origin resource sharing) restrictions that are used by other types of web requests. The biggest vulnerability that this exposes is a cross-site request forgery (CSRF) attack. In a CSRF attack, a different website controlled by the attacker initiates a request to your application. The attacker may be able to use this connection as if they were the user, receiving private data about the user or making changes to the user's data.

There are strategies for avoiding this type of attack vector. One is to check the origin of all connection requests—your application should only allow connections from domains that it knows about. A different strategy is to include a CSRF token that proves that the user visited the application in the proper way.

The strategy that we'll use in this book is to not use cookies when authenticating our WebSocket. Instead, we'll use a signed token to provide a user session to our Socket. Our front-end client will pass a securely signed token in the connection parameters upon connection to a Socket. Our application will then verify that the token originated from one of its servers and that the token was generated within a given period of time.

We will code a Socket authentication example by laying out the skeleton of our Socket and then implementing the authentication logic. First, let's add our new Socket to our Endpoint. Enter this code after the existing socket/3 function call:

```
hello_sockets/lib/hello_sockets_web/endpoint.ex
socket "/auth_socket", HelloSocketsWeb.AuthSocket,
  websocket: true,
  longpoll: false
```

The Endpoint module contains the definition of our application's web interface. We added our socket definition here, so the necessary WebSocket endpoints will be defined.

Next, create the AuthSocket module. You do not need to change the existing UserSocket when you add this module.

```
hello_sockets/lib/hello_sockets_web/channels/auth_socket.ex
defmodule HelloSocketsWeb.AuthSocket do
  use Phoenix.Socket
  require Logger

  channel "ping", HelloSocketsWeb.PingChannel
  channel "tracked", HelloSocketsWeb.TrackedChannel
```

```elixir
  def connect(%{"token" => token}, socket) do
    case verify(socket, token) do
      {:ok, user_id} ->
        socket = assign(socket, :user_id, user_id)
        {:ok, socket}

      {:error, err} ->
        Logger.error("#{__MODULE__} connect error #{inspect(err)}")
        :error
    end
  end

  def connect(_, _socket) do
    Logger.error("#{__MODULE__} connect error missing params")
    :error
  end
end
```

Our AuthSocket is a pretty typical skeleton of a Socket. We are using our existing PingChannel to demonstrate that for the associated Channel to work, it doesn't need to know about the Socket's validation. (We've changed nothing about PingChannel and it will work for our example.) We haven't defined our verify/2 function yet, but you can see by the case statement that it will turn our token string into a tuple indicating that the user's session is valid or that there was an error with the token.

It's a good practice to always log when a Socket or Channel connection error happens. There may be a bug somewhere in the system, and knowing if a client cannot connect is great for debugging.

hello_sockets/lib/hello_sockets_web/channels/auth_socket.ex
```elixir
@one_day 86400

defp verify(socket, token),
  do:
    Phoenix.Token.verify(
      socket,
      "salt identifier",
      token,
      max_age: @one_day
    )
```

We use Phoenix.Token.verify/4 to verify our secret token. The "salt identifier" string provides additional cryptographic protection for the token. This value can be anything as long as it remains the same between the token being signed and verified. You can generate a random string and either write it directly into your code or through a Mix.Config value. You can use the same salt for all users—it acts like a namespace for the token and is not a per-user salt.

Phoenix.Token uses a separate secret key to sign all data. This key, called secret_key_base, is automatically extracted from our socket, but it could be provided through other means as well. This secret key should always be unique for your application and should be securely stored in production environments, possibly in an environment variable. You should *not* store your production secret_key_base value in source control. Anyone that has this secret can generate a valid token that could be used to access your system. Protect it! You can provide this value in a system environment variable that is stored in a secure location, separate from an application's source code.

hello_sockets/config/config.exs
```
secret_key_base: "generate this with mix phx.gen.secret",
```

The secret is present in the Endpoint configuration and can be generated with a helpful CLI generator.

```
$ mix phx.gen.secret
dwP08dxRJnVuGM1oxi7Sbo2+v7drAyxJ/+7vnsuIUbOsc4k2Ea15zd7s6mHlayZl
```

Phoenix.Token signs messages to prevent tampering but it does *not* encrypt data. It's important to prevent tampering so a malicious client cannot grant itself access to the system that it would not normally have. You can keep information that a user can see, such as an ID, in the signed message. However, you should not keep anything sensitive in the signed message, such as a password or personally identifying information, because this data can be read by anyone who has access to the user's client.

The final step for AuthSocket is to define an identifier for the Socket. This is completely optional; we could return nil, but it is a best practice to identify a Socket when it's for a particular user. We can do things like disconnecting a specific user or use the Socket identifier in other parts of the system. Let's add an Id/1 function to AuthSocket now.

hello_sockets/lib/hello_sockets_web/channels/auth_socket.ex
```
def id(%{assigns: %{user_id: user_id}}),
  do: "auth_socket:#{user_id}"
```

We now have an AuthSocket that requires a signed token to connect to it. Let's try connecting to it without a token, with an invalid token, and with a valid token. Start the server with iex -S mix phx.server to get started.

Let's first connect to the socket without a token.

```
$ wscat -c 'ws://localhost:4000/auth_socket/websocket?vsn=2.0.0'
error: Unexpected server response: 403
```

You will see in your server logs a connect error with the message "connect error missing params". This lines up with our connect/2 function clause for when there is no "token" parameter present. Now, let's add in a fake token value.

```
$ wscat -c 'ws://localhost:4000/auth_socket/websocket?vsn=2.0.0&token=x'
error: Unexpected server response: 403
```

Our client still receives an invalid connection, but our error log now says "connect error :invalid". Phoenix.Token.verify/4 is being called and is now returning that our token is not valid. Let's fix that by generating a real token and connecting.

```
iex(3)> Phoenix.Token.sign(HelloSocketsWeb.Endpoint, "salt identifier", 1)
"SFMyNTY.g3QAAAACZA...vlHU0EM0FZFo3O_QiM"
```

Our first step is to generate a valid token for ID 1. We use Phoenix.Token.sign/3 to do so. The function signature is very similar to verify/4 in our AuthSocket except that we are providing the data and Endpoint. We can take this token and copy it into our connection URL to see a successful connection.

```
$ wscat -c 'ws://localhost:4000/auth_socket/websocket?vsn=2.0.0&token=SF..iM'
connected (press CTRL+C to quit)
> ["1","1","ping","phx_join",{}]
< ["1","1","ping","phx_reply",{"response":{},"status":"ok"}]

> ["1","2","ping","ping",{}]
< ["1","2","ping","phx_reply",{"response":{"ping":"pong"},"status":"ok"}]
```

Use the generated token to connect to the Socket and you'll now see a successful connection! You have connected to the PingChannel and can send messages to it like we can with our non-authenticated Socket. The Socket authentication we added hasn't affected our Channel in any way.

We used Phoenix.Token in this example, but you can use any secure format you want. Next, we'll discuss an alternative to Phoenix.Token and when you may want to use it.

Different Types of Tokens

Phoenix.Token provides a great way to integrate authentication into an Elixir application, but it is an Elixir-specific solution. Sometimes we need a cross-language solution to tokens. For example, we may need a solution where the message contents can be used from JavaScript, to view the contents and expiration independent of the server, or we could need to generate a token in a microservice that uses Ruby (or any other language) in order to allow access to our real-time application.

Alternatives to Phoenix.Token can help us in these situations. A very common web standard for authentication is the JSON Web Token (JWT).[1] JWTs are cryptographically secure but not encrypted (an encrypted variant called JWE does exist), so they meet the same security standard as Phoenix.Token. One large difference, however, is that JWT is a standardized format that can be consumed easily in nearly any language, including the front-end client. You can use this in your client code to detect if a JWT has expired before the credential is sent to the server. You'll have to do a bit more work to use JWTs as compared to Phoenix.Token because JWT support is not included out-of-the-box with Phoenix. JWTs are not a proper replacement for cookie-based authentication. They should only be used to pass a user session between different parts of an application.

Joken[2] is my go-to library for handling JWTs in Elixir. I use it in all my Elixir projects and highly recommend it. We'll use Phoenix.Token in this book as it is already included and set up for our project. However, consider looking into JWT if you need a cross-language solution or if you need strongly secured tokens through standards such as RSA encryption.

Whether you're using Phoenix Tokens, JWT, or another technology, it's important to set the token's expiration to a low-enough value. A token is the user's way to get into your system, and a user has access for the duration of the token. Pick a token duration that is long enough to be convenient, but short enough to provide security for your users—I usually default to 10 minutes. There are techniques that can invalidate tokens before they're expired, such as token blocklists, but we won't cover them in this book.

Socket authentication provides a nice layer of security, but it doesn't cover everything. It is also important to secure private topics at the Channel level.

Add Authorization to Channels

Socket authentication is not always enough to fully secure our applications. For example, we could have a Socket that stores the authenticated user ID in Socket state and allows a connection to occur. When a client attempts to join "user:1" Channel, but they are user ID 2, we should reject the Channel join request. The client should only have access to topics that are relevant to them. We can do that with Channel authorization.

---

1.   https://jwt.io/introduction
2.   https://github.com/joken-elixir/joken

When a client joins a Channel, the Channel's join/3 function is invoked. You can add authorization to your Channel by making this function check for a valid token. There are two options for how to add Channel authorization:

- Parameter based—Parameters can optionally be sent when a Channel topic is joined. The client's authentication token is sent via these parameters and the Channel can authorize the topic using the data encoded into the token.

- Socket state based—You can store information about the current connection, such as the connected user's ID or token, when a Socket connection occurs. This state becomes available in Socket.assigns and can be used in your Channel's join/3 function. You fully control the state at this point, so it is trusted.

There are advantages to the Socket state-based approach that make it the best choice most of the time. You can secure your application by passing a single token to the Server on Socket connection, rather than passing the token on every Channel join. This makes it much easier to write the code powering your authorization.

We'll use Socket state-based authorization in the next examples. Let's start by looking at how to secure a topic based on the topic's name matching the provided user ID.

hello_sockets/lib/hello_sockets_web/channels/auth_socket.ex
```
channel "user:*", HelloSocketsWeb.AuthChannel
```

We use our previously written AuthSocket, but extend it by adding a new Channel route for "user:*" topics. You can use any topic name in a Socket—we're using "user:*" here to make it clear that the authorization is for users.

Now we can build our AuthChannel to correspond with this. Let's start with an example where the user ID information is stored in Socket state and is not provided by the client's join parameters.

hello_sockets/lib/hello_sockets_web/channels/auth_channel.ex
```
defmodule HelloSocketsWeb.AuthChannel do
  use Phoenix.Channel

  require Logger

  def join(
        "user:" <> req_user_id,
        _payload,
        socket = %{assigns: %{user_id: user_id}}
      ) do
```

```
    if req_user_id == to_string(user_id) do
      {:ok, socket}
    else
      Logger.error("#{__MODULE__} failed #{req_user_id} != #{user_id}")
      {:error, %{reason: "unauthorized"}}
    end
  end
end
```

Our join/3 function is set up to match on topics that look like "user:*". Everything after the : is extracted into a string variable, the requested user ID. We use the assigns property of the Socket to retrieve the user_id that was provided by the token that we connected with. We make the decision of whether the join is allowed or not by comparing the requested user ID with our authenticated user ID. The req_user_id variable is a string, so we convert the numeric user_id variable to a string when we do our comparison.

Let's manually test our Channel code by trying an incorrect and then a correct join. Use the same command we used previously to generate a Phoenix.Token. Make sure that the provided data is 1 in order to line up with the example.

```
iex(3)> Phoenix.Token.sign(HelloSocketsWeb.Endpoint, "salt identifier", 1)
"SFMyNTY.g3QAAAACZA...vlHU0EM0FZFo3O_QiM"
```

Provide this token to the connection and then connect to the private user topics.

```
$ wscat -c 'ws://localhost:4000/auth_socket/websocket?vsn=2.0.0&token=SF..iM'
connected (press CTRL+C to quit)
> ["1","1","user:2","phx_join",{}]
< ["1","1","user:2","phx_reply",{"response":
  {"reason":"unauthorized"},"status":"error"}]

> ["1","1","user:1","phx_join",{}]
< ["1","1","user:1","phx_reply",{"response":{},"status":"ok"}]
```

Once connected, you will receive a reason of unauthorized when you try to join the "user:2" topic. You are able, however, to join the "user:1" topic that corresponds to your signed token ID. Try generating your signed request with user ID 2 to see the "user:2" topic work.

The client subscription message to the Channel did not involve using the token in any way. The token's information was previously exchanged and kept in the Socket's state, which is then passed into the Channel. This allows our client code to be much simpler, as the token is only used for connection and then discarded. This is completely safe because the Socket's state is set by our application in a trusted way; it can't be tampered with by a client.

We used Socket state authorization in this example. You are able to use parameter-based authorization by passing the token parameter when the Channel is joined, then using that token in the Channel join function. In practice, it is more cumbersome to send an authorization token with each topic join. Check to see if your problem fits a Socket authorization model before doing token verification in your join/3 function.

Next, let's connect our JavaScript client to our authenticated Socket and Channel.

Use Authentication from JavaScript

Clients that connect to our secured Socket must be able to pass the authentication parameters on connection. Phoenix's JavaScript client provides a simple way to add the right authentication parameters.

We wrote an AuthSocket that accepts a "token" parameter and verifies it using a known secret. We'll complete the client side of this flow by including the token with the socket connection. This task boils down to a few key parts:

- Controller—generate a token when our page loads and write it into the page's JavaScript

- JavaScript—send the token parameter with the Socket connection

- Socket—use the token in our Socket

We'll generate an authentication token in the Controller that renders our page view. We've worked entirely in the default generated files so far, meaning we haven't even looked at the Controller yet, but our change will not be very complex. Replace the existing index/2 function with the following code:

```
hello_sockets/lib/hello_sockets_web/controllers/page_controller.ex
def index(conn, _params) do
  fake_user_id = 1

  conn
  |> assign(:auth_token, generate_auth_token(conn, fake_user_id))
  |> assign(:user_id, fake_user_id)
  |> render("index.html")
end

defp generate_auth_token(conn, user_id) do
  Phoenix.Token.sign(conn, "salt identifier", user_id)
end
```

A token is generated in every request and assigned to the conn before rendering. The token is generated with Phoenix.Token.sign/3. Let's use this assigned variable in the template. Place this next script at the top of the template file.

hello_sockets/lib/hello_sockets_web/templates/page/index.html.eex

```
<script>
  window.authToken = "<%= assigns[:auth_token] %>";
  window.userId = "<%= assigns[:user_id] %>";
</script>
```

We placed the assigned variable auth_token in a JavaScript window variable in our specific page view. But it could be placed in a layout so every loaded page had access to it. It would be good practice, if every page required it, to place the token generation in a Plug that is placed in the pipeline for every request.

hello_sockets/assets/js/socket.js

```
const authSocket = new Socket("/auth_socket", {
  params: { token: window.authToken }
})

authSocket.onOpen(() => console.log('authSocket connected'))
authSocket.connect()
```

We complete our example by passing authentication params into our new authSocket. We leverage the onOpen callback of the client Socket in order to know that we successfully established the Socket connection. You will see the successful connection when you refresh the web page.

Great! You have a secured Socket connection through your web page! Adding authentication and authorization is a very simple way to ensure that the wrong party doesn't get access to your application. If you do find yourself wanting to add topic-level authentication (where the token is provided with the topic join request), it's possible to add a params argument that contains the token to socket.channel(channel, params).

Let's look at when to write a new Socket versus using a new Channel.

When to Write a New Socket

We've written two Sockets so far, UserSocket and AuthSocket, and we wrote Channels for each of them. This raises the question of when we should create a new Socket versus using the same topic and adding a new Channel. You'll make this decision based primarily on the authentication needs of your application. There are also performance costs to adding new Sockets; let's look at these costs first.

Each connected Socket adds one connection to the server, but each connected Channel adds zero new connections to the server. Channels do take up a slight amount of memory and CPU because there is a process associated with each, but you can consider Channels nearly free because processes are cheap in Elixir. Sockets are a bit more expensive due to network connections and the heartbeat process.

Each Socket must maintain a heartbeat to the server. If four Channels are open on a single Socket connection, that means that there is one heartbeat process occurring:

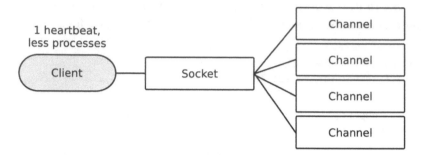

If four Channels are open on four socket connections, then there are four heartbeat processes occurring over the four connections:

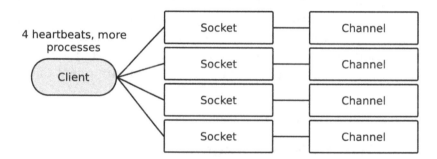

The heartbeat and additional connections mean that the cost of many idle Channels is less than the cost of many idle Sockets.

While there are some performance differences, you should primarily consider the authentication needs of your application when deciding whether to add a new Socket or use an existing one when adding a new Channel topic. When you are writing a system that has separate real-time features or pages for users and admins, you would add a new Socket. This is because users would not have the ability to connect to admin-specific features and so should be rejected from connecting to the Socket. Separating the Socket authentication like this leads to simpler code further down in the system. You would add to an existing Socket when the authentication needs are the same.

As a general rule of thumb, use multiple Channels with a single Socket. Use multiple Sockets if your application has different authentication needs between different parts of the application. This approach leads to a system architecture with the lowest resource usage.

Wrapping Up

It is necessary to restrict access to Sockets and Channels in order to keep your application safe. There are two different ways to secure the Channels of your application—either by authenticating when a client connects to a Socket or when a client joins a Channel. Socket authentication is useful when the client should have no access at all to the part of the application served by the Socket. Use Channel authorization to keep user-specific data safe from the incorrect user.

Phoenix provides ways to add access restriction out-of-the-box by using a signed Phoenix.Token. A signed token gives the Socket and Channel a way to know which user is connecting and whether they are properly authenticated. There are other options for adding authentication, such as JWTs, that can be used to implement different types of authentication requirements.

Access restriction significantly informs the creation of a new Socket or Channel. If you're adding a new real-time feature and it has different access requirements, such as the user needing to be an admin, then reach for a new Socket. If you're adding a new feature that is tied to an existing access requirement, then a new Channel is probably best.

We've been progressing into more advanced Channels concepts throughout the last few chapters. We'll dive a bit deeper in the next chapter and cover Channel concepts that are important when building production applications. You'll implement custom Channel behavior, design for unreliable client connections, configure Channels to run in a cluster of servers, and write tests for Sockets and Channels.

## CHAPTER 5

Dive Deep into Phoenix Channels

In the last chapter, you learned how to restrict access to a Channel-based application using authentication. We've covered enough to build basic Channel applications, but there's still more you need to know to build full-featured Channel applications. In this chapter, we're going to look at concepts such as Channels in a cluster of servers, how to customize Channel behavior, and how to write tests for Channels.

We'll first cover the unreliable nature of internet connections and consider how we can build applications that survive the strange things that can happen with real users. Flaky internet connections, bugs in an application, and server restarts can all lead to connection trouble for users.

You'll then learn about different challenges that come up when using Channels with multiple servers. You'll see different patterns that can be used to customize the behavior of Channels. These patterns enable us to build more complex flows when we have complex application requirements. We'll finish off this chapter by writing tests for our Socket and Channel code. Let's jump into the challenges of unreliable connections now.

Design for Unreliable Connections

Clients connect to our real-time application using a long-lived connection. The client's connection can close or fail at any point; we need to consider this and write code to recover from this when it happens.

There are certainly expected reasons for a connection to disconnect, such as a user leaving the application, changing pages, or closing their laptop while the application is loaded. There are also more unpredictable reasons that cause a connection to (erroneously) disconnect. A few examples of this are:

- A client's internet connection becomes unstable and drops their connection without any other changes.

- A bug in the client code causes it to close the connection.

- The server restarts due to a routine deploy or operational issue.

These are just some of the things that can go wrong in our application. Some of these disconnection reasons are preventable, but some are the result of the unreliable nature of internet connections. Users expect that an application will continue to work in an intuitive way, even when an interruption of some sort occurs. An example of this is that an application could remain in a usable state even if the connected user's network connection is poor. There is a limit to this, however, as you can't make an internet application work when there is no internet connection available.

We'll cover different aspects of reliability in this section. First, we'll look at how Channels manage their subscriptions throughout disconnection events. We'll then look at different techniques to avoid losing critical data when a client disconnects. Finally, we'll cover Phoenix's message-delivery guarantees. Let's jump into Channel subscription management now.

Channel Subscriptions

In Channels, on page 31, we covered how clients subscribe to topics that create associated Channel processes. The record of these Channel subscriptions is kept in memory. In the event of a client disconnecting, the Channel subscriptions are no longer present on the server because the memory is collected. For example, a client could be connected to one Socket and three Channels. If the client became disconnected from the server, then the server has zero Sockets and zero Channels. When the client reconnects to the server, the server has one Socket and zero Channels. In this scenario all of the Channel information has been lost from the server, which means that our application would not be working properly.

Throughout this scenario, the client knows that it's supposed to be connected to the server and which Channel topics it should be connected to. This means that the client can reconnect to the server (creating one Socket) and then resubscribe to all of the topics (creating three Channels). This puts the client back in a correct state, with an amount of downtime based on how long it took to establish the connection and subscriptions.

The official Phoenix JavaScript client handles this reconnection scenario for us automatically. If you're using a non-standard client implementation, then you need to specifically consider this event to prevent your clients from ending up in an incorrect state after reconnection.

Let's look at another aspect of protecting unreliable clients: keeping our critical data alive in any circumstance.

Keeping Critical Data Alive

The processes that power our real-time application can shut down or be killed at any point. When a client disconnects, for example, all of the processes that power that client's real-time communication layer (Socket and Channels) are shut down. The data that is stored in a process is lost when the process shuts down. We do not have any important information in the real-time communication processes by default, but we often will enrich our Channel processes with custom state that powers our application.

When we store custom state in a process in our application, we must consider what happens when the process shuts down. There is a useful rule of thumb that we can use when designing our systems: all business-related data should be stored in persistent stores that can withstand system restarts.

Let's use an example to understand this further. In a typical e-commerce shop, we store the contents of the user's shopping cart on the server. In Elixir, we may choose to store this information in a process. If that process is shut down, then we must store the data somewhere else, or it is lost forever. If the server reboots, then we must have that data stored somewhere off the server, or it is lost forever. We can avoid the loss of this important data by storing our user's shopping cart data in a persistent store, such as a database.

You can follow these best practices to set yourself up for the most success:

- Utilize a persistent source of truth that the Channel interacts with, such as a database, for business data.

- Create a functional core that maintains boundaries between the communication layer and the business logic, like in *Designing Elixir Systems with OTP [IT19]*.

- Consider the life cycle of any processes linked to or otherwise associated with your Channel process.

These practices will help you focus on the true responsibility of a Channel—real-time communication—and avoid custom business logic being implemented in your Channels. In Chapter 8, Break Your Application with Acceptance Tests, on page 141, you will see how our application reacts when we randomly kill processes.

These rules do not mean that you are unable to store critical business data in process memory. Doing so can have significant speed and scalability benefits. You should, however, be able to recover the current state of the data if the process is killed at any point.

One final aspect of protecting unreliable clients is to understand how our application's messages are delivered.

Message Delivery

Channels deliver messages from the server to a client with some limited guarantees about how these messages are delivered. These guarantees will often be okay for your applications, but you should understand the limitations to know if they will not work for you.

Phoenix Channels use an at-most-once strategy to deliver messages to clients. This means that a given message will either appear zero or one time for a client. A different approach is at-least-once message delivery, where a message will be delivered one or more times. It is not possible to have exactly-once message delivery, due to uncertainty in distributed systems.

Phoenix's at-most-once message delivery is a bit of a problem on the surface: how can we work with a system that may not deliver a message? This is a trade-off that Phoenix makes in how it implements real-time messaging. By having an at-most-once guarantee with message delivery, Phoenix prevents us from needing to ensure that every message can be processed multiple times, which is potentially a much more complex system requirement.

Phoenix's at-most-once delivery is good in many use cases, such as:

- Application flows where the loss of a message won't break the flow

- Applications that are willing to trade off an occasional failure for writing less code (You can exert a significant amount of effort to do guaranteed message delivery correctly.)

- Applications with clients that can recover from a missed message manually

The at-most-once strategy can be seen in action when we observe how PubSub is used in broadcasting messages across our cluster. PubSub has a local component that is very likely to always succeed in broadcasting the message to the local node. PubSub also has a remote component that sends a message when a broadcast occurs. PubSub will try only once to deliver the message and does not have the concept of acknowledgment or retries. If the message is not delivered for some reason, then that message would not make it to remotely connected clients.

We also see this strategy at work when we observe how Phoenix delivers messages to the client. Phoenix sends messages to connected clients but doesn't look for any type of acknowledgment message. If you want guaranteed at-least-once delivery, then you will need to write code to add acknowledgment, something we aren't going to cover due to its complexity. The important thing to know is that you are able to fully customize this behavior if you need to. In practice, however, you usually want the at-most-once strategy that comes standard with Phoenix.

Unreliable connections and servers is a topic that you must constantly consider when building your real-time application. Next, let's look at a component of a production system that can sometimes contribute to this problem, but also helps make applications much more scalable: multi-server distribution.

Use Channels in a Cluster

It is critical to run multiple servers when you are deploying a production application. Doing so provides benefits for scalability and error tolerance. For example, the ability to double the number of servers in the event of higher load is much more powerful than doubling the number of cores on the single server. It can take a few minutes (or less!) to add more machines but could take much longer to move the application to a different machine with more cores. There may also be a time when a single machine is fully utilized, and you cannot add more CPU cores or memory.

Elixir makes connecting a cluster of BEAM nodes very easy. However, we have to ensure that we're building our application to run across multiple nodes without error. Phoenix Channels handles a lot of this for us due to PubSub being used for all message broadcasts, which we'll look at next.

Connecting a Local Cluster

Let's jump right in by starting a local Elixir node (instance of our application) with a name:

```
$ iex --name server@127.0.0.1 -S mix phx.server
[info] Access HelloSocketsWeb.Endpoint at http://localhost:4000
iex(server@127.0.0.1)1>
```

We use the --name switch to specify a name for our node. You can see the name on the input entry line; ours is located at server@127.0.0.1. Let's start a second node:

```
$ iex --name remote@127.0.0.1 -S mix
Interactive Elixir (1.6.6) - press Ctrl+C to exit (type h() ENTER for help)
iex(remote@127.0.0.1)1> Node.list()
[]
```

We started a second node that doesn't run a web server by starting mix instead of mix phx.server. We used a different name, remote@127.0.0.1, which gives us two nodes running on the same host domain. You can use Node.list/0 to view all currently connected nodes and see that there are none. Let's correct that:

```
iex(remote@127.0.0.1)1> Node.list()
[]
iex(remote@127.0.0.1)2> Node.connect(:"server@127.0.0.1")
true
iex(remote@127.0.0.1)3> Node.list()
[:"server@127.0.0.1"]
```

We run Node.connect/1 from our remote node to connect to the server node. This creates a connected cluster of nodes that can be verified by running Node.list/0 again. Try running Node.list/0 on the server node; you will see it contains the remote node name.

This is all that we have to do to take advantage of Phoenix PubSub's standard distribution strategy powered by pg2. We can broadcast a message from our remote node, which is incapable of serving Sockets, and see it on a client that is connected to a Socket on our main server. Let's try this out:

First, connect to the ping topic to establish the connection.

```
$ wscat -c 'ws://localhost:4000/socket/websocket?vsn=2.0.0'
> ["1","1","ping","phx_join",{}]
< ["1","1","ping","phx_reply",{"response":{},"status":"ok"}]
```

Next, broadcast a message *from the remote node.*

```
iex(r@127)> HelloSocketsWeb.Endpoint.broadcast("ping", "request_ping", %{})
:ok
```

Finally, you can see that the ping request made it to the client:

```
< [null,null,"ping","send_ping",{"from_node":"server@127.0.0.1"}]
```

The node that sent the message to the client is server@127.0.0.1, but we sent our broadcast from remote@127.0.0.1. This means that the message was distributed across the cluster and intercepted by the PingChannel on our server node.

This demo shows that we can have a message originate anywhere in our cluster, and the message will make it to the client. This is critical for a correctly working application that runs on multiple servers, and we get it for very low cost by using Phoenix PubSub.

In practice, our remote node would be serving Socket connections, and the entire system would be placed behind a tool that balances connections between the different servers. You could emulate this locally by changing the HTTP port in the application configuration, then connecting to the new port with wscat.

hello_sockets/config/dev.exs
```
config :hello_sockets, HelloSocketsWeb.Endpoint,
  http: [port: String.to_integer(System.get_env("PORT") || "4000")],
```

You can now start the remote server in HTTP serving mode by prepending PORT=4001 to the command. You will need to restart the original server@127.0.0.1 server as well.

```
$ PORT=4001 iex --name remote@127.0.0.1 -S mix phx.server
[info] Running Web.Endpoint with cowboy 2.6.3 at 0.0.0.0:4001 (http)
[info] Access Web.Endpoint at http://localhost:4001
iex(remote@127.0.0.1)1>
```

You can experiment with sending messages between the different nodes to confirm that they are delivered in either direction. You'll learn about cluster deployments in greater detail in Chapter 11, Deploy Your Application to Production, on page 221.

Channel distribution is very powerful and easy to get started with out-of-the-box. However, there are some challenges with it, which we'll explore next.

Challenges with Distributed Channels

Distribution provides immense benefits to the scalability of our application, but it comes with costs as well. A distributed application has potential problems that a single-node application won't experience. A single-node application may be the right call in some circumstances, such as a small internal application, but we often must deliver our applications to many users that require the performance and stability that are provided by distribution.

Here are a few of the challenges that we'll face when distributing our application. These problems are not specific to Elixir—you would experience the same problems when building a distributed system in any language.

- We cannot be sure that we have fully accurate knowledge of the state of remote nodes at any given time. We can use techniques and algorithms to reduce uncertainty, but not completely remove it.

- Messages may not be transmitted to a remote node as fast as we'd expect, or at all. It may be fairly rare for messages to be dropped completely, but message delays are much more common.

- Writing high-quality tests becomes more complicated as we have to spin up more complex scenarios to fully test our code. It is possible to write tests in Elixir that spin up a local cluster to simulate different environments.

- Our clients may disconnect from a node and end up on a different node with different internal state. We must accommodate this by having a central source of truth that any node can reference; this is most commonly a shared database.

The easiest principle to get started with is having a central source of truth that all nodes can read from when a process, such as a Channel, starts. We will use this technique throughout the book. The other challenges involve using proven data structures and algorithms for key tasks of our distributed application. In part II, you'll learn about Phoenix Tracker for distributed process tracking, and you have already learned about PubSub's mesh approach to message broadcasting.

Let's look at different ways to customize Channel behavior. These exercises get into a bit more code than we've seen so far, which makes them quite fun!

Customize Channel Behavior

A Phoenix Channel is backed by a GenServer that lets it receive messages and store state. We can take advantage of this property of Channels to customize the behavior of our Channel on a per-connection level. This allows us to build flows that are not possible (or would be much more complex) with standard message broadcasting, which can't easily send messages to a single client.

We can't customize the behavior of Sockets as much due to their process structure. We'll focus our attention strictly on Channel-level customization for these examples by walking through several different patterns that use Phoenix.Socket.assign/3 and message sending.

Send a Recurring Message

We sometimes need to send data to a client in a periodic way. One use case of this is to refresh an authentication token every few minutes to ensure that a client always has a valid token. This is useful because it is possible to overwhelm a server if all clients ask for a token at the same time.

Our Channel will send itself a message every five seconds by using Process.send_after/3. This flow will be started when the Channel process initializes, but it would be possible to start the flow in our handle_in callback as well, in response to a client-initiated message.

First, add a new "recurring" Channel route to the AuthSocket module.

hello_sockets/lib/hello_sockets_web/channels/auth_socket.ex
```
channel "recurring", HelloSocketsWeb.RecurringChannel
```

This Channel route makes our new Channel available. Let's create the RecurringChannel.

hello_sockets/lib/hello_sockets_web/channels/recurring_channel.ex
```
defmodule HelloSocketsWeb.RecurringChannel do
  use Phoenix.Channel

  @send_after 5_000

  def join(_topic, _payload, socket) do
    schedule_send_token()
    {:ok, socket}
  end

  defp schedule_send_token do
    Process.send_after(self(), :send_token, @send_after)
  end
end
```

We leverage our join callback in order to schedule a message to self() for five seconds in the future. This starts a timer that will cause the message :send_token to be delivered. Now, let's define the :send_token message handler.

hello_sockets/lib/hello_sockets_web/channels/recurring_channel.ex
```
def handle_info(:send_token, socket) do
  schedule_send_token()
  push(socket, "new_token", %{token: new_token(socket)})
  {:noreply, socket}
end

defp new_token(socket = %{assigns: %{user_id: user_id}}) do
  Phoenix.Token.sign(socket, "salt identifier", user_id)
end
```

We use handle_info/2, as we would in a standard GenServer, to handle the :send_token message. The first thing we do is schedule another message so the flow will run forever. We then use push/3 to send a newly signed Phoenix.Token to the client.

The Socket.assigns.user_id property set in AuthSocket.connect/2 provides the user information needed when we sign our token. Socket.assigns is a great way to bridge the gap between the initial connection and ongoing business logic, as it allows us to pass information that was initially provided in the connection request to the Channel.

Now let's add a subscription to RecurringChannel in our JavaScript:

```
hello_sockets/assets/js/socket.js
const recurringChannel = authSocket.channel("recurring")

recurringChannel.on("new_token", (payload) => {
  console.log("received new auth token", payload)
})

recurringChannel.join()
```

We are using our JavaScript client to observe this example, as we previously configured it to connect to the AuthSocket. Refresh your web page to see that the client is receiving a new unique token every five seconds. You will see log statements in your console, like this:

```
received new auth token ▸ {token: "SFMyNTY.g3QAAAACZAAEZGF0YWEBZAAGc2lnbmVkbgYAmxWNX2oB.-_uA9Fo7pTlr76FqXf0dNTV_Ve8A3_VA8adgrCnGAe0"}
received new auth token ▸ {token: "SFMyNTY.g3QAAAACZAAEZGF0YWEBZAAGc2lnbmVkbgYAJCmNX2oB.h_L67yxPKUyJIGeuxYDYHFxVAORan3MISEXZGOl50Qw"}
received new auth token ▸ {token: "SFMyNTY.g3QAAAACZAAEZGF0YWEBZAAGc2lnbmVkbgYArTyNX2oB._olX_bqfjpGG3eRh7u4LAzKEUAbh4mRHdFnGwzEB1A0"}
received new auth token ▸ {token: "SFMyNTY.g3QAAAACZAAEZGF0YWEBZAAGc2lnbmVkbgYANlCNX2oB.W8O79A4RcZ5RfGS-4HbSoZw_cHQTKdgUNLgXJ_GIDoc"}
received new auth token ▸ {token: "SFMyNTY.g3QAAAACZAAEZGF0YWEBZAAGc2lnbmVkbgYAv2ONX2oB.Dbp-1OI7MrZfOOfNvdlpq0NfiBi-B8lX-TZlJsoPLtA"}
> |
```

This will continue forever because our Channel does not have any logic to stop it. We are sending a message every five seconds for observation purposes, but we would normally set this duration closer to the expiration time of our token.

Let's look at a more advanced Channel customization that intercepts outgoing messages.

Deduplicate Outgoing Messages

Preventing duplicate outgoing messages is a great exercise in Channel customization. The solution to this problem must be implemented as close to the client as possible, because that way we can be certain of what messages have been sent to a particular client. Channels are the lowest-level process we control between a single client and our server; this makes them the perfect location for us to achieve this task.

In the last example, we used Socket.assigns to store state that is relevant to our Socket. In this example, we'll be using Socket.assigns to store state that is relevant to our Channel.

We can put anything we want in Socket.assigns. Any data that we add to Socket.assigns is for our Channel process only and won't be seen by other Channel processes, even Channels that use the same Socket. This is something that can be confusing at first but makes sense when you consider that Elixir is functional and generally side-effect free. If we modify the state of a Channel process, other processes in the system are not affected.

Let's start by adding a new Channel route.

hello_sockets/lib/hello_sockets_web/channels/user_socket.ex
```elixir
channel "dupe", HelloSocketsWeb.DedupeChannel
```

We make a new Channel by adding a route in our Socket. We are using the UserSocket because we don't need authentication for this example.

hello_sockets/lib/hello_sockets_web/channels/dedupe_channel.ex
```elixir
defmodule HelloSocketsWeb.DedupeChannel do
  use Phoenix.Channel

  def join(_topic, _payload, socket) do
    {:ok, socket}
  end
end
```

Our join function doesn't have any logic in it. All of this Channel's logic will be in handle_out.

hello_sockets/lib/hello_sockets_web/channels/dedupe_channel.ex
```elixir
intercept ["number"]

def handle_out("number", %{number: number}, socket) do
  buffer = Map.get(socket.assigns, :buffer, [])
  next_buffer = [number | buffer]

  next_socket =
    socket
    |> assign(:buffer, next_buffer)
    |> enqueue_send_buffer()

  {:noreply, next_socket}
end
```

We intercepted the event "number" and defined a handle_out callback for when we receive this event. Our handle_out function is different than normal because we're not invoking push in it. We can do this because there's nothing that requires us to push a message to the client when we intercept a message.

We use a buffer to store a list of numbers that have been given to the Channel. This buffer is put into the Channel's Socket.assigns state and is persisted between messages. The buffer will place the newest messages at the front, which means our messages would normally arrive in reverse order to the client. Adding to the buffer this way, to the beginning of a list, is a constant-time operation. Adding to the end of a list takes increasingly more time based on the size of the list; this means that adding to the beginning of a list is faster.

Let's enqueue a message that allows our buffer to be "flushed" to the client.

hello_sockets/lib/hello_sockets_web/channels/dedupe_channel.ex
```
defp enqueue_send_buffer(socket = %{assigns: %{awaiting_buffer?: true}}),
  do: socket

defp enqueue_send_buffer(socket) do
  Process.send_after(self(), :send_buffer, 1_000)
  assign(socket, :awaiting_buffer?, true)
end
```

We schedule a message to the Channel when it receives a new number for the first time. The handling of this message is where our buffer will be deduplicated and sent to the client. The state awaiting_buffer? is used to prevent multiple send_buffer messages from being enqueued during a single time period.

hello_sockets/lib/hello_sockets_web/channels/dedupe_channel.ex
```
def handle_info(:send_buffer, socket = %{assigns: %{buffer: buffer}}) do
  buffer
  |> Enum.reverse()
  |> Enum.uniq()
  |> Enum.each(&push(socket, "number", %{value: &1}))

  next_socket =
    socket
    |> assign(:buffer, [])
    |> assign(:awaiting_buffer?, false)

  {:noreply, next_socket}
end
```

The buffer, a list of numbers, is made unique by passing the list to Enum.uniq/1. Each unique number is then individually pushed to the client. We could optionally roll all of the numbers into a single message to reduce the number of messages sent. We reverse the buffer before it's made unique to preserve number ordering, due to our buffer being stored in reverse order.

The state is reset to an initial value so the process can continue. We'll write a helper function so we can quickly enqueue a large number of messages to the topic.

hello_sockets/lib/hello_sockets_web/channels/dedupe_channel.ex
```
def broadcast(numbers, times) do
  Enum.each(1..times, fn _ ->
    Enum.each(numbers, fn number ->
      HelloSocketsWeb.Endpoint.broadcast!("dupe", "number", %{
        number: number
      })
    end)
  end)
end
```

We broadcast a single message for each number. This means that every broadcast causes handle_out to be called a single time. If we enqueue [1, 2] 20 times, then there would be 40 broadcasts handled by the Channel.

A simple JavaScript client change can be made to demo our example.

hello_sockets/assets/js/socket.js
```
const dupeChannel = socket.channel("dupe")

dupeChannel.on("number", (payload) => {
  console.log("new number received", payload)
})

dupeChannel.join()
```

Your server should be started with iex -S mix phx.server so we can run our broadcast command easily. You can load the web page and then send numbers using HelloSocketsWeb.DedupeChannel.broadcast/2.

```
iex> HelloSocketsWeb.DedupeChannel.broadcast([1, 2, 3], 100)
iex> :ok
```

You can then check your JavaScript console to see the messages arriving.

```
js> new number received {value: 1}
js> new number received {value: 2}
js> new number received {value: 3}
```

The messages will always arrive in this order, one second after they are broadcast. Try enqueuing a larger number of messages to see what happens. If you enqueue 1_000_000 iterations, you will see that multiple rounds of messages will be delivered to the client. This is because our buffer flushing runs after one second, even if new messages are occurring, and it takes over one second to process that many messages.

We've built strong foundations for customizing Channel behavior. You're able to leverage these building blocks in order to tailor your Channels to what is needed for your application. Next, let's write tests for our different Channels, including our DedupeChannel.

Write Tests

If there is one thing that every developer probably has an opinion about, it's testing. You may believe in test-driven development, where you write tests before writing any of your implementation code. Or maybe you follow the practice of "code first, test second." We won't open up any testing philosophy questions in this book. Instead, we'll look at the available mechanisms for testing our real-time code—and you can apply them using your preferred methodology.

Tests provide us with a higher sense of confidence in the code we're writing. We are able to trap complex bugs in robust tests that withstand the test of time. In the ideal world, we can capture any bug in a test and prevent it from happening again in the future.

Phoenix provides a simple and powerful way to write Channel tests. A few basic primitives allow us to easily write tests of our entire real-time communication stack. We don't have to worry about the challenges of WebSockets or long polling when we write our tests. Instead, we only have to write tests for the Socket and Channel implementations, which we'll cover in this section.

Testing Sockets

Every Phoenix application generated with mix phx.new includes a few different test helpers found in test/support. One of these helpers is called ChannelCase; ours takes the name HelloSocketsWeb.ChannelCase. We do not have to worry about customizing this file at this point as we will not be doing anything out of the ordinary.

Our UserSocket and AuthSocket are able to connect and identify a Socket. We'll first write a test for UserSocket because it has no logic in it. Our tests will assert that we can connect to this Socket. The tests for AuthSocket will be similar but also slightly more complex because of the connection logic in it.

You can run these tests using mix test. You should run that now to verify that your test environment is properly set up. After you see that working, let's move into writing our UserSocket tests.

hello_sockets/test/hello_sockets_web/channels/user_socket_test.exs
```elixir
defmodule HelloSocketsWeb.UserSocketTest do
  use HelloSocketsWeb.ChannelCase
  alias HelloSocketsWeb.UserSocket
end
```

We use a test module that imports our HelloSocketsWeb.ChannelCase to provide all of its testing ability.

Note that the file name must end in _test.exs and the test module name should end in Test. The module name isn't a requirement, but I have spent many hours debugging broken tests when the problem turned out to be defining a test module as HelloSocketsWeb.UserSocket instead of HelloSocketsWeb.UserSocketTest, causing the original module being tested to be overwritten by the test module.

Let's connect to our UserSocket now.

hello_sockets/test/hello_sockets_web/channels/user_socket_test.exs
```
describe "connect/3" do
  test "can be connected to without parameters" do
    assert {:ok, %Phoenix.Socket{}} = connect(UserSocket, %{})
  end
end
```

Phoenix.ChannelTest also provides a connect/3 function that accepts the Socket handler (UserSocket) as well as any connection parameters. We are not using the optional third argument, but it would be useful if you include specific HTTP information as part of your Socket connection.

Our Socket can never have an error in connection, because we don't have any logic. This means we don't need to write many test cases. Our id test looks similar, but with an additional assertion.

hello_sockets/test/hello_sockets_web/channels/user_socket_test.exs
```
describe "id/1" do
  test "an identifier is not provided" do
    assert {:ok, socket} = connect(UserSocket, %{})
    assert UserSocket.id(socket) == nil
  end
end
```

The Phoenix.Socket structure that is returned by the connect/2 function makes it very easy to write tests that require a valid Socket, such as the id/1 function.

Run these tests with mix test and you'll see green! Let's write some more interesting tests for our AuthSocket now.

hello_sockets/test/hello_sockets_web/channels/auth_socket_test.exs
```
defmodule HelloSocketsWeb.AuthSocketTest do
  use HelloSocketsWeb.ChannelCase
  import ExUnit.CaptureLog
  alias HelloSocketsWeb.AuthSocket
end
```

This is exactly like UserSocketTest. The import of CaptureLog provides the capture_log/1 function, which will test that our code is properly logging output.

Let's write an authentication helper function that makes the rest of our test simpler.

hello_sockets/test/hello_sockets_web/channels/auth_socket_test.exs
```
defp generate_token(id, opts \\ []) do
  salt = Keyword.get(opts, :salt, "salt identifier")
  Phoenix.Token.sign(HelloSocketsWeb.Endpoint, salt, id)
end
```

The generate_token/2 function will help our tests by creating a valid or invalid token in a very simple and concise way.

```
hello_sockets/test/hello_sockets_web/channels/auth_socket_test.exs
describe "connect/3 success" do
  test "can be connected to with a valid token" do
    assert {:ok, %Phoenix.Socket{}} =
             connect(AuthSocket, %{"token" => generate_token(1)})

    assert {:ok, %Phoenix.Socket{}} =
             connect(AuthSocket, %{"token" => generate_token(2)})
  end
end
```

We have written a test that looks very similar to UserSocket but now uses the params map to provide a token to the Socket. The user ID doesn't matter in this case because any valid user is allowed to connect.

Both of these tests pass after connecting to our Socket, because each has been given a valid authentication token. It's a good practice to see a test "go red" if you're writing it after the code. Try breaking these tests by changing the implementation of AuthSocket in some way. You should then restore the tests back to green.

This next test looks long but it's really just one type of test repeated a few times.

```
hello_sockets/test/hello_sockets_web/channels/auth_socket_test.exs
describe "connect/3 error" do
  test "cannot be connected to with an invalid salt" do
    params = %{"token" => generate_token(1, salt: "invalid")}

    assert capture_log(fn ->
             assert :error = connect(AuthSocket, params)
           end) =~ "[error] #{AuthSocket} connect error :invalid"
  end

  test "cannot be connected to without a token" do
    params = %{}

    assert capture_log(fn ->
             assert :error = connect(AuthSocket, params)
           end) =~ "[error] #{AuthSocket} connect error missing params"
  end

  test "cannot be connected to with a nonsense token" do
    params = %{"token" => "nonsense"}

    assert capture_log(fn ->
             assert :error = connect(AuthSocket, params)
           end) =~ "[error] #{AuthSocket} connect error :invalid"
  end
end
```

Here, we are testing a variety of different scenarios that could occur during connection. These tests are similar to each other, with most of the code being identical setup functions. We now know that our Socket can withstand invalid or missing parameters gracefully.

We use capture_log/1 to verify that our log statements worked properly. You should write tests for any code that uses log statements, even though it seems unimportant, because these logs may end up being critical to tracking down production issues.

Let's test our Socket id now.

```
hello_sockets/test/hello_sockets_web/channels/auth_socket_test.exs
describe "id/1" do
  test "an identifier is based on the connected ID" do
    assert {:ok, socket} =
             connect(AuthSocket, %{"token" => generate_token(1)})

    assert AuthSocket.id(socket) == "auth_socket:1"

    assert {:ok, socket} =
             connect(AuthSocket, %{"token" => generate_token(2)})

    assert AuthSocket.id(socket) == "auth_socket:2"
  end
end
```

Our id/1 test uses a successful Socket connection to verify that the Socket is identified with the user ID authentication information.

Try adding IO.inspect(socket) at the end of this test. You will see assigns: %{user_id: 2}. The IO.inspect/1 function can be very helpful for debugging complex state flows because it shows you the current state.

The simple techniques in this section let us test any standard Socket implementation. Next, we'll see a few more techniques to deal with the increased business logic in Channels.

Testing Channels

Channels contain much more application logic than Sockets do. This means they will be a bit more involved to test than Sockets. We'll write tests for our WildcardChannel and DedupeChannel to capture a wide range of testing needs. The amount of testing primitives is fairly low but can still be confusing at first. Keep in mind during our tests that message passing is at the heart of Channels, and that the test module uses messages to verify data is sent and received properly between the test process and a Channel process.

Let's add tests for our WildcardChannel's custom join implementation. Then we'll test that a message can be received and replied to.

hello_sockets/test/hello_sockets_web/channels/wildcard_channel_test.exs
```elixir
defmodule HelloSocketsWeb.WildcardChannelTest do
  use HelloSocketsWeb.ChannelCase
  import ExUnit.CaptureLog
  alias HelloSocketsWeb.UserSocket
end
```

Our initial skeleton will look very similar for a majority of tests that we write. This sets up all the dependencies for our test.

hello_sockets/test/hello_sockets_web/channels/wildcard_channel_test.exs
```elixir
describe "join/3 success" do
  test "ok when numbers in the format a:b where b = 2a" do
    assert {:ok, _, %Phoenix.Socket{}} =
             socket(UserSocket, nil, %{})
             |> subscribe_and_join("wild:2:4", %{})

    assert {:ok, _, %Phoenix.Socket{}} =
             socket(UserSocket, nil, %{})
             |> subscribe_and_join("wild:100:200", %{})
  end
end
```

The socket/3 function returns a Phoenix.Socket struct that would be created if the given handler, id, and assigned state were provided to our Socket implementation. This is a useful convenience function allowing us to set up initial state without going through the process of connecting our real Socket.

We use subscribe_and_join/3 to join the given topic with certain params. The correct Channel to use is inferred by matching the topic with the provided Socket implementation. This ensures that our Socket has the appropriate Channel routes defined, which adds to our test coverage.

hello_sockets/test/hello_sockets_web/channels/wildcard_channel_test.exs
```elixir
describe "join/3 error" do
  test "error when b is not exactly twice a" do
    assert socket(UserSocket, nil, %{})
           |> subscribe_and_join("wild:1:3", %{}) == {:error, %{}}
  end

  test "error when 3 numbers are provided" do
    assert socket(UserSocket, nil, %{})
           |> subscribe_and_join("wild:1:2:3", %{}) == {:error, %{}}
  end
end
```

Our topic only subscribes properly in a particular format. These tests try out other formats that don't match in order to ensure that the Channel is not started.

We are using == in these tests, rather than pattern matching, because we care that the reply of the join function is exactly {:error, %{}}. If we used pattern matching, then a return value like {:error, %{reason: "invalid"}} would incorrectly pass the test.

hello_sockets/test/hello_sockets_web/channels/wildcard_channel_test.exs
```
describe "join/3 error causing crash" do
  test "error with an invalid format topic" do
    assert capture_log(fn ->
              socket(UserSocket, nil, %{})
              |> subscribe_and_join("wild:invalid", %{})
            end) =~ "[error] an exception was raised"
  end
end
```

It's possible to crash the WildcardChannel by sending an incorrectly formatted string. This is okay for our example, but it's a good idea to test this behavior to show that we understand and accept it.

We cause the crash to occur by passing in a topic that doesn't have numbers separated by a colon. This highlights one of the challenges of writing tests in Elixir: if we use the built-in assert_raise/2 function, our test would fail because the ArgumentError happens in a process other than our test process. We get around this challenge by using the Logger to verify our assertions.

In production, we would want to write code that doesn't crash. Try making this test pass by asserting a {:error, %{}} return value rather than capturing the crash log. To do so, you will make the test red first and then modify the Channel implementation so that the test becomes green.

Our next test will ensure that our Channels respond to "ping" events with a "pong" response.

hello_sockets/test/hello_sockets_web/channels/wildcard_channel_test.exs
```
describe "handle_in ping" do
  test "a pong response is provided" do
    assert {:ok, _, socket} =
              socket(UserSocket, nil, %{})
              |> subscribe_and_join("wild:2:4", %{})

    ref = push(socket, "ping", %{})
    reply = %{ping: "pong"}
    assert_reply ref, :ok, ^reply
  end
end
```

We start by joining our Socket like we did in our previous tests. This could be extracted into a helper function if we were repeating it many times.

The push/3 function is used to invoke handle_in on the Channel. The function arguments correspond to the connected Channel state, event name, and payload. We receive a reference back from this function. The reference is simply a unique value that ensures the reply is sent correctly.

We use assert_reply/3 to ensure we received the expected response back from our Channel. This function is both deceptively powerful and sometimes confusing due to pattern matching. We are using ^reply to pin a map value to the reply we receive. If we didn't use ^reply and just left the response inline in the arguments, then values such as %{ping: "pong", extra: true} would still cause our tests to pass. Pattern matching would allow us to ignore the full or partial payload by using underscore variables, but it can also cause false positives in our test suite.

Our WildcardChannel is now fully tested. Our final and most exciting test will be for DedupeChannel.

Testing DedupeChannel

Our DedupeChannel module contains more complex logic in it than WildcardChannel does. We will leverage both Channel and Elixir testing patterns to develop complete tests for our Channel's logic. Our tests will use message broadcasting to and from the DedupeChannel. This is the last technique we'll cover for writing Channel tests.

Our join/3 function is very simple in DedupeChannel, so we won't add tests for it. We'll start with tests to check that our Channel state changes when we broadcast a new number to our Channel. Let's write a few helper functions that will make our tests much easier to write and read.

```
hello_sockets/test/hello_sockets_web/channels/dedupe_channel_test.exs
defmodule HelloSocketsWeb.DedupeChannelTest do
  use HelloSocketsWeb.ChannelCase
  alias HelloSocketsWeb.UserSocket

  defp broadcast_number(socket, number) do
    assert broadcast_from!(socket, "number", %{number: number}) == :ok
    socket
  end
end
```

We use broadcast_from!/3 to trigger handle_out of our Channel. The broadcast function invokes the PubSub callbacks present in the Phoenix.Channel.Server module.

Our helper function accepts socket as the first parameter and returns it as the lone return value. This will allow us to use a pipeline operator to chain together our helper functions, as you'll see soon.

```
hello_sockets/test/hello_sockets_web/channels/dedupe_channel_test.exs
defp validate_buffer_contents(socket, expected_contents) do
  assert :sys.get_state(socket.channel_pid).assigns == %{
            awaiting_buffer?: true,
            buffer: expected_contents
          }

  socket
end
```

We use :sys.get_state/1 to retrieve the contents of our Channel.Server process that is created by the test helper. This creates a tight coupling between the process being spied on and the calling process, so you should limit its usage. It can be valuable when used sparingly in tests because it gives all the information about a process.

Next, add a helper function to create the Socket.

```
hello_sockets/test/hello_sockets_web/channels/dedupe_channel_test.exs
defp connect() do
  assert {:ok, _, socket} =
            socket(UserSocket, nil, %{})
            |> subscribe_and_join("dupe", %{})

  socket
end
```

I mentioned previously that you could extract the Channel connection into a helper if it became cumbersome. We do that here to make our tests easier to read.

All our helper functions are returning the socket reference. This pattern allows us to use pipeline function invocation. It turns complex testing code into elegant code like this:

```
hello_sockets/test/hello_sockets_web/channels/dedupe_channel_test.exs
test "a buffer is maintained as numbers are broadcasted" do
  connect()
  |> broadcast_number(1)
  |> validate_buffer_contents([1])
  |> broadcast_number(1)
  |> validate_buffer_contents([1, 1])
  |> broadcast_number(2)
  |> validate_buffer_contents([2, 1, 1])

  refute_push _, _
end
```

We use our helper functions to repeatedly broadcast messages to our Channel and then check its internal state. We ensure that no message has been sent to the client by using refute_push/2 with very loose pattern matching.

Next, let's test that our buffer drains correctly.

```
hello_sockets/test/hello_sockets_web/channels/dedupe_channel_test.exs
test "the buffer is drained 1 second after a number is first added" do
  connect()
  |> broadcast_number(1)
  |> broadcast_number(1)
  |> broadcast_number(2)

  Process.sleep(1050)

  assert_push "number", %{value: 1}, 0
  refute_push "number", %{value: 1}, 0
  assert_push "number", %{value: 2}, 0
end
```

We are using Process.sleep/1 in order to wait long enough for our Channel to have drained the buffer. This can cause the test suite to be slower, although there are slightly more complex alternatives. If you placed a configurable timeout for draining the buffer in the test suite, you would be able to sleep for much less time. Alternatively, you could develop a way to ask the Channel process how many times it has drained and then wait until it increases. The sleep function is great for this test because it keeps the code simple.

assert_push/3 and refute_push/3 delegate to ExUnit's assert_receive and refute_receive functions with a pattern that matches the expected Phoenix.Socket.Message. This means the Channel messages are located in our test process's mailbox and can be inspected manually when necessary. We are providing a timeout of 0 for these functions, as we have already waited enough time for the processing to have finished.

The push assertion functions are very useful when writing most tests, but they remove the ability to test that the messages are in a certain order. This matters for our Channel, so we will inspect the process mailbox manually.

```
hello_sockets/test/hello_sockets_web/channels/dedupe_channel_test.exs
test "the buffer drains with unique values in the correct order" do
  connect()
  |> broadcast_number(1)
  |> broadcast_number(2)
  |> broadcast_number(3)
  |> broadcast_number(2)

  Process.sleep(1050)
```

```
assert {:messages,
      [
        %Phoenix.Socket.Message{
          event: "number",
          payload: %{value: 1}
        },
        %Phoenix.Socket.Message{
          event: "number",
          payload: %{value: 2}
        },
        %Phoenix.Socket.Message{
          event: "number",
          payload: %{value: 3}
        }
      ]} = Process.info(self(), :messages)
end
```

We are able to leverage pattern matching to ensure the messages are in the correct order while still maintaining tests that care about the minimum possible state structure. With that, we have fully covered our DedupeChannel's logic with tests.

Your testing toolbox is now complete. It is important to have quality tests in a scalable application—you'll use these tools throughout the rest of the book.

The Importance of Tests

Tests that are easy to read and modify are an important part of having an application that can be maintained by any teammate in the future. These tests also help identify errors in code. When I originally created the DedupeChannel, I discovered a bug where the pushes would happen in the wrong order. The tests that I wrote revealed the bug to me. The value of well-written tests never decreases, even for experienced programmers.

Wrapping Up

Writing real-time applications requires you to consider the unreliable nature of long-lived connections. Users can disconnect at any time, so your applications must be developed with this in mind. A source of truth that lives outside of the connection life cycle is one of the best ways to combat the challenges of unreliable connections.

Applications in production should always have multiple servers to ensure uptime, even when something goes wrong. Channels are usable across multiple servers with only a small amount of work necessary to make sure everything works as expected. Distributing your application over multiple servers adds new challenges, but it can significantly improve scalability and reliability.

It's possible to both write and test complex business logic in Channels. Phoenix gives you the right foundations so you can develop robust Channel tests while only needing to learn a handful of functions. These tests are able to ensure that complex logic such as asynchronous message processing and state is correctly implemented in a Channel.

One of the most important aspects of a scalable real-time application is ensuring that performance is good, even with a large number of simultaneous users. In the next chapter, you will see a variety of performance pitfalls and how to avoid them.

## CHAPTER 6

Avoid Performance Pitfalls

You now have the tools and knowledge to build a real-time application using Phoenix Channels. However, you will need to run this application for real users in order for it to be useful. Your application needs to be able to operate efficiently so that requests do not time out, encounter errors, or otherwise not work correctly.

This chapter looks at several common scaling challenges and best practices to help avoid performance issues as you develop and ship your application. We're covering these topics before we build a real application (in part II) because it's important to consider them at the design stage of the development process, and not after the application is already written.

The following performance pitfalls are a collection of common problems that can affect applications. You'll experience many other challenges when building and shipping an application, but we'll focus on these three, because they are applicable to all real-time applications.

Unknown application health

  We need to know if our deployed application is healthy. When our application experiences a problem, we're able to identify root cause by looking at all of our metrics. You'll see how to add measurements to our Elixir applications using StatsD.

Limited Channel throughput

  Channels use a single process on the server to process incoming and outgoing requests. If we're not careful, we can constrain our application so that long running requests prevent the Channel from processing. We'll solve this problem with built-in Phoenix functions.

Unintentional data pipeline

> We can build a pipeline that efficiently moves data from server to user. We should be intentional in our data pipeline design so that we know the capabilities and limitations of our solution. We'll use GenStage to build a production-ready data pipeline.

We'll walk through each pitfall in detail throughout this chapter—you'll see solutions to each as we go. Let's start by looking at how to measure our Elixir applications.

Measure Everything

A software application is made up of many interactions and events that power features. The successful combination of all the different events in a feature's flow cause it to work properly and quickly. If even a single step of our application encounters an issue or slowdown, the rest of that flow is affected. We need to be aware of everything that happens in our application to prevent and identify problems.

It is impossible to effectively run a decently sized piece of software without some form of measurement. Software becomes a black box once deployed, and having different view ports into the application lets us to know how well things are working. This is so useful that a class of tools has emerged called Application Performance Monitoring (APM). While they usually cost money, these tools are a good way to start measuring your applications. Even if you use an APM tool, the content in this chapter will apply because not everything can be automatically handled.

We will cover a few different types of measurements that we can use in our application. These measurements can be collected by many different open-source tools. We'll work with one of these tools and see how to use it in our code, but first we'll cover a few types of measurements that are useful for most applications.

Types of Measurements

The best way to know if our application is behaving correctly is to place instrumentation on as many different events and system operations as possible. There are a large number of things you can measure and ways that you could measure them. Here are a few of the simple but effective ways that you can measure things:

- Count occurrences—The number of times that an operation happens. We could count every time a message is pushed to our Channel, or we could count every time a Socket fails to connect.

- Count at a point in time—The value of a component of our system at a moment of time. The number of connected Sockets and Channels could be counted every few seconds. This is commonly called a gauge in many measurement tools.

- Timing of operation—The amount of time that it takes for an operation to complete. We could measure the time taken to push an event to a client after the event is generated.

Each measurement type is useful in different situations, and there isn't a single type that's superior to the others. A combination of different measurements combined into a single view (in your choice of visualization tool) can help to pinpoint an issue. For example, you may have a spike in new connection occurrences that lines up with an increase in memory consumption. All of this could contribute to an increase in message delivery timing. Each of these measurements on its own would tell you something, but not the full picture. The combination of all of them contribute to understanding how the system is stressed.

Measurements are usually collected with some identifying information. At a minimum, each measurement has a name and value, but some tools allow for more structured ways of specifying additional data, such as with tags. We are able to attach additional metadata to our measurements to help tell our application's story. For example, shared online applications often use the concept of "tenant" to isolate a customer's data. We could add a tenant_id=XX tag to all metrics to understand the current system health from the perspective of a single tenant.

Now, let's see how to collect these measurements in using StatsD.

Collect Measurements using StatsD

We can use a number of different tools to take measurements in our code. A commonly used tool is StatsD, and that's what we'll use throughout this book. StatsD is a daemon that aggregates statistics; it takes measurements sent by our application and aggregates them into other back ends that collect the stats. Many APMs provide a StatsD back-end integration; this makes StatsD a great choice for collecting measurements.

There are other tools you can use to collect measurements. StatsD is commonly used and easy to understand. If you prefer a different tool, then you should use that. The important thing is that you are collecting measurements.

It is easy to get started with StatsD in Elixir by using the Statix[1] library. This library has a simple interface with functions that correspond to StatsD measurement types. We'll use Statix in this book to capture measurements in our application.

Let's capture various measurements in our HelloSockets application by using Statix and a local StatsD server. We'll use a fake StatsD server for development that simply logs any packets to the Elixir application console.

Let's start by adding Statix and a fake StatsD logger to our application.

```
hello_sockets/mix.exs
{:statix, "~> 1.2"},
{:statsd_logger, "~> 1.1", only: [:dev, :test]},
```

Run mix deps.get to fetch these dependencies. We must configure Statix to work in our application.

```
hello_sockets/config/dev.exs
config :statsd_logger, port: 8126

config :statix, HelloSockets.Statix, port: 8126
```

We're using the non-standard StatsD port of 8126 for our development. This will help ensure that our StatsD example works even if you have another StatsD server on your computer already.

We can use Statix after configuring a simple module for our application.

```
hello_sockets/lib/hello_sockets/statix.ex
defmodule HelloSockets.Statix do
  use Statix
end
```

We will use the HelloSockets.Statix module in our application any time we want to capture a StatsD measurement.

Finally, we must connect Statix to our StatsD server. Add the following code to the top of the start function.

```
hello_sockets/lib/hello_sockets/application.ex
def start(_type, _args) do
  :ok = HelloSockets.Statix.connect()
```

---

1. https://github.com/lexmag/statix

We can now try out Statix to make sure it's working. Let's try out Statix in an iex session:

```
$ iex -S mix
iex(1)> alias HelloSockets.Statix
iex(1)> Statix.increment("test")
StatsD metric: test 1|c
:ok
iex(2)> Statix.increment("test", 1, tags: ["name:1", "success:true"])
:ok
StatsD metric: test 1|c|#name:1,success:true
```

The StatsD metric lines indicate that the metric was successfully sent over UDP to the StatsD server. Tags are not native to the StatsD protocol, but they have become popular with a variety of StatsD tools. We'll use them throughout this book because of their usefulness.

We now have a working way to collect metrics in our application! Let's capture valuable metrics in our application's Sockets and Channels. We will start by counting the number of Socket connections that occur in a Socket.

```
hello_sockets/lib/hello_sockets_web/channels/stats_socket.ex
defmodule HelloSocketsWeb.StatsSocket do
  use Phoenix.Socket

  channel "*", HelloSocketsWeb.StatsChannel

  def connect(_params, socket, _connect_info) do
    HelloSockets.Statix.increment("socket_connect", 1,
      tags: ["status:success", "socket:StatsSocket"]
    )

    {:ok, socket}
  end

  def id(_socket), do: nil
end
```

This Socket is mostly boilerplate, which you've already seen. We've added an increment/3 call to emit a StatsD event each time a Socket is connected. This event will tell us the number of attempts to connect to our Socket. You can use this information to know when an abnormal number of new connections occur in a customer-facing application.

It is useful to compare Channels joined versus Sockets connected in order to know if clients are properly configured. Add the following code to the StatsChannel module to capture join metrics on the Channel level:

hello_sockets/lib/hello_sockets_web/channels/stats_channel.ex

```elixir
defmodule HelloSocketsWeb.StatsChannel do
  use Phoenix.Channel

  def join("valid", _payload, socket) do
    channel_join_increment("success")
    {:ok, socket}
  end

  def join("invalid", _payload, _socket) do
    channel_join_increment("fail")
    {:error, %{reason: "always fails"}}
  end

  defp channel_join_increment(status) do
    HelloSockets.Statix.increment("channel_join", 1,
      tags: ["status:#{status}", "channel:StatsChannel"]
    )
  end
end
```

We have defined two different topics: "valid" and "invalid". This allows us to simulate valid and invalid Channel joins.

You benefit from recording metadata such as status or Channel name in your metric tags because you can drill deeper into the data. For example, you may see an increase in Channel join events in your application. Is this due to legitimate user traffic, or is there a bug that's preventing proper joins? Capturing the join status in your tags means you have the correct data for answering this question.

Let's write another example that measures the performance of a request in our StatsChannel.

hello_sockets/lib/hello_sockets_web/channels/stats_channel.ex

```elixir
def handle_in("ping", _payload, socket) do
  HelloSockets.Statix.measure("stats_channel.ping", fn ->
    Process.sleep(:rand.uniform(1000))
    {:reply, {:ok, %{ping: "pong"}}, socket}
  end)
end
```

The measure/2 function accepts a function that it will both execute and time. The time taken by the function will be reported to StatsD as a metric and the return value of the function is returned. This means we can measure different parts of our code very quickly by wrapping our code in the measure function.

Taking measurements of key code paths will allow you to better understand if the code path is slow or becomes slow in the future. One final step before we can use our new Socket is to add it to our Endpoint.

```
hello_sockets/lib/hello_sockets_web/endpoint.ex
socket "/stats_socket", HelloSocketsWeb.StatsSocket,
  websocket: true,
  longpoll: false
```

Now that our Socket is configured, let's try out StatsSocket and StatsChannel to see our metrics being sent to StatsD. Start by configuring our JavaScript to connect to and use our Socket.

```
hello_sockets/assets/js/socket.js
const statsSocket = new Socket("/stats_socket", {})
statsSocket.connect()

const statsChannelInvalid = statsSocket.channel("invalid")
statsChannelInvalid.join()
  .receive("error", () => statsChannelInvalid.leave())

const statsChannelValid = statsSocket.channel("valid")
statsChannelValid.join()

for (let i = 0; i < 5; i++) {
  statsChannelValid.push("ping")
}
```

We connect to the Socket one time and connect to each topic. We then send five "ping" messages. This allows us to see multiple timing events.

Run our application with mix phx.server and then visit http://localhost:4000. You will see the following in your terminal output each time you refresh the web page. This may be mixed together with our other logs:

```
StatsD Metric: socket_connect 1|c|#status:success,socket:StatsSocket
StatsD Metric: channel_join 1|c|#status:fail,channel:StatsChannel
StatsD Metric: channel_join 1|c|#status:success,channel:StatsChannel
StatsD Metric: stats_channel.ping 712|ms
StatsD Metric: channel_join 1|c|#status:fail,channel:StatsChannel
StatsD Metric: stats_channel.ping 837|ms
StatsD Metric: stats_channel.ping 503|ms
StatsD Metric: stats_channel.ping 8|ms
StatsD Metric: stats_channel.ping 429|ms
StatsD Metric: channel_join 1|c|#status:fail,channel:StatsChannel
```

We now have a working Socket and Channel instrumentation. You can add measurements to critical paths of your application in order to know how these paths are being used, and whether they are healthy or not.

You need to view and interact with your measurements, no matter the tool you use to capture them. Next, we'll cover what you can do with measurements and how having them can help you avoid performance problems.

Visualizing Measurements

We are emitting our StatsD measurements, but we are not yet able to make use of them. We need a tool for that. There are many commercial and open-source tools that operate on StatsD metrics. It is outside of the scope of this book to learn how to use these tools, but here's what you can ultimately do with these metrics.

Visualize metrics with graphs

> You can create graphs of your different measurements. You can even combine and compare graphs to correlate potential problems.

Produce dashboards for your team

> You can combine graphs and other visualizations into a "single pane of glass." This allows you to quickly see the health of your system, maybe from a shared monitor in your office.

Get alerted to problems

> Many metrics systems allow you to set up alerts on values of your measurements. For example, you may want to get an alert when your Channel begins taking a certain amount of time to respond to a particular request.

Detect anomalies

> Some metrics systems are capable of detecting anomalies in your metrics without you configuring known thresholds. This can be useful in identifying unexpected problems. For example, a metric system could automatically detect that your metric values are outside of several standard deviations and then alert you to a potential problem.

All of these features allow you to understand more about the state of your system, closing one of the performance pitfalls. You can respond to any issues or plan capacity for your system when you have this knowledge. You should add measurements early in your application's development so you can identify potential problems early—before a problem affects users.

Measurement and instrumentation are crucial for knowing about our application's performance, but knowledge doesn't improve our application's performance. We need to take action on this knowledge with techniques that can improve the performance of our Channels.

Keep Your Channels Asynchronous

Elixir is a parallel execution machine. Each Channel can leverage the principles of OTP design to execute work in parallel with other Channels, since the BEAM executes multiple processes at once. Every message processed by a

Channel, whether incoming or outgoing, must go through the Channel process in order to execute. It's possible for this to stop working well if we're not careful about how our Channel is designed. This is easiest to see when we have an example of the problem in front of us.

We'll leverage our existing StatsChannel to see the effect of process slowness. Let's add a new message handler that responds very slowly.

```
hello_sockets/lib/hello_sockets_web/channels/stats_channel.ex
def handle_in("slow_ping", _payload, socket) do
  Process.sleep(3_000)
  {:reply, {:ok, %{ping: "pong"}}, socket}
end
```

We have copied our existing ping handler but have made every request to it take a full three seconds to complete. We can add this into our JavaScript to see how slow it is.

```
hello_sockets/assets/js/socket.js
const slowStatsSocket = new Socket("/stats_socket", {})
slowStatsSocket.connect()

const slowStatsChannel = slowStatsSocket.channel("valid")
slowStatsChannel.join()

for (let i = 0; i < 5; i++) {
  slowStatsChannel.push("slow_ping")
    .receive("ok", () => console.log("Slow ping response received", i))
}
console.log("5 slow pings requested")
```

When you load http://localhost:4000, you will start seeing messages each time that the "slow_ping" message receives a response. Notice that all five responses occur over 15 seconds. This means there is no parallelism present, even though we're using one of the most parallel languages available!

The root cause of this problem is that our Channel is a single process that can handle only one message at a time. When a message is slow to process, other messages in the queue have to wait for it to complete. We artificially added slowness into our handler, but something like a database query or API call could cause this problem naturally.

Phoenix provides a solution for this problem. We can respond in a separate process that executes in parallel with our Channel, meaning we can process all messages concurrently. We'll use Phoenix's socket_ref/1 function to turn our Socket into a minimally represented format that can be passed around. Let's make this change in our StatsChannel.

hello_sockets/lib/hello_sockets_web/channels/stats_channel.ex
```elixir
def handle_in("parallel_slow_ping", _payload, socket) do
  ref = socket_ref(socket)

  Task.start_link(fn ->
    Process.sleep(3_000)
    Phoenix.Channel.reply(ref, {:ok, %{ping: "pong"}})
  end)

  {:noreply, socket}
end
```

We spawn a linked Task that starts a new process and executes the given function. The ref variable used by this function is a stripped-down version of the socket. We pass a reference to the Socket around, rather than the full thing, to avoid copying potentially large amounts of memory around the application.

Task is used to get a Process up and running very quickly. In practice, however, you'll probably be calling into a GenServer. You should always pass the socket_ref to any function you call.

Finally, we use Phoenix.Channel.reply/2 to send a response to the Socket. This serializes the message into a reply and sends it to the Socket transport process. Once this occurs, our client receives the response as if it came directly from the Channel. The outside client has no idea that any of this occurred.

Let's update our client to try out our asynchronous Channel.

hello_sockets/assets/js/socket.js
```javascript
const fastStatsSocket = new Socket("/stats_socket", {})
fastStatsSocket.connect()

const fastStatsChannel = fastStatsSocket.channel("valid")
fastStatsChannel.join()

for (let i = 0; i < 5; i++) {
  fastStatsChannel.push("parallel_slow_ping")
    .receive("ok", () => console.log("Parallel slow ping response", i))
}
console.log("5 parallel slow pings requested")
```

If you load the page at http://localhost:4000, you will see all five messages load after a three-second wait. This means that all messages were processed in parallel and our client does not experience a slowdown.

You shouldn't reach for reply/2 for all of your Channels right away. If you have a use case where a potentially slow database query is being called, or if you are leveraging an external API, then it's a good fit. As with most things, there are benefits and trade-offs to using reply/2. We have seen the benefit of increased parallelism already. A trade-off, though, is that we lose the ability to slow down a client (back-pressure) if it is asking too much of our system. We could write code to support a maximum amount of concurrency per Channel if needed. This would give us increased performance and ability to back-pressure, at a cost of increased complexity.

Asynchronous Channel responses help to close a pitfall of accidentally limiting our Channel throughput. There is no silver bullet for writing code that is fully immune to these slowdowns. Keep an eye out for times when your code is going through a single process, whether it be a Channel or another process.

We'll next look at how to build a scalable data pipeline. This will help us deliver real-time messages as quickly as possible.

Build a Scalable Data Pipeline

Our real-time application keeps our users up to date with the latest information possible. This means we have to get data from our server to our clients, potentially a lot of data, as quickly and efficiently as possible. Delays or missed messages will cause users to not have the most current information in their display, affecting their experience. We must be intentional in designing how the data of our application flows due to the importance of this part of our system. The mechanism that handles outgoing real-time data is a data pipeline.

A data pipeline should have certain traits in order to work quickly and reliably for our users. We'll cover these traits before writing any code. You'll then see how to use the Elixir library GenStage to build a completely in-memory data pipeline. You'll learn about GenStage's features that are important for a data pipeline but would be difficult to build traditionally.

We'll measure our pipeline in order to know that it's working properly. Finally, you'll see what makes GenStage such a powerful base for a data pipeline. Let's start by going over the traits of a production-grade data pipeline.

Traits of a Data Pipeline

Our data pipeline should have a few traits no matter what technology we choose. Our pipeline can scale from both a performance and maintainability perspective when it exhibits these traits.

Deliver messages to all relevant clients
> This means that a real-time event will be broadcast to all our connected Nodes in our data pipeline so they can handle the event for connected Channels. Phoenix PubSub handles this for us, but we must consider that our data pipeline spans multiple servers. We should never send incorrect data to a client.

Fast data delivery

Our data pipeline should be as fast as possible. This allows a client to get the latest information immediately. Producers of data should also be able to trigger a push without worrying about performance.

As durable as needed

Your use case might require that push events have strong guarantees of delivery, but your use case can also be more relaxed and allow for in-memory storage until the push occurs. In either case, you should be able to adjust the data pipeline for your needs, or even completely change it, in a way that doesn't involve completely rewriting it.

As concurrent as needed

Our data pipeline should have limited concurrency so we don't overwhelm our application. This is use-case dependent, as some applications are more likely to overwhelm different components of the system.

Measurable

It's important that we know how long it takes to send data to clients. If it takes one minute to send real-time data, that reduces the application's usability.

These traits allow us to have more control over how our data pipeline operates, both for the happy path and failure scenarios. There has always been debate over the best technical solution for a data pipeline. A good solution for many use cases is a queue-based, GenStage-powered data pipeline. This pipeline exhibits the above traits while also being easy to configure.

Next, we'll walk through writing a data pipeline powered by GenStage.

GenStage Powered Pipeline

GenStage[2] helps us write a data pipeline that can exchange data from producers to consumers. GenStage is not an out-of-the-box data pipeline. Instead, it provides a specification on how to pass data, which we can then implement in our application's data pipeline.

GenStage provides two main stage types that are used to model our pipeline:

- Producer—Coordinates the fetching of data items and then passes to the next consumer stage. Producers can fetch data from a database, or they can keep it in memory. In this chapter, our data pipeline will be completely in memory.

---

2. https://github.com/elixir-lang/gen_stage

- Consumer—Asks for and receives data items from the previous producer stage. These items are then processed by our code before more items are received.

We model our pipeline in a very sequential way. We start with a producer stage that is connected to a consumer stage. We could continue to link together as many stages as needed to model our particular data pipeline—a consumer can also be a producer to other consumers. We'll use the simplest pipeline possible with only one producer and one consumer stage.

Let's jump right into building a data pipeline. The pipeline that we'll end up with at the end of this chapter is generic and can be used for many use cases. I often start with the same base configuration and add to it as necessary. Here's what we'll be building:

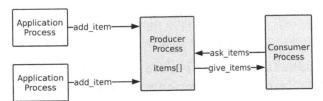

We will start by writing a GenStage producer that provides data to a GenStage consumer. Any process in our application will be able to write new items to the GenStage producer.

hello_sockets/mix.exs

```
{:gen_stage, "~> 0.14.1"}
```

We first add the gen_stage package to our application. As always, run mix deps.get after adding this package definition.

We can now create a basic Producer module.

hello_sockets/lib/hello_sockets/pipeline/producer.ex

```
defmodule HelloSockets.Pipeline.Producer do
  use GenStage

  def start_link(opts) do
    {[name: name], opts} = Keyword.split(opts, [:name])
    GenStage.start_link(__MODULE__, opts, name: name)
  end

  def init(_opts) do
    {:producer, :unused, buffer_size: 10_000}
  end

  def handle_demand(_demand, state) do
    {:noreply, [], state}
  end
end
```

We are using GenStage almost as if it were a GenServer. This allows it to feel very familiar to us when compared to other Elixir code we write. The init/1 function returns {:producer, state} tuple to tell GenStage that we are writing a producer.

Our handle_demand/2 callback isn't doing anything, because in this case, GenStage's internal buffer manages our entire data flow for us.

Next, we will write the function that adds items to our producer.

```
hello_sockets/lib/hello_sockets/pipeline/producer.ex
def push(item = %{}) do
  GenStage.cast(__MODULE__, {:notify, item})
end

def handle_cast({:notify, item}, state) do
  {:noreply, [%{item: item}], state}
end
```

We use GenStage.cast/2 in order to cast a message to our producer process. The handle_cast callback returns a tuple that includes the item in a list.

GenStage will take the items we provide it (there could be several at once) and either sends them to waiting consumer stages or buffers them in memory. We are using GenStage's internal buffer in our pipeline to hold and send data.

This is a non-traditional use of GenStage, but allows us to have an item buffer while writing no buffering code of our own. This, combined with other features of GenStage that we'll cover, gives us a lot of power for very little code.

Let's write a consumer to use our producer's data.

```
hello_sockets/lib/hello_sockets/pipeline/consumer.ex
defmodule HelloSockets.Pipeline.Consumer do
  use GenStage

  def start_link(opts) do
    GenStage.start_link(__MODULE__, opts)
  end

  def init(opts) do
    subscribe_to =
      Keyword.get(opts, :subscribe_to, HelloSockets.Pipeline.Producer)

    {:consumer, :unused, subscribe_to: subscribe_to}
  end
end
```

Our consumer is very similar to the producer, except we are telling GenStage that this is a different stage type and that this process will need to subscribe to a particular producer. Leaving this option configurable gives us the ability to configure the consumer at the supervisor level, which we'll do shortly.

Every consumer must have a callback function to handle items. We won't do any real work in it yet, but will use log statements in order to see what is happening.

hello_sockets/lib/hello_sockets/pipeline/consumer.ex
```elixir
def handle_events(items, _from, state) do
  IO.inspect(
    {__MODULE__, length(items), List.first(items), List.last(items)}
  )

  {:noreply, [], state}
end
```

Our handle_events callback receives multiple items at once; we must always treat the items as a list and not a single item. All that we're doing is logging so we can see how GenStage dispatches items.

The last stage is to configure our producer and consumer in our application tree.

hello_sockets/lib/hello_sockets/application.ex
```elixir
alias HelloSockets.Pipeline.{Consumer, Producer}
```

hello_sockets/lib/hello_sockets/application.ex
```elixir
children = [
  {Producer, name: Producer},
  {Consumer,
   subscribe_to: [{Producer, max_demand: 10, min_demand: 5}]},
  HelloSocketsWeb.Endpoint,
]
```

We add each stage to our application before our Endpoint boots. This is very important because we want our data pipeline to be available before our web endpoints are available. If we didn't do this, we would sometimes see "no process" errors.

The min/max demand option helps us configure our pipeline to only process a few items at a time. This should be configured to a low value for in-memory workloads. It is better to have higher values if using an external data store as this reduces the number of times we go to the external data store.

Let's see what happens when we push items into our producer.

```elixir
$ iex -S mix
iex(1)> alias HelloSockets.Pipeline.Producer
iex(2)> Producer.push(%{})
:ok
{HelloSockets.Pipeline.Consumer, 1, %{item: %{}}, %{item: %{}}}

iex(3)> Enum.each((1..53), & Producer.push(%{n: &1}))
{HelloSockets.Pipeline.Consumer, 1, %{item: %{n: 1}}, %{item: %{n: 1}}}
{HelloSockets.Pipeline.Consumer, 1, %{item: %{n: 2}}, %{item: %{n: 2}}}
...
```

```
{HelloSockets.Pipeline.Consumer, 1, %{item: %{n: 9}}, %{item: %{n: 9}}}
{HelloSockets.Pipeline.Consumer, 5, %{item: %{n: 10}}, %{item: %{n: 14}}}
...
{HelloSockets.Pipeline.Consumer, 5, %{item: %{n: 40}}, %{item: %{n: 44}}}
{HelloSockets.Pipeline.Consumer, 5, %{item: %{n: 45}}, %{item: %{n: 49}}}
{HelloSockets.Pipeline.Consumer, 1, %{item: %{n: 50}}, %{item: %{n: 50}}}
{HelloSockets.Pipeline.Consumer, 3, %{item: %{n: 51}}, %{item: %{n: 53}}}
```

Your output may look slightly different than this—the important thing to see
is the grouping of messages.

You will immediately see a consumer message after the first push/1 call. Things
get more interesting when we send many events to the producer in a short
time period. The consumer starts by processing one item at a time. After ten
are processed, the items are processed five at a time until the items are all
processed.

This pattern appears a bit unusual because we never see ten items processed
at once, and we also see many single items processed. A GenStage consumer
splits events into batches based on the max and min demand. Our values
are ten and five, so the events are split into a max batch size of five. The single
items are an implementation detail of how the batching works—this isn't a
big deal for a real application.

For most use cases, you won't need to worry about that internals of the
buffering process. GenStage takes care of the entire process of managing the
buffer and demand of consumers. You only need to think about writing data
to the producer and the rest will be managed for you.

This introductory example shows that it's easy to get set up with GenStage.
Let's look at how to easily add concurrency and Channel broadcasts into our
pipeline. This will give us a useful pipeline that pushes data to our Channels.

Adding Concurrency and Channels

A scalable data pipeline must handle multiple items at the same time; it must
be concurrent. GenStage has a solution for adding concurrency to our pipeline
with the ConsumerSupervisor module. This module allows us to focus on defining
the pipeline and letting the library take care of how the concurrency will be
managed.

ConsumerSupervisor is a type of GenStage consumer that spawns a child process
for each item received. The amount of concurrency is controlled via setup
options, and it otherwise behaves exactly like a consumer. Every item spawns
a new process; they're not re-used, but this is cheap to do in Elixir.

A quick note on concurrency versus parallelism. You make your system concurrent by creating processes that run work. The BEAM then makes that system parallel by taking the concurrent work and running it over multiple cores at the same time. All of the concern around how parallel execution happens is completely handled by the BEAM.

Our final result in this chapter will look like this:

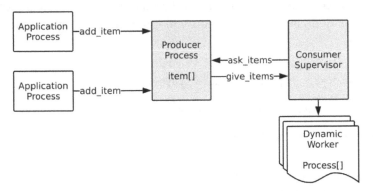

Our Consumer has been replaced by a ConsumerSupervisor, which has the ability to dynamically spawn worker processes. Let's walk through adding Consumer-Supervisor to our pipeline.

hello_sockets/lib/hello_sockets/pipeline/consumer_supervisor.ex
```elixir
defmodule HelloSockets.Pipeline.ConsumerSupervisor do
  use ConsumerSupervisor

  alias HelloSockets.Pipeline.{Producer, Worker}

  def start_link(opts) do
    ConsumerSupervisor.start_link(__MODULE__, opts)
  end

  def init(opts) do
    subscribe_to = Keyword.get(opts, :subscribe_to, Producer)
    supervisor_opts = [strategy: :one_for_one, subscribe_to: subscribe_to]

    children = [
      %{id: Worker, start: {Worker, :start_link, []}, restart: :transient}
    ]

    ConsumerSupervisor.init(children, supervisor_opts)
  end
end
```

This ConsumerSupervisor module is, fittingly, a mix of common Supervisor and Consumer process setup. We configure our module to subscribe to the correct producer stage like we did for the regular Consumer. The biggest difference here is that we define what the children of our ConsumerSupervisor are.

We have to set up our new ConsumerSupervisor stage before we can try it out. The setup is exactly like our Consumer from earlier. Replace the previous Producer and Consumer alias with our new module.

hello_sockets/lib/hello_sockets/application.ex
```
alias HelloSockets.Pipeline.Producer
alias HelloSockets.Pipeline.ConsumerSupervisor, as: Consumer
```

This alias change swaps out our existing Consumer for our new ConsumerSupervisor. If you run the code at this point, you will encounter an error that our Worker doesn't exist.

```
$ iex -S mix
iex(1)> HelloSockets.Pipeline.Producer.push(%{})
:ok
iex(2)> [error] ConsumerSupervisor failed to start child
```

Let's define our Worker module now.

hello_sockets/lib/hello_sockets/pipeline/worker.ex
```
defmodule HelloSockets.Pipeline.Worker do
  def start_link(item) do
    Task.start_link(fn ->
      process(item)
    end)
  end
end
```

We are using Task.start_link/1 to start a new Process that runs our item-handler code. This simplifies our Worker because we don't have to worry about setting up a new GenServer.

hello_sockets/lib/hello_sockets/pipeline/worker.ex
```
defp process(item) do
  IO.inspect(item)
  Process.sleep(1000)
end
```

For now, we're simply printing out the item and sleeping for a bit. This will demonstrate how the ConsumerSupervisor processes our items. Don't worry, we'll fill this function with real work shortly.

Let's observe what happens when we push work through our pipeline:

```
$ iex -S mix
iex(1)> Enum.each((1..50), & HelloSockets.Pipeline.Producer.push(%{n: &1}))
:ok
[group of 1-10]
[group of 11-20]
[group of 21-30]
```

```
[group of 31-40]
[group of 41-50]
```

You'll see that the jobs run ten at a time with a delay in between. The items always group together the same way, but the group itself can come in any order. This is because our tasks are running fully parallel with each other and order is no longer guaranteed.

In our earlier example, with a regular Consumer, the items were processed in batches of five. In this example, the items were processed ten at a time. The GenStage batch size hasn't changed, but the ConsumerSupervisor is able to start up max_demand (ten) workers at a time. Each worker handles a single item, so the end result is that ten items are processed in parallel. You should tune the max_demand to the maximum amount of processes that you want to run in parallel, based on your use case.

ConsumerSupervisor is very powerful. We added concurrent execution to our data pipeline in only a small amount of code, and most of it was boilerplate. This scales to a very large number of jobs with very little issue, thanks to the power of Elixir and the BEAM. One of the biggest advantages of how we added our concurrency is that the BEAM manages parallel execution of our work. If we doubled our CPU cores, we'd double the execution parallelism of our pipeline.

Let's change our Worker module to do some real work. We'll push items for a particular user from our server to our AuthChannel. Replace the process/1 function with the following code:

hello_sockets/lib/hello_sockets/pipeline/worker.ex
```elixir
defp process(%{item: %{data: data, user_id: user_id}}) do
  Process.sleep(1000)
  HelloSocketsWeb.Endpoint.broadcast!("user:#{user_id}", "push", data)
end
```

We are using our Endpoint's broadcast! function to deliver a message to a particular user. The pushed data and user ID are passed via the data pipeline item.

The final step is to connect to our private user topic and listen for the push event.

hello_sockets/assets/js/socket.js
```javascript
const authUserChannel = authSocket.channel(`user:${window.userId}`)

authUserChannel.on("push", (payload) => {
  console.log("received auth user push", payload)
})

authUserChannel.join()
```

With this, we're able to do an end-to-end test of our data pipeline. Start the server with iex -S mix phx.server and load http://localhost:4000. Run the following code to see the items come through to the front end; you may need to copy/paste this code in because our iex terminal is very noisy.

```
$ iex -S mix phx.server
iex(1)> alias HelloSockets.Pipeline.Producer
iex(2)> push = &(Producer.push(%{data: %{n: &1}, user_id: 1}))
iex(3)> Enum.each((1..50), push)
```

You will see all 50 messages arrive in your JavaScript console, roughly in groups of ten. Try changing the max_demand option in order to change the amount of concurrency. You will see the grouping change when you do this. You can even change it to 1 to see it process a single item at a time. If you change the user_id property, you will no longer see the events because they are not delivered to this topic.

We now have a working end-to-end data pipeline capable of pushing data to our Channels. We'll use this pipeline in part II to deliver e-commerce updates to our clients.

We may have a working pipeline, but we're lacking measurements and tests for it. Let's cover that next.

Measuring our Pipeline

The ultimate question of running software is "how do I know it's working?" Our data pipeline is no different. We need to be able to answer questions about the health of our pipeline so that we can fix any problems that occur. We'll achieve this by adding measurement for how long our Worker takes to process and how long it takes to broadcast our message.

We can use our stats knowledge to capture a timing event for our Worker process. We'll trigger a manual timing event in order to measure the time that it takes between item generation and push delivery. Let's jump right into our Worker process.

Replace our current Worker.start_link function with this new timed one:

```
hello_sockets/lib/hello_sockets/pipeline/worker.ex
def start_link(item) do
  Task.start_link(fn ->
    HelloSockets.Statix.measure("pipeline.worker.process_time", fn ->
      process(item)
    end)
  end)
end
```

That wasn't very exciting; all we did was add a measure around our existing code! This is the beauty of taking measurements: it doesn't have to be hard. This simple two-line addition allows us keep track of a critical part of our pipeline health. It does feel a bit low-value to capture this single-function timing. However, it quickly becomes important as we add more logic or servers.

Adding a measurement of our total delivery time is a bit more complex. We aren't able to wrap that in a function because it occurs over our entire pipeline. However, we're able to capture the current time when we enqueue an item to our pipeline. We'll then intercept the outgoing event in our Channel and make a measurement of the current time minus the event's time. This difference tells us how long the pipeline and Channel took to process the item. Let's start by writing the current time when an item is added to our pipeline.

`hello_sockets/lib/hello_sockets/pipeline/timing.ex`
```
defmodule HelloSockets.Pipeline.Timing do
  def unix_ms_now() do
    :erlang.system_time(:millisecond)
  end
end
```

This helper allows us to get the current unix time in milliseconds. We'll use this at the entry and exit points of our data pipeline. There are different ways[3] to measure time in the BEAM, but we are using the system time because a real-time app often runs across multiple servers. If we used :erlang.monotonic_time/0, we would have drastically inaccurate timing information. However, there is some inaccuracy with system time as well because two servers will often have slightly different times.

We must add the current time to the item as it gets enqueued through the producer:

`hello_sockets/lib/hello_sockets/pipeline/producer.ex`
```
alias HelloSockets.Pipeline.Timing

def push_timed(item = %{}) do
  GenStage.cast(__MODULE__, {:notify_timed, item, Timing.unix_ms_now()})
end

def handle_cast({:notify_timed, item, unix_ms}, state) do
  {:noreply, [%{item: item, enqueued_at: unix_ms}], state}
end
```

Our push_timed function provides the current time with the items when it casts to the GenStage producer process. This is important because it's possible for

---

3. https://adoptingerlang.org/docs/development/hard_to_get_right/#handling-time

the notify message to be delayed if there are many items in the producer's message queue. If we captured the current time in the handle_cast function, then our measurement won't represent the entire pipeline.

We will change our Worker to pass enqueued_at in the broadcasted message.

```
hello_sockets/lib/hello_sockets/pipeline/worker.ex
defp process(%{
      item: %{data: data, user_id: user_id},
      enqueued_at: unix_ms
    }) do
  HelloSocketsWeb.Endpoint.broadcast!("user:#{user_id}", "push_timed", %{
    data: data,
    at: unix_ms
  })
end
```

This function must be defined above (or in place of) the existing process function or else it won't be used due to pattern matching. This is a pretty simple unit of code that writes to unix_ms in the broadcast.

Our previous Worker broadcast relied on Phoenix to directly send the data to the client. This won't work anymore because we need to run custom logic after the data is pushed. We'll make a change to intercept the outgoing message "push_timed" in order to add measurements.

```
hello_sockets/lib/hello_sockets_web/channels/auth_channel.ex
intercept ["push_timed"]

alias HelloSockets.Pipeline.Timing

def handle_out("push_timed", %{data: data, at: enqueued_at}, socket) do
  push(socket, "push_timed", data)

  HelloSockets.Statix.histogram(
    "pipeline.push_delivered",
    Timing.unix_ms_now() - enqueued_at
  )

  {:noreply, socket}
end
```

AuthChannel will intercept outgoing "push_timed" events now. Our handle_out callback will run, and it immediately pushes the data to the client. We capture the elapsed milliseconds by taking the difference between now and enqueued_at. We are using a histogram metric type to capture statistical information with our metric. Histograms aggregate several attributes of a given metric, such as percentiles, count, and sum. You will often use a histogram type when capturing a timing metric.

One last change is needed to run this example end-to-end. Let's add this new event type to our JavaScript client.

```
hello_sockets/assets/js/socket.js
authUserChannel.on("push_timed", (payload) => {
  console.log("received timed auth user push", payload)
})
```

You should start your server with iex -S mix phx.server and load http://localhost:4000. You'll see a histogram metric appear if you use the new Producer.push_timed function.

```
$ iex -S mix phx.server
iex(1)> alias HelloSockets.Pipeline.Producer
iex(1)> Producer.push_timed(%{data: %{n: 1}, user_id: 1})
:ok
StatsD metric: pipeline.worker.process_time 0|ms
StatsD metric: pipeline.push_delivered 0|h
```

Try enqueueing a lot of messages to see the difference in time.

```
$ iex -S mix phx.server
iex(1)> alias HelloSockets.Pipeline.Producer
iex(2)> push = &(Producer.push_timed(%{data: %{n: &1}, user_id: 1}))
iex(3)> Enum.each((1..500), push)
:ok
StatsD metric: pipeline.push_delivered 0|h
...
StatsD metric: pipeline.push_delivered 25|h
```

In this example, you will see a total pipeline time of several milliseconds for the very last item. This demonstrates that our data pipeline has to work through all 499 messages before getting to the last one. This is going to take a small amount of time; we wouldn't expect to see 0ms for both the first and last item.

You can play around with the max_demand in Application to see how it affects the timing. When I go from 10 to 1 max_demand, the timing doubled from 25ms to 50ms. When I go from 10 to 100 max_demand, the timing only decreased to 23ms. Your machine is capable of a maximum amount of parallel execution, based on the number of cores, which could change these numbers and how the amount of concurrency impacts performance.

There is one disclaimer for this measurement technique that is worth repeating: our data pipeline spans multiple servers, so the data could originate on a different server than where it finishes. Two servers usually have a slight amount of clock difference that would either add or remove milliseconds to the difference. In practice, we can accept this because the difference will usually be small, and we aren't basing application logic on the times.

There is one final piece of developing a strong data pipeline that we haven't covered yet: tests. Let's write an integration-level test to ensure our application can move data the whole way through our pipeline.

Test our Data Pipeline

Good production code includes tests for verification. We are able to test our data pipeline to ensure that everything is wired up correctly. Data should move from beginning to end without any error.

There are a few different ways to approach the testing methodology for our pipeline. We could write unit tests for every part of the pipeline or integration tests for the entire pipeline. We'll look at how to integration test our pipeline to see all pieces work together. This serves us well because we don't have complex logic in our data pipeline. If we had more complex functions in our Worker, then we would most likely also want unit tests.

We will write our integration test in a new test file. Phoenix's ChannelCase helper will simulate a connected socket.

```
hello_sockets/test/integration/pipeline_test.exs
defmodule Integration.PipelineTest do
  use HelloSocketsWeb.ChannelCase, async: false

  alias HelloSocketsWeb.AuthSocket
  alias HelloSockets.Pipeline.Producer

  defp connect_auth_socket(user_id) do
    {:ok, _, %Phoenix.Socket{}} =
      socket(AuthSocket, nil, %{user_id: user_id})
      |> subscribe_and_join("user:#{user_id}", %{})
  end

  test "event are pushed from begining to end correctly" do
    connect_auth_socket(1)

    Enum.each(1..10, fn n ->
      Producer.push_timed(%{data: %{n: n}, user_id: 1})
      assert_push "push_timed", %{n: ^n}
    end)
  end
end
```

We use our Producer module to enqueue an event that will eventually make its way to the Channel as an outgoing message. Everything behaves exactly the same as it did in our Channel tests that didn't use the pipeline. We have to use a synchronous test, denoted by async: false, because our data pipeline is globally available to the test suite. Using a synchronous test prevents random test failures.

We should always include a negative test to go with our positive test. Let's add a test for ensuring that users don't receive each other's data.

hello_sockets/test/integration/pipeline_test.exs
```
test "an event is not delivered to the wrong user" do
  connect_auth_socket(2)

  Producer.push_timed(%{data: %{test: true}, user_id: 1})
  refute_push "push_timed", %{test: true}
end
```

Finally, we should test that our pipeline emits a StatsD metric at the end of processing. We will use StatsDLogger in a special test mode to write this test–it will forward any stats to the test process rather than the StatsD server. Let's configure our test environment for StatsD and then write our test.

hello_sockets/config/test.exs
```
config :statix, HelloSockets.Statix, port: 8127
```

hello_sockets/test/integration/pipeline_test.exs
```
test "events are timed on delivery" do
  assert {:ok, _} = StatsDLogger.start_link(port: 8127, formatter: :send)
  connect_auth_socket(1)

  Producer.push_timed(%{data: %{test: true}, user_id: 1})

  assert_push "push_timed", %{test: true}
  assert_receive {:statsd_recv, "pipeline.push_delivered", _value}
end
```

When you run mix test, you will see all the tests passing. We now have a working integration test!

Testing doesn't have to be complex to be powerful. This integration test doesn't flex every nook and cranny of our data pipeline, but it covers close to all of it. Now that we have these tests, we would learn immediately if our pipeline became misconfigured.

Before we wrap up this data pipeline section, let's cover how GenStage can serve us through changing or complex requirements.

The Power of GenStage

Our applications must grow and adapt to changing requirements or lessons learned over time. We find ourselves in the best position when we can implement new requirements by changing very little code. The power of GenStage is that it can grow with our application. We start simple and add as needed over time.

Let's look at a few examples of how our application may change over time. We'll think about how GenStage can help us achieve these goals.

Enforce stricter delivery guarantees for messages

One of the biggest trade-offs with a fully in-memory approach is that a server crash or restart will lose all current in-memory work. We can use a data store such as a SQL database, Redis, or Kafka to store every outgoing message. This would reduce data loss potential when a server restarts.   GenStage helps us here because its core purpose is to handle data requesting and buffering from external data stores. We could adapt our pipeline's Producer module in order to read from the data store.

You may get pretty far with an in-memory, no-persistence solution. There is a great saying in software architecture: "Our software architecture is judged by the decisions we are able to defer." This means that you're able to tackle the important things up-front and leave yourself open to tackle currently less important things in the future—such as pipeline persistence.

Augment an outgoing message with data from a database

Our GenStage-powered pipeline exposes a Worker module that can do *anything* you want it to do. For example, it's possible to augment messages with data from an external API or database. These external resources often have a maximum throughput, so the maximum concurrency option helps us to avoid overwhelming these external data providers. We could also leverage the concept of a GenStage ProducerConsumer to achieve the goal of data augmentation.

Equitable dispatching between users

Our GenStage-based pipeline will currently send items on a first-come-first-served basis. This is great for most applications, but it could be problematic in an environment where a single user (or team of users) has significantly more messages than other users. In this scenario, all users would become slower due to the effect of a single user.

GenStage allows us to write a custom Dispatcher module capable of routing messages in any way we want. We could leverage this to isolate users that are taking over the system's capacity onto a single worker. We wouldn't need to change any existing part of our application other than our Producer and Consumer modules.

This is an advanced use case, but it shows that GenStage can achieve fairly complex requirements with little code change.

We don't *have* to do any of these things until it's the right time. We're able to defer those decisions and focus on the behavior that is most important for *now*.

GenStage is a great choice for writing a data pipeline. It's efficient, well-designed with OTP principles, and easy to adapt to new requirements over time.

We've covered all of The Performance Pitfalls! We'll think about these things as we develop our application in part II.

Wrapping Up

The Performance Pitfalls are common problems that affect our application development. We're able to get a head start on our application's performance by considering them early in the development process. The key aspect of overcoming these pitfalls is to be intentional. We must think about how to overcome performance problems throughout the development life cycle; it's not good enough to consider performance at the beginning or end only.

We need to know if our application is running and healthy. We can use a metrics protocol like StatsD, combined with a data visualization service, to provide measurements of our running application. It is easy to add metrics to your applications, so always do it!

Elixir is designed around concurrency, but we must still consider how our code runs. Channels are not concurrent because they are a single process. This affects a Channel's throughput, but this can be counteracted with development techniques. We're able to spawn processes to handle requests. This gives our Channel the ability to process multiple requests at the same time for a connected client.

Moving data from server to client is one of the key tasks of our real-time application. Genstage is used to develop a real-time data pipeline that provides us with a scalable and well-featured way to process data. We will often use the same basic GenStage setup to configure our application's data pipeline, so we don't reinvent the wheel for every real-time application we develop.

Next, we build a real-world application from the ground up. All of our Channel and real-time application knowledge will be used as we develop simple to more advanced features throughout part II.

Part II

Building a Real-Time Application

We have the fundamentals of Phoenix Channels down and have seen some of the challenges that real-time applications can bring. We will build a larger, real-world application that spans many large requirements in order to solidify our knowledge in a practical way.

## CHAPTER 7

Build a Real-Time Sneaker Store

In part I, we covered the topics necessary for building real-time applications powered by Phoenix Channels. Your toolbox has been assembled and is now ready for action. In part II, we'll use all the tools we have to build a real-world application. Throughout these next chapters, you'll build an e-commerce store with a twist. We'll implement new features in each chapter until we have a fairly complete product.

There is a fine line when writing a book between wanting to show everything and keeping the book concise. And there is a lot of value in building a Phoenix application from the ground up, from mix phx.new to a working product, but it takes up time that would be better spent on the book's main topic. Rather than starting from a completely empty project, you'll be using an application base that already has a functional core and data models for our e-commerce application.

Our project will use a few concepts that you might not be familiar with. We'll use Ecto to interact with a database, create a distributed system for scalability, and we'll write a GenServer to give us fast access to local data. All of these tools are regularly used in real projects, but don't worry if you're not familiar with them yet. We'll walk through each step and cover what is happening. The project base will also make it easy to breeze through these unfamiliar concepts.

We'll start by covering the requirements and goals of our online shoe store. The project looks simple enough on the surface, but the need to serve thousands of simultaneous users shopping for a limited selection of items adds complexity. We'll leverage the power of Phoenix and OTP to build a fast, real-time e-commerce store. You'll write a simple Phoenix controller, add real-time features to the application, and then run the application across multiple servers. Let's jump into the product requirements!

From Product Requirements to a Plan

We've been contacted by a local sneaker store, Sneakers23, that is looking to better manage how they release new shoes online. Some of their shoe launches have sold out in 30 seconds and are hotly contested by thousands of shoppers wanting to buy a pair. Shoppers have given feedback that the current system doesn't let them know what's still available until it's too late to adjust. We're going to solve these problems by creating an online shoe release site for Sneakers23.

Sneakers23 would like the ability to launch different shoes at specific times, with each launch getting thousands of visitors and finishing within a minute. Each size will indicate the current stock levels (low, medium, high, out) in real-time to each visitor. Shoppers will be able to add up to two items into their cart and will be alerted if any of their items sell out.

We'll use a simple visual design throughout this project in order to focus on the behavior of the system, so don't worry if you aren't familiar with web design.

The result at the end of this chapter will look like this:

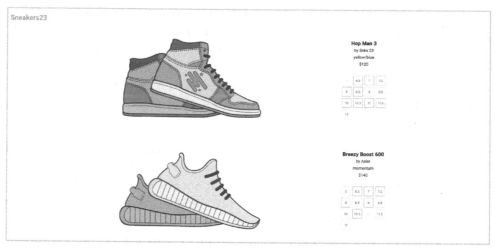

Let's cover the specific goals for the first phase of this project.

Phase 1 Goals

Our first phase focuses on establishing the basic pages of the system. We'll add two different real-time features to complete a working demo. We'll be able to extend the application with additional features in future chapters. To start, you'll build an application that fulfills these requirements:

- Display a single page containing all current products to the shopper.

- Show the shopper all shoe sizes available as well as the current stock levels.
- Update the products and availability during the launch.
- Run multiple servers at the same time without issue.

In the next few chapters, we'll add features like a checkout process and an admin section.

Let's start with the data model and system architecture.

Modeling the Data

Sneaker23 has a fairly simple e-commerce data model. We'll build specifically to the needs of this store, rather than trying to build a generic e-commerce platform, which would be much more complex. The e-commerce structure breaks down as follows:

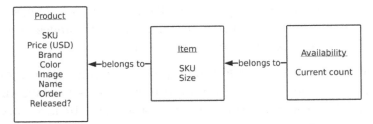

Products are the highest-level data model and consist of the attributes of a particular type of shoe. A product is not directly sellable on its own. Instead, each product is sold through individual SKU-size pairings called items. An item has availability and cannot be sold when the available count is 0. The item availability is stored in a separate table, which is just an implementation detail of this project.

These database schemas have been implemented for you using Ecto. You'll download this application base in the next section.

Developing a System Architecture

We must pick a system architecture that can handle thousands of simultaneous data requests while also still being easy to write and maintain. A useful technique, which we'll leverage in this project, is to use an Elixir process that holds the current application state. The local state must be kept in sync with other servers, it must be recoverable in case of crashes, and it should not be used in operations that must be exactly correct, such as checking out. The figure on page 124 is what our system will look like at the end of this chapter.

A shopper's web page connects to a Phoenix controller that reads the current data from the inventory process. The shopper then connects to a Channel for

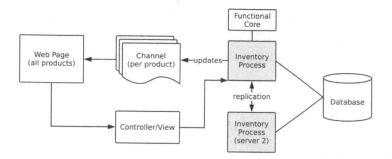

each product they're viewing. This Channel doesn't receive any data from the shopper, but it keeps track of all inventory updates. The inventory process is powered by a functional core and handles replication to other servers. Finally, the database is the source of truth for our data and is used when loading the inventory and in operations like checking out. Our servers will use a replication process to send data about inventory changes to each other, allowing them to always reflect the correct state.

It's not always necessary to add a data process to your application. In the case of our store, the number of simultaneous requests for data will be very high and the database could prove to be a bottleneck. The inventory process acts like a cache that contains correct (or close to correct) data about the inventory. Also, the inventory and replication processes will give you the experience of implementing a GenServer in Elixir, which is one of the most useful programming constructs in Elixir.

Now that you've seen the project requirements and architecture, it's time to jump into coding. You'll need to set up the project first, in order to get the database schemas and functional core.

Set Up the Project

If you have not yet downloaded the book's code, following the instructions found in Introduction, on page xi, then do so now—you'll need the project base in order to start this chapter. You should copy the base project into a working folder, like so. You'll need to substitute code/location with the folder of the extracted code:

```
$ cp -R code/location/sneakers_23_base ~/sneakers_23
$ cd ~/sneakers_23
$ git init && git add . && git commit -m "initial commit (from base)"
```

The project base is now set up in a folder that you can work from. You can verify that everything is working by running the test suite.

```
$ mix deps.get && mix ecto.setup && mix test
Compiling 2 files (.ex)
Generated sneakers_23 app
...............
$ npm --prefix assets install

Finished in 0.1 seconds
15 tests, 0 failures
```

Finally, let's test that the web view is working properly. Use the following commands to seed the database and then start the server.

```
$ mix ecto.reset && mix run -e "Sneakers23Mock.Seeds.seed!()"
$ iex -S mix phx.server
```

When you visit http://localhost:4000, you will see a "coming soon..." page. This changes when you release one of the products using a helper function.

```
$ iex -S mix phx.server
iex(1)> Sneakers23.Inventory.mark_product_released!(1)
:ok
```

When you refresh the page, you will see that the size selector is available. It has randomized data that makes each seed slightly different. Finally, you can ensure that the front end updates as shoes are sold. This application is not yet real-time, so you'll need to refresh to see the size selector display when sizes are sold out. It will become a bit noisy when you run this command due to SQL logging, but keep refreshing the page until it's done.

```
$ iex -S mix phx.server
iex(2)> Sneakers23Mock.InventoryReducer.sell_random_until_gone!(500)
...
[info] Elixir.Sneakers23Mock.InventoryReducer sold out!
```

As you refresh, the size selector on the front end will change colors and then become disabled once the InventoryReducer finishes.

You're all set to continue with this chapter! We'll jump right into making the application real-time.

Render Real-Time HTML with Channels

There are two major real-time features of our store. The first is to mark a shoe as released and to update all connected shoppers with the released shoe. We'll use HTML replacement for this feature by swapping out "coming soon" with our size selector. This approach makes it easy to ensure that a user interface looks the same before and after a real-time update occurs.

Adding the application's real-time features is usually less work than the other parts of writing the application due to Channel's abstractions. In this chapter, we'll write a small amount of code compared to the size of the project base that exists already. Real-time features are often added on top of other features, so it does make sense that you'll spend more time building the features and less time enhancing them to be real-time.

Our front end currently isn't connected to a Channel that could provide it with real-time updates. To start, we'll add a very simple Socket and Channel, and then connect our storefront to it. We'll leverage a Channel to send data from the server to a client. We don't need to add authentication because this is a public feature that anyone can see. There is no user-sensitive data in any of the Channels that we'll build in this chapter. Let's start by updating our Endpoint with a new Socket.

sneakers_23/lib/sneakers_23_web/endpoint.ex

```
socket "/product_socket", Sneakers23Web.ProductSocket,
  websocket: true,
  longpoll: false
```

You can replace the existing UserSocket definition with this one. UserSocket is one of the generated files that comes with Phoenix. You can optionally delete the channels/user_socket.ex file now. Let's define ProductSocket now.

sneakers_23/lib/sneakers_23_web/channels/product_socket.ex

```
defmodule Sneakers23Web.ProductSocket do
  use Phoenix.Socket

  ## Channels
  channel "product:*", Sneakers23Web.ProductChannel

  def connect(_params, socket, _connect_info) do
    {:ok, socket}
  end

  def id(_socket), do: nil
end
```

This is a very standard Socket defined without any authentication, because the feature is publicly accessible. Our ProductChannel will be equally simple for now.

sneakers_23/lib/sneakers_23_web/channels/product_channel.ex

```
defmodule Sneakers23Web.ProductChannel do
  use Phoenix.Channel

  alias Sneakers23Web.{Endpoint, ProductView}

  def join("product:" <> _sku, %{}, socket) do
    {:ok, socket}
  end
end
```

We're not doing anything exciting in this Channel yet. Let's change that by defining a broadcast function. This is a fairly interesting function because we're going to render our size selector HTML for a given product.

sneakers_23/lib/sneakers_23_web/channels/product_channel.ex

```
def notify_product_released(product = %{id: id}) do
  size_html = Phoenix.View.render_to_string(
    ProductView,
    "_sizes.html",
    product: product
  )

  Endpoint.broadcast!("product:#{id}", "released", %{
    size_html: size_html
  })
end
```

This technique allows us to render full pages or templates from anywhere in our Elixir application. This is a big advantage because all the template logic lives in Elixir, rather than being duplicated in JavaScript. We should write a test for this function.

sneakers_23/test/sneakers_23_web/channels/product_channel_test.exs

```
Line 1  defmodule Sneakers23Web.ProductChannelTest do
   -      use Sneakers23Web.ChannelCase, async: true
   -      alias Sneakers23Web.{Endpoint, ProductChannel}
   -      alias Sneakers23.Inventory.CompleteProduct
   5
   -      describe "notify_product_released/1" do
   -        test "the size selector for the product is broadcast" do
   -          {inventory, _data} = Test.Factory.InventoryFactory.complete_products()
   -          [_, product] = CompleteProduct.get_complete_products(inventory)
  10
   -          topic = "product:#{product.id}"
   -          Endpoint.subscribe(topic)
   -          ProductChannel.notify_product_released(product)
   -
  15          assert_broadcast "released", %{size_html: html}
   -          assert html =~ "size-container__entry"
   -          Enum.each(product.items, fn item ->
   -            assert html =~ ~s(value="#{item.id}")
   -          end)
  20        end
   -      end
   -  end
```

Our test subscribes to the notified topic, on line 12, so that any broadcasted messages will be received by the test process. This lets assert_broadcast check that the right message was broadcast. On line 18, our test ensures that each item of the product is accounted for in the HTML.

This function will be called whenever our item is released, which happens in the Inventory context. We'll use our Sneakers23Web module as our web context and will define a function that delegates to the ProductChannel. Elixir gives us a built-in way to do this.

sneakers_23/lib/sneakers_23_web.ex
```
defdelegate notify_product_released(product),
  to: Sneakers23Web.ProductChannel
```

The defdelegate macro[1] is incredibly useful for building a context module because it lets you separate implementation from exposure in a very quick and easy way. We now have to use this delegate function in our Inventory context. Without it, a product release event will not be broadcast to connected clients. Add the following test at the end of the existing describe block.

sneakers_23/test/sneakers_23/inventory_test.exs
```
test "the update is sent to the client", %{test: test_name} do
  {_, %{p1: p1}} = Test.Factory.InventoryFactory.complete_products()
  {:ok, pid} = Server.start_link(name: test_name, loader_mod: DatabaseLoader)
  Sneakers23Web.Endpoint.subscribe("product:#{p1.id}")

  Inventory.mark_product_released!(p1.id, pid: pid)
  assert_received %Phoenix.Socket.Broadcast{event: "released"}
end
```

You'll see this test fails when you run mix test. This is because the Inventory.mark_product_released!/2 function doesn't call notify_product_released/1. Let's fix that now.

sneakers_23/lib/sneakers_23/inventory.ex
```
def mark_product_released!(id), do: mark_product_released!(id, [])
def mark_product_released!(product_id, opts) do
  pid = Keyword.get(opts, :pid, __MODULE__)

  %{id: id} = Store.mark_product_released!(product_id)
  {:ok, inventory} = Server.mark_product_released!(pid, id)
  {:ok, product} = CompleteProduct.get_product_by_id(inventory, id)
  Sneakers23Web.notify_product_released(product)

  :ok
end
```

You can use default options in the function definition, like mark_product_released!(product_id, opts \\ []), instead of writing two separate function definitions. However, this book will often omit that type of definition.

All of the tests will now pass. This means that the back end is fully working. The Inventory context provides a function that marks the product as released

---

1. https://hexdocs.pm/elixir/Kernel.html#defdelegate/2

in the database, changes it locally in the Inventory.Server process, then pushes the new state to any connected clients.

Now that our back end is configured, let's connect our front end by using the Phoenix Channel JavaScript client. Our strategy will be to grab the data-product-id attributes off of our HTML DOM elements and then connect to a Channel per matching product ID.

```
sneakers_23/assets/js/app.js
import css from "../css/app.css"
import { productSocket } from "./socket"
import dom from './dom'

const productIds = dom.getProductIds()

if (productIds.length > 0) {
  productSocket.connect()
  productIds.forEach((id) => setupProductChannel(productSocket, id))
}

function setupProductChannel(socket, productId) {
  const productChannel = socket.channel(`product:${productId}`)
  productChannel.join()
    .receive("error", () => {
      console.error("Channel join failed")
    })
}
```

This isn't a runnable example yet because we need to define our dom.js and socket.js files. However, the flow that we'll follow is complete. We'll soon add additional setup operations into setupProductChannel/1, which is why that function ends without closing.

```
sneakers_23/assets/js/socket.js
import { Socket } from "phoenix"

export const productSocket = new Socket("/product_socket")
```

This file simply makes the productSocket available for import. It's a good idea to keep the code separated with exported modules to help increase the focus of a particular file, even if there's no logic in the file now. It also gives us a place to add more Socket-specific logic in the future, if needed. We still need to define our DOM operations.

```
sneakers_23/assets/js/dom.js
const dom = {}

function getProductIds() {
  const products = document.querySelectorAll('.product-listing')
  return Array.from(products).map((el) => el.dataset.productId)
}
```

```
dom.getProductIds = getProductIds
```

export default dom

This function will grab the matching .product-listing elements and return each pro-ductId attribute. At this point, everything is complete for our Socket to connect. Try it out by starting mix phx.server and visiting http://localhost:4000. You should see a Socket request in the "Network" tab as well as Channel join messages for product:1 and product:2. We're ready to wire up our product release message.

Start your server with iex -S mix phx.server so you can trigger the release message. Do so like this:

```
$ iex -S mix phx.server
iex(1)> {:ok, products} = Sneakers23.Inventory.get_complete_products()
iex(2)> List.last(products) |> Sneakers23Web.notify_product_released()
:ok
```

You can run this as many times as you want because it doesn't modify data. Try to watch the network message tab while you execute it. You should see the "released" message come through with an HTML payload. If you don't see it, make sure that you're inspecting the product_socket connection and not the live_reload connection.

Our front end needs to listen for this event in order to display the HTML.

sneakers_23/assets/js/app.js
```
function setupProductChannel(socket, productId) {
  const productChannel = socket.channel(`product:${productId}`)
  productChannel.join()
    .receive("error", () => {
      console.error("Channel join failed")
    })

  productChannel.on('released', ({ size_html }) => {
    dom.replaceProductComingSoon(productId, size_html)
  })
}
```

Our setup function is now adding a handler for the "released" event from the Channel. When the event is received, the DOM elements will be replaced with the new HTML. We'll add that function into our dom module, above the bottom export.

sneakers_23/assets/js/dom.js
```
function replaceProductComingSoon(productId, sizeHtml) {
  const name = `.product-soon-${productId}`
  const productSoonEls = document.querySelectorAll(name)

  productSoonEls.forEach((el) => {
    const fragment = document.createRange()
                        .createContextualFragment(sizeHtml)
```

```
    el.replaceWith(fragment)
  })
}

dom.replaceProductComingSoon = replaceProductComingSoon
```

We're not using jQuery or a similar library in this project. If we were, we could replace this HTML with something a bit simpler. This function lets the DOM turn HTML into the appropriate node types, and then swaps out the original element for the new node.

This is one of the more exciting parts of the demo! Our first real-time message is working end-to-end. Trigger notify_product_released/1 in the console when you have the page loaded. You will see the "coming soon" text instantly replaced by the shoe size selector, complete with the right colors. Type the following commands into your terminal.

```
$ mix ecto.reset && mix run -e "Sneakers23Mock.Seeds.seed!()"
$ iex -S mix phx.server
iex(1)> Sneakers23.Inventory.mark_product_released!(1)
iex(2)> Sneakers23.Inventory.mark_product_released!(2)
```

Take a moment to commit all of your current changes. The feature to release our product is fully implemented. This is a great time to make sure that you fully understand the code powering Sneakers23.Inventory.mark_product_released!/1 before moving on.

Next, you will implement another real-time feature in JavaScript, without HTML. This provides some variety in the way that you implement real-time features.

Update a Client with Real-Time Data

In the last section, we used a Channel broadcast to replace content by swapping out the HTML. We could use this same technique for item stock level updates, but we will take a different approach. Instead of sending the client server-rendered HTML, our real-time message will include details about the new stock level. The JavaScript client will use this data to change the relevant parts of the DOM in order to affect the view. Our message "stock_change" will include the product ID, item ID, and the new stock level.

Our ProductChannel will be modified to define the new broadcast function. This function will broadcast if the stock level has changed, or it will skip the broadcast if it's identical. This prevents unnecessary data being sent to connected clients.

Let's add the stock level change function to the ProductChannel module.

```
sneakers_23/lib/sneakers_23_web/channels/product_channel.ex
Line 1  def notify_item_stock_change(
          previous_item: %{available_count: old},
          current_item: %{available_count: new, id: id, product_id: p_id}
        ) do
   5      case {
          ProductView.availability_to_level(old),
          ProductView.availability_to_level(new)
        } do
          {same, same} when same != "out" ->
  10          {:ok, :no_change}

          {_, new_level} ->
            Endpoint.broadcast!("product:#{p_id}", "stock_change", %{
              product_id: p_id,
  15          item_id: id,
            level: new_level
          })

          {:ok, :broadcast}
  20    end
      end
```

A case statement is used on line 5 to prevent duplicate updates from being
sent to a client. There is one exception to this—we want to ensure that "out"
is never missed by a client, so we aren't stopping duplicate broadcasts for it.
If the availability level has changed between the old and new items, then the
stock_change event is broadcast on line 13. Let's see this in action by writing a
test for it.

```
sneakers_23/test/sneakers_23_web/channels/product_channel_test.exs
describe "notify_item_stock_change/1" do
  setup _ do
    {inventory, _data} =
      Test.Factory.InventoryFactory.complete_products()

    [product = %{items: [item]}, _] =
      CompleteProduct.get_complete_products(inventory)

    topic = "product:#{product.id}"
    Endpoint.subscribe(topic)

    {:ok, %{product: product, item: item}}
  end

  test "the same stock level doesn't broadcast an event", %{item: item} do
    opts = [previous_item: item, current_item: item]
    assert ProductChannel.notify_item_stock_change(opts)
      == {:ok, :no_change}

    refute_broadcast "stock_change", _
  end
end
```

This test uses a setup block to reduce the amount of code copied between our tests. We're ensuring that the same stock level doesn't broadcast duplicate events.

We also need to write a test for the change scenario. Add the following test inside of the notify_item_stock_change/1 describe block.

```
sneakers_23/test/sneakers_23_web/channels/product_channel_test.exs
test "a stock level change broadcasts an event",
  %{item: item, product: product} do
  new_item = Map.put(item, :available_count, 0)
  opts = [previous_item: item, current_item: new_item]
  assert ProductChannel.notify_item_stock_change(opts)
    == {:ok, :broadcast}

  payload = %{item_id: item.id, product_id: product.id, level: "out"}
  assert_broadcast "stock_change", ^payload
end
```

These tests show that our broadcast function is working as expected. We could add tests for all the different scenarios, and most likely would in a professional project, but we'll leave those unwritten to save time.

Let's add this function to our web context so that it can be used in other parts of our application.

```
sneakers_23/lib/sneakers_23_web.ex
defdelegate notify_item_stock_change(opts),
  to: Sneakers23Web.ProductChannel
```

We're now ready to connect our front end so we can try out this message. We'll write code similar to our "released" message handler. This next code snippet should be placed at the bottom of setupProductChannel/1.

```
sneakers_23/assets/js/app.js
productChannel.on('stock_change', ({ product_id, item_id, level }) => {
  dom.updateItemLevel(item_id, level)
})
```

All of our work is performed by dom. We will remove any "size-container__entry--level-*" CSS class and add our new class of "size-container__entry--level-NEW_LEVEL". In addition, we need to disable the size button if the item is now out-of-stock.

```
sneakers_23/assets/js/dom.js
function updateItemLevel(itemId, level) {
  Array.from(document.querySelectorAll('.size-container__entry')).
    filter((el) => el.value == itemId).
    forEach((el) => {
      removeStockLevelClasses(el)
      el.classList.add(`size-container__entry--level-${level}`)
```

```
      el.disabled = level === "out"
    })
}

dom.updateItemLevel = updateItemLevel

function removeStockLevelClasses(el) {
  Array.from(el.classList).
    filter((s) => s.startsWith("size-container__entry--level-")).
    forEach((name) => el.classList.remove(name))
}
```

It's amazing how far we can get with plain JavaScript these days. You can, of course, use a library that makes DOM manipulation easier if you want to.

Once this is written, you can test it end-to-end. Start your server with iex -S mix phx.server and then run the following script.

```
$ iex -S mix phx.server
iex(1)> {:ok, products} = Sneakers23.Inventory.get_complete_products()
iex(2)> %{items: items} = List.first(products)
iex(3)> items |> Enum.take(6) |> Enum.each(fn item ->
          out_item = Map.put(item, :available_count, 0)
          opts = [previous_item: item, current_item: out_item]
          Sneakers23Web.notify_item_stock_change(opts)
        end)
```

This script will mark the first six items as out-of-stock. However, you will notice that the front end reverts back to the previous state when refreshed. This is because we haven't used the Inventory.item_sold!/2 function that marks the item as sold in the database.

Let's update the item_sold! function to use the notify_item_stock_change function.

sneakers_23/lib/sneakers_23/inventory.ex

```
Line 1  def item_sold!(id), do: item_sold!(id, [])
  -     def item_sold!(item_id, opts) do
  -       pid = Keyword.get(opts, :pid, __MODULE__)
  -
  5       avail = Store.fetch_availability_for_item(item_id)
  -       {:ok, old_inv, inv} = Server.set_item_availability(pid, avail)
  -       {:ok, old_item} = CompleteProduct.get_item_by_id(old_inv, item_id)
  -       {:ok, item} = CompleteProduct.get_item_by_id(inv, item_id)
  -       Sneakers23Web.notify_item_stock_change(
 10         previous_item: old_item, current_item: item
  -       )
  -
  -       :ok
  -     end
```

Lines 7–11 are new to this function and are used to provide the old and new item to the notify_item_stock_change! function. The Store function, on line 5, retrieves the item availability from the database. On the next line, the item's availability is updated in the GenServer that keeps a copy of the inventory. Finally, the old_item is then retrieved. This is necessary for the notify_item_stock_change function.

You can now test that the application updates item stock levels and saves them in the database.

```
$ mix ecto.reset && mix run -e "Sneakers23Mock.Seeds.seed!()"
$ iex -S mix phx.server
iex(1)> Sneakers23.Inventory.mark_product_released!(1)
iex(2)> Sneakers23.Inventory.mark_product_released!(2)
iex(3)> Sneakers23Mock.InventoryReducer.sell_random_until_gone!()
```

You will see the items on the page at http://localhost:4000 start to disappear after you run this. When you refresh, the items stay the way they are. You can even shut down the server with ctrl-c then a, and the items will remain the same after you start the server again.

We have developed two different approaches to real-time features. These features are relatively simple in their business objective, but they significantly improve the user experience for customers. Next, we'll look at how to change our code so that the application can run across multiple server instances.

Run Multiple Servers

To deal with the large scale of Sneakers23's online operation, we'll need to run multiple servers at once. Running multiple servers can be difficult when in-memory data structures are used because updates are not automatically sent across the cluster. However, the scalability is certainly worth it. We have already discussed how Phoenix deals with this by broadcasting messages to all connected nodes, and we'll use a similar solution to broadcast our Inventory changes across the cluster. Let's start by demonstrating the particular problem we're facing.

The Challenge of Distribution

Running multiple servers exposes a problem. The current Inventory.Server process only knows about its own transactions. This means that if an item is released or sold on another node, it won't update until the server reboots. We can discover this ourselves by running a local test with two nodes.

```
$ mix ecto.reset && mix run -e "Sneakers23Mock.Seeds.seed!()"
$ iex --name app@127.0.0.1 -S mix phx.server
```

Open http://localhost:4000 in order to get the connection started. In another shell, run the following iex session and commands.

```
$ iex --name back@127.0.0.1 -S mix
iex(1)> Node.connect(:"app@127.0.0.1")
true
iex(2)> Sneakers23.Inventory.mark_product_released!(1)
:ok
```

When you view the web page, everything looks good! The products are there and all is well...until you refresh. Once you refresh, you are right back to a "coming soon" state. This is because there are two different Inventory.Server processes running, and only the "back" node received the update. The real-time message was broadcast because of Phoenix, but the underlying data was not updated in the Inventory.Server process. As you can imagine, this would also occur for item sales. We can solve this problem by adding replication.

Add Replication of Inventory Events

Phoenix PubSub can be used for more than Channel messages. At its core, it lets any process subscribe to a particular event type. We will use PubSub to power the replication events for our Inventory. You'll need to spin up a new GenServer to handle the events, as well as a context to dispatch the events.

Replication is not without its own challenges—it's possible for nodes to become out of sync from this replicated approach. For non-critical data, the benefits of scalability are often worth the trade-off of potential data incorrectness. In Sneakers23, we never use the replicated data as a source of truth for important operations, such as the purchase process. Instead, we use the database to ensure that these operations are consistent.

We'll first write the GenServer and then work our way up through the various layers.

```
sneakers_23/lib/sneakers_23/replication/server.ex
Line 1  defmodule Sneakers23.Replication.Server do
  -       use GenServer
  -
  -       alias Sneakers23.Inventory
  5
  -       def start_link(opts) do
  -         GenServer.start_link(__MODULE__, opts, name: __MODULE__)
  -       end
  -
  10      def init(_opts) do
```

```
        Phoenix.PubSub.subscribe(Sneakers23.PubSub, "inventory_replication")
        {:ok, nil}
      end

15    def handle_info({:mark_product_released!, product_id}, state) do
        Inventory.mark_product_released!(product_id, being_replicated?: true)
        {:noreply, state}
      end

20    def handle_info({:item_sold!, id}, state) do
        Inventory.item_sold!(id, being_replicated?: true)
        {:noreply, state}
      end
    end
```

Phoenix.PubSub makes this code very clean and simple. Our process subscribes to the "inventory_replication" event on line 11. Any message that is sent to this topic will be received by the process as messages. Each message type will need to be handled by using a handle_info callback.

On lines 16 and 21, we are calling the appropriate Inventory context functions, but we also indicate that this is due to a replication event with the being_replicated?: true option. This allows us to modify our context functions so they do not broadcast messages when handling a replication message. Our nodes would end up in an infinite loop in this case, which is never good!

We'll next define the Replication context so that other parts of our code can cleanly emit replication events.

sneakers_23/lib/sneakers_23/replication.ex
```
Line 1  defmodule Sneakers23.Replication do
          alias __MODULE__.{Server}

          defdelegate child_spec(opts), to: Server

5         def mark_product_released!(product_id) do
            broadcast!({:mark_product_released!, product_id})
          end

10        def item_sold!(item_id) do
            broadcast!({:item_sold!, item_id})
          end

          defp broadcast!(data) do
15          Phoenix.PubSub.broadcast_from!(
              Sneakers23.PubSub,
              server_pid(),
              "inventory_replication",
              data
20          )
```

```
      end

      defp server_pid(),
        do: Process.whereis(Server)
25  end
```

We use PubSub.broadcast_from! on line 15 to send a message to all processes except the local process. In our case, only remote nodes will receive replication events. This makes sense because we've already handled the message locally if we're broadcasting the message to other nodes. Let's add this new GenServer to our Application module.

sneakers_23/lib/sneakers_23/application.ex
```
children = [
  Sneakers23.Repo,
  Sneakers23Web.Endpoint,
  Sneakers23.Inventory,
  Sneakers23.Replication,
]
```

Now that our Replication functions are defined and the process is added, we'll need to put them to use in the Inventory context functions.

sneakers_23/lib/sneakers_23/inventory.ex
```
Line 1  alias Sneakers23.Replication

        def mark_product_released!(id), do: mark_product_released!(id, [])
        def mark_product_released!(product_id, opts) do
5         pid = Keyword.get(opts, :pid, __MODULE__)
          being_replicated? = Keyword.get(opts, :being_replicated?, false)

          %{id: id} = Store.mark_product_released!(product_id)
          {:ok, inventory} = Server.mark_product_released!(pid, id)
10
          unless being_replicated? do
            Replication.mark_product_released!(product_id)
            {:ok, product} = CompleteProduct.get_product_by_id(inventory, id)
            Sneakers23Web.notify_product_released(product)
15        end

          :ok
        end
```

We have essentially the same function as before, except with a replication check on line 11 that will only run when the function isn't being called from the replication context. We invoke the Replication.mark_product_released!/1 function in order to trigger the replication. We'll follow an identical pattern for item_sold!/2.

sneakers_23/lib/sneakers_23/inventory.ex
```
def item_sold!(id), do: item_sold!(id, [])
def item_sold!(item_id, opts) do
```

```
  pid = Keyword.get(opts, :pid, __MODULE__)
  being_replicated? = Keyword.get(opts, :being_replicated?, false)

  avail = Store.fetch_availability_for_item(item_id)
  {:ok, old_inv, inv} = Server.set_item_availability(pid, avail)

  unless being_replicated? do
    Replication.item_sold!(item_id)
    {:ok, old_item} = CompleteProduct.get_item_by_id(old_inv, item_id)
    {:ok, item} = CompleteProduct.get_item_by_id(inv, item_id)
    Sneakers23Web.notify_item_stock_change(
      previous_item: old_item, current_item: item
    )
  end

  :ok
end
```

The changes we've made are close to identical as with the previous function. Now, we actually have a completely connected replicated system. Take a moment to make the final git commit for this chapter.

Verify Multiple Server Behavior

We already performed an experiment to show that distribution was not working. We can do this same demo again to show that replication is working. Re-seed your database and then execute the following demo—make sure to close any running instances of the server before doing this.

```
$ mix ecto.reset && mix run -e "Sneakers23Mock.Seeds.seed!()"
$ iex --name app@127.0.0.1 -S mix phx.server
```

In another shell, run the following commands. Keep http://localhost:4000 loaded and view it after each command. To ensure that the replication occurred, you can refresh the page. If you ever see a different result before and after the refresh, something may have gone wrong with your replication code.

```
$ iex --name back@127.0.0.1 -S mix
iex(1)> Node.connect(:"app@127.0.0.1")
iex(2)> Sneakers23.Inventory.mark_product_released!(1)
iex(2)> Sneakers23.Inventory.mark_product_released!(2)
iex(3)> Sneakers23Mock.InventoryReducer.sell_random_until_gone!()
```

You can even run sell_random_until_gone!/0 on the server node at the same time, since it runs on the back node. You'll end up with all items at exactly 0 availability and the front end will display all items as sold out, without the need to refresh. Try running this example again with multiple pages open side-by-side to ensure that they receive updates at the same time.

Wrapping Up

Phoenix Channels provide the backbone for our application's real-time messaging. Our application is only sending messages from server to client right now, but we still benefit from the simplicity and reliability of the Channel library. We sent HTML directly from server to client as well as JSON payloads that were processed by a JavaScript front end. The flexibility of using either HTML replacement or JavaScript event handling gives you several different ways to approach the same problem.

Phoenix also provides the PubSub feature that powers our real-time replication. We were able to enhance the existing GenServer implementation with replication across a cluster. This was necessary to ensure that our application could run across multiple servers without having data consistency issues.

We're going to step back from building an application in our next chapter. We'll explore how to *break* an application that we've built. The quality assurance process is very important for becoming confident that our application won't break in production.

## CHAPTER 8

Break Your Application
with Acceptance Tests

In the last chapter, we used Phoenix Channels to add real-time features to an application. You tested the application locally to ensure that everything worked as expected. However, we didn't really test the application to the extent that would be expected of a business application—we only tested the happy-path. In this chapter, we'll try to break the application through a variety of front-end and back-end techniques. By the end of this chapter, we'll have gained confidence that the system works as expected. We will use the techniques covered in this chapter when we add more complex features in the rest of part II.

Real-time systems can be difficult to write correctly due to challenges caused by persistent connections and long-running applications. Many software engineers take pride in their work, and they may be optimistic about bugs not existing in their code—I have been guilty of this. However, it's an ever-present possibility that code we write has bugs. Always test your application in order to ensure that it works in normal and out-of-the-ordinary situations. It is also important to test that library code works in many situations, even if there are tests covering the library's code.

In this chapter, we'll first cover why acceptance tests—tests that use the entire application stack—are useful for real-time applications. We'll try to break last chapter's application through manual acceptance tests. We'll use a different set of techniques to crash parts of the app that are hidden from the user, such as Elixir processes or the database. Finally, we'll look at using Hound to automate acceptance tests.

Let's explore some challenges of real-time application development, and why it's important to thoroughly test them.

The Power of Acceptance Testing

It is a challenge to write and run real-time systems, although Phoenix handles many of the hard parts. Real-time systems use persistent connections to optimize the speed and efficiency of sending data to clients. As we covered in Design for Unreliable Connections, on page 67, persistent connections are less forgiving than traditional web requests and require additional code to cover scenarios that can happen to users.

Let's look at some of the reasons why this is the case and how acceptance tests can help us gain confidence in our application. Acceptance tests are tests that use the entire application stack, from browser to server. They can be manual or automated, which we'll cover later in this chapter. We can recreate the following challenging scenarios with acceptance tests.

Applications may be open for long periods of time
> Users can leave web pages open for hours, days, or even weeks. Browsers vary in how they handle this, but many will actually leave the page resident in memory and restore without fetching a new copy of the page from the server. If your application uses Channels to provide new data to users as it is available, users are even less likely to refresh the page because their view updates in real-time. You want to ensure that an application you build works just as well after being open for five hours as it does after being open for five seconds.

> Problems that can occur to long-lived applications are a bit inobvious at first and may be unrelated to the real-time connection itself. For example, signed tokens, which are usually only signed for a short amount of time, need to be re-obtained in order to stay fresh. Memory leaks, a completely different problem, are more likely because the application is not resetting all of its memory like it would on a page load.

Persistent connections must be maintained across failures
> Failures will occur when an application is open for a long period of time. A failure can be from a bad internet connection, computer hibernation, or any other event that interrupts the connection while the page is still loaded. It is critical that the client establishes the connection again after it becomes disconnected.

> When the real-time communication layer is disconnected, events are not being sent nor received from the application. It could take many reconnection attempts in order to successfully connect back to the server. You

should test the different ways that a connection could be severed in order to be confident that your code handles disconnection correctly.

A good goal to keep: if the user has an internet connection and the server is up, they're connected to the server via a WebSocket. We may need to add small delays, in practice, but any disconnection duration should be minimized.

Servers must maintain open connections

Servers may be restarted when an application is deployed, causing the open connections to disconnect. The back-end servers would then receive an influx of new connections in a short period of time after the servers restart. This could become expensive depending on whether the server is doing work when a Socket connection opens or Channel join occurs.

This is not an exhaustive list of what can go wrong with a real-time application. As you gain experience with building and running real-time applications, you will discover which situations are most relevant to your users. The bugs you encounter can be caused by bugs in your code or in a software library's code. However, it's more likely that you will encounter a bug in an application's usage of a library, rather than in the library itself.

Acceptance tests allow us to verify that our application works as expected in many different scenarios, both common and uncommon. When we perform an acceptance test, we check that the system works as our users and our business expects. The biggest difference between this style of testing and unit or integration testing is that the system is not simulated or mocked when we do these tests—you execute acceptance tests against a real instance of an application. You can also automate acceptance tests using a tool that controls a web browser. We'll see examples of manual and automated acceptance tests in this chapter.

First, we'll try to break last chapter's application with manual acceptance tests. We will throw some of the above scenarios at it, such as different connection failures, in order to make sure it works in any situation.

Break Your App Like a User

Users put themselves into all kinds of strange scenarios, often without even trying. We need to put ourselves in the shoes of a user as we test real-time applications to ensure we cover as many scenarios as possible. We should try to keep as much of our system identical to what our users use—browsers, operating systems, and network stability can all affect how an application works.

We're going to try different manual acceptance testing scenarios to ensure that our application works properly in each. We become more confident that users will not encounter problems when we try to break our application, but cannot. One scenario that we will execute in this section will actually reveal a very subtle problem in our existing application. We'll try out different techniques that are common for users to do, such as using forward/backward page navigation or experiencing a network disconnection.

The Phoenix JavaScript client handles many of the cases we'll see in this section, so we often don't need to implement code to handle them. However, you should still test the scenarios that Phoenix handles for you. This ensures the provided solutions work for your application's use case. Ultimately, you and your team are responsible for your application working as expected, and acceptance tests are a great way to find problems before an application is deployed to production.

Let's look at how to design a test scenario.

Define the Correct Behavior

You should write your expectations of a manual acceptance test before you start the test. This helps you stay honest with yourself, but it also makes it easier to spot anything that goes against what you expect to happen. A simple, but effective technique is to write down the test you're performing, how to run the test, and what you expect to happen. You can then confirm that the test did what you expected. You or a teammate will also be able to easily repeat the test in the future.

Our store application has a very simple feature set right now. We're not sending data from the client up to the server, and the amount of data being sent down to the client is fairly low. The chance of something going wrong is slim because of the small amount of code powering our application. Problems will occur more frequently as a codebase becomes larger and changes over time. Changes to old code, new features, or library upgrades can all introduce new defects in an application.

In this section, we'll walk through tests that ensure our application works for a variety of user situations. We'll follow a standard template for each test. For each scenario, we'll write a high-level definition of the test. Then, we'll write detailed steps for how to execute the test. Finally, we'll record what we expect to happen. This simple pattern will make sure each test feels simple and straightforward to execute.

It's a good idea to get another teammate to provide a second set of eyes on any test plans you write. This helps ensure that edge cases are not missed and also ensures that other team members are able to execute the manual acceptance tests.

Let's perform our first test.

Page Related Actions

Users click buttons, navigate to different pages, and submit forms in order to get things done. The most obvious type of testing is to follow what a user will do. We're going to focus on a seemingly safe user action: moving forward and backward in an application.

Web pages follow a well-established life cycle flow.[1] This flow drives page loads, cache usage, and much more. It can vary across browsers, as we'll discuss below. One optimization that we have to be aware of is that forward and backward events use cached versions of pages that are placed in different caches by the browser.

Here's a test plan for testing user navigation in our application. We are going to run into a bug when we run this test. In the real-world, you wouldn't know whether a bug exists or not, so you would be testing different scenarios to see what happens.

Define the test
>   A shopper should be able to start on the "coming soon" screen, receive an event that shows the product release, go to a new web page, then use the back button in the browser to get back to Sneakers23 home page. The shopper should see the released product and not the "coming soon" text.

Write steps for the test
1. Start the server in a freshly seeded state.
2. Load http://localhost:4000 in Google Chrome.
3. Release sneaker with ID 1 while viewing the page.
4. Navigate to https://www.pragprog.com in the same tab.
5. Go "back" to the previous page.

Write expectations for the test
- The shopper should see all "coming soon" shoes after step 2.
- The shopper should see the size selector for product with ID 1 after step 3.
- The shopper should see the size selector for product with ID 1 after step 5.

---

1. https://developers.google.com/web/updates/2018/07/page-lifecycle-api

Let's run this test now to see what happens. Perform the following steps:

```
$ mix ecto.reset && mix run -e "Sneakers23Mock.Seeds.seed!()" # (step 1)
$ iex -S mix phx.server
# Load the page now (step 2)
iex(1)> Sneakers23.Inventory.mark_product_released!(1) # (step 3)
:ok
```

We have followed steps 1, 2, and 3 so far. At this point, you will have verified that the first two expectations are correct. Next, follow step 4 and 5 in your browser.

If everything worked correctly, you will see that the web page says "coming soon" instead of showing the size selector—a clear bug. The reason for this is that the original web page content was placed in a local cache on the first load. Our product release process sent new HTML over the Channel, but it didn't invalidate the cached page. This process is managed completely by the browser—we did not implement caching in our example in any way. You will see the correct page data when you refresh the page.

This bug doesn't affect all browsers, such as Safari, due to Safari having a back-forward cache. Depending on when you run this test, you may not be able to reproduce the bug in Chrome either, because back-forward cache is being implemented there as well. This caching technique places the JavaScript and page in memory until it's deemed out of scope—a technique that introduces challenges of its own when the cache entry is old. We would need to run our test in major browsers to fully test all possibilities, but we must always consider that browsers can change the implementation of the page life cycle over time.

There are a few ways to fix this particular bug, although the most important takeaway is that such bugs exist and can affect real-time applications that update content. One way to fix this bug is to tell the browser to not cache the page. You can do this by setting the "Cache-Control" header to a value of "no-store, must-revalidate" in the ProductController, like so:

```
sneakers_23/lib/sneakers_23_web/controllers/product_controller_fixed.ex
def index(conn, _params) do
  {:ok, products} = Sneakers23.Inventory.get_complete_products()

  conn
  |> assign(:products, products)
➤ |> put_resp_header("Cache-Control", "no-store, must-revalidate")
  |> render("index.html")
end
```

This has the trade-off of increasing the number of hits to the page. As an alternative, you can use JavaScript to fetch the current state of the dynamic content pieces when the page loads. The trade-off here is increased complexity and a request via the ProductChannel. The best solution for a bug depends on how comfortable you are with the impact of the bug and the trade-offs of the solution.

Next, let's look at how losing your internet connection could break an application.

Internet Related Actions

Internet connections are flaky. Connections can randomly fail when you're on a laptop or desktop, and it's more common than it should be to have a low-quality data connection on cell phones. We need to ensure that our application is able to properly reconnect a user's connection, even if the page has been open for a long time.

The official Channels JavaScript client handles reconnection attempts for us. It uses a back-off algorithm that starts with frequent retries and ends up waiting a few seconds between attempts. You can change the reconnection algorithm to be more or less aggressive if needed, but the default one will work well for most applications. We'll execute a test case to ensure that users can reconnect to the store when they become disconnected.

Define the test

A shopper should initially connect to the Channel when they load the application. The shopper should quickly reconnect to the Channel if they become disconnected. Once reconnected, the store should work as if the shopper was never disconnected. The shopper will miss any messages for the time that they are disconnected.

Write steps for the test

1. Start the server in a freshly seeded state.
2. Load http://localhost:4000.
3. Kill the server to simulate a disconnection.
4. Bring the server back online after one second.
5. Release sneaker with ID 1 while viewing the page.
6. Repeat all instructions with a wait time of five seconds and 30 seconds.

Write expectations for the test

- The shopper sees "coming soon" shoes after step 2.
- The shopper's WebSocket connection is disconnected after step 3.
- The shopper's WebSocket connection is connected after step 4.
- The shopper sees the released shoe's size selector after step 5.

We have a local server, so disconnecting our internet connection won't have an impact on our WebSocket connection. If this application was deployed, you would run these tests by disconnecting the internet rather than shutting down the server. Let's run through these tests now. Follow these instructions and observe what happens.

```
$ mix ecto.reset && mix run -e "Sneakers23Mock.Seeds.seed!()" # (step 1)
$ iex -S mix phx.server
# Load the page here (step 2)
iex(1)> # Type ctrl-c
BREAK: (a)bort (c)ontinue (p)roc info (i)nfo (l)oaded
       (v)ersion (k)ill (D)b-tables (d)istribution
# Type a and then enter (step 3)
# Wait 1 second (step 4)
$ iex -S mix phx.server
iex(1)> Sneakers23.Inventory.mark_product_released!(1) # (step 5)
:ok
```

At this point, you should see that the product selector is visible on the front end. This shows that the JavaScript client will attempt to reconnect to the server. Another possibility is that you don't see the front end change. This could happen if you executed mark_product_released/1 during the few seconds of delay of the reconnection process.

One strategy to solve the issue of missing messages during a disconnection is to send the most up-to-date data when a Channel loads. This would solve both the caching issue and missing message issue that we've seen in this chapter, at the cost of additional processing by the server. We won't implement that strategy in this book, but it is a useful technique to know about.

One other scenario to test in your production application is putting your computer in hibernation when it's connected to a server. If you tested this, you would want to ensure that the server is not running on the computer that is being put into hibernation.

We're going to move onto a different class of potential errors now—server-side errors.

Break Your App Like a Server

Errors do not always happen from user initiated actions—different processes and tools can fail on the server. Your application may experience network disconnections between servers, database slowness or downtime, and crashed processes due to bugs or a large amount of work. It's nearly impossible to consider everything that can go wrong in an application, so you often won't realize that there is a problem with failure handling until it's too late. You can simulate many types of problems locally and in staging environments before experiencing them in production.

In this section, we'll test what happens to our application during database downtime and when different processes crash on the server. We'll utilize the observer tool that ships with Erlang/OTP to view our application's supervision tree. We will kill various processes to ensure that our application doesn't reach an incorrect state. A good rule of thumb is to make sure that any custom GenServers, custom Supervisors, and your Ecto Repo can be killed without your application crashing. We'll be performing manual acceptance tests throughout this section. However, our tests will be doing things outside of what a normal user could do.

Simulate Database Downtime

A database outage is a serious issue. The database of an application is often the source of truth, so any operation that requires strong consistency *should* fail. Operations that don't perform updates or don't require strong consistency may still work in the event of a database outage.

This type of test is pretty advanced for a normal QA process, but is useful when you are testing flows that involve money or other important resources. It's good to know how your application will respond when a database disconnects, although hopefully you won't see that happen very frequently.

Define the test

A shopper is initially connected to the store, waiting for a shoe to release. The application database restarts during this time. The shopper should be able to reload the page without error but should not see a shoe release during this time. From an application admin perspective, the application will disallow the release of a sneaker.

The server should serve pages during this time, but the server will not work if restarted.

Write steps for the test

1. Start the server in a freshly seeded state.
2. Load http://localhost:4000.
3. Stop your database to simulate a downtime event.
4. Refresh http://localhost:4000 several times.
5. Attempt to release sneaker with ID 1.
6. Start your database.
7. Release sneaker with ID 1 while viewing the page.

Write expectations for the test
- The shopper sees "coming soon" after step 2.
- The shopper can refresh the page without issue at step 4.
- The release process should fail at step 5.
- The release process should succeed at step 7.
- The shopper sees the released shoe's selector after step 7.

You will need to discover how to stop your database locally in order to perform this test. I am using brew to power my Postgres installation, so I can run brew services stop postgresql. You may need to use a different command depending on your operating system and the way that you installed Postgres. Let's run through our test now.

```
$ mix ecto.reset && mix run -e "Sneakers23Mock.Seeds.seed!()" # (step 1)
$ iex -S mix phx.server
# Load the page now (step 2)
# Stop your database now (step 3)
# Refresh the page several times (step 4)
iex(1)> Sneakers23.Inventory.mark_product_released!(1) # (step 5)
** (Postgrex.Error) FATAL 57P01 (admin_shutdown)...
    (ecto_sql) lib/ecto/adapters/sql.ex:621: Ecto.Adapters...
    (ecto_sql) lib/ecto/adapters/sql.ex:554: Ecto.Adapters...
# Start your database now (step 6)
iex(2)> Sneakers23.Inventory.mark_product_released!(1) # (step 7)
:ok
```

You might have had a hard time interpreting your console during this test because of all of the red text. Ecto is not happy with the lack of a database connection, and it will work very hard to try to reconnect—each failure produces a red error in your console. This is a good sign because it means that Ecto will keep attempting to reconnect. Eventually the database will come back online and Ecto will regain connectivity.

All the expectations pass for our test scenario. The server is able to serve the main page during this time because all the data for rendering the product page comes from processes in our application. This is one of the benefits of the replicated data approach in our application, although it's certainly not without trade-offs. One of those trade-offs is the inability for the Inventory process to start while the database is offline.

For a final test, try to restart the iex -S mix phx.server process while the database is down. In this case, the product page will receive errors because the processes are not able to start properly. If you start the database while this is going on, you will see everything become correctly initialized and the product page is able to be served again.

A database outage is among the worst errors that can happen to your applications—it really is an all-hands-on-deck scenario. Let's look at a different type of error next: process crashes.

Kill BEAM Processes with Observer

The BEAM is a resilient virtual machine. Supervisor processes are used to monitor child processes and can be configured to handle failure differently based on the needs of the application. The most common configuration is to simply restart any failed child process, using the one_for_one supervisor option. The child process then initializes itself back to a healthy state. You can see this in the handle_continue callback of our Sneakers23.Inventory.Server process. If it were to crash, it would pull the current inventory from the database and continue in a healthy state. There are other restart strategies[2] that are not covered in this book. The restart strategy you should use depends on the supervision structure of your application.

It can be tricky to design a process tree that is guaranteed to come back online correctly. You should test the initialization of processes with automated tests, but the QA process can also help us guarantee the correctness of our processes in practice. In the next scenario, we will kill various processes in our system with the observer tool. Any process that we kill should re-initialize in a healthy state, with very little interruption to connected shoppers.

Define the test
> A shopper is initially connected to the store, waiting for a shoe to release. Many processes in the application then crash. The system restores itself to a healthy state and the shopper will see the shoe release.

Write steps for the test
> 1. Start the server in a freshly seeded state.
> 2. Load http://localhost:4000.
> 3. Kill the Sneakers23.Inventory, Sneakers23.Replication.Server, Sneakers23.Repo processes.
> 4. Release sneaker with ID 1 while viewing the web page.

Write expectations for the test
> • The shopper sees "coming soon" after step 2.
> • The shopper is not affected after step 3.
> • The shopper sees the sneaker selector for shoe 1 after step 4.

---

2. https://hexdocs.pm/elixir/Supervisor.html#module-strategies

The processes that we'll kill were selected because they're custom processes built for this application. It's more likely that these processes could have bugs that would prevent graceful restarts. I've added in the database as well, because databases are known to go down in production.

We will use observer to actually kill the processes listed above. You could do this on the command line, but it's useful to visualize the process tree during the test. After you start the observer in the instructions below, find the "Applications" tab at the top—you will see a large sideways tree. The processes to kill are all named, so you should be able to find them without issue. They're all in the same column, close to the left-hand side of the tree. You will see the following view when you right-click a process and select "Kill process":

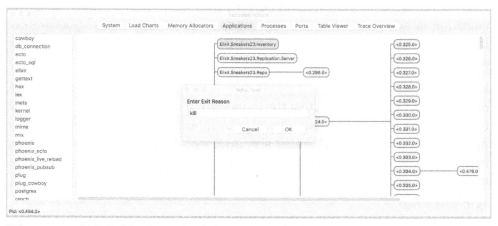

When you click "ok", the selected process will be killed. You can verify that a process is killed by looking at the pid in the bottom left corner of the observer window. When you click a different process and then back onto the one that you killed, you will see the pid change. Let's jump into the scenario.

```
$ mix ecto.reset && mix run -e "Sneakers23Mock.Seeds.seed!()" # (step 1)
$ iex -S mix phx.server
# Load the page now (step 2)
iex(1)> :observer.start
:ok
# Find and kill the first processes in step 3
iex(2)> Sneakers23.Inventory.mark_product_released!(1) # (step 4)
:ok
```

You could kill the processes from the iex session, instead of the observer. However, you'll benefit from knowing how to use observer.

You will see that each expectation passes during the test. This demonstrates the power of the BEAM and Supervisors when it comes to fault tolerance. Processes do not crash unless something goes wrong, but it is comforting to know that a process crash will not cause our application to run in an incorrect state.

We've executed several manual QA tests so far. We'll switch things up by writing automated acceptance tests next.

Automate Acceptance Tests With Hound

Manual acceptance tests are powerful, but they are also cumbersome to run. You performed tests in this chapter that took several minutes to execute, at a minimum, and were prone to error if you missed any of the steps. We can improve on manual acceptance tests by automating them.

Automated acceptance tests are extremely powerful because they let you run hundreds or thousands of acceptance tests without a person being involved. If each acceptance test takes one minute to execute (a very conservative estimate), then one thousand tests would take over 16 hours of non-stop testing! It would be extremely costly to fully cover a large application with manual acceptance tests. Automated acceptance tests improve on this by both being able to run on a dedicated server, without a person involved, and by allowing fast setup of a test scenario. A thousand automated acceptance tests may be able to run in an hour or less, which is a reasonable amount of time.

We'll leverage WebDriver and Hound in this section to write automated acceptance tests. You'll write tests that feel like standard ExUnit tests, but are actually full-stack acceptance tests. We will not port the manual tests we ran earlier to automated tests. It is possible to port those tests over, but we're going to stick with simpler tests for this section.

The Power of WebDriver and Hound

WebDriver[3] is an interface to automate browsers. You can use a WebDriver implementation to build an automated test suite against a real browser. There are many different types of WebDrivers that can be used to control a variety of major browsers. We'll be using ChromeDriver to write automation tests against Chrome.

Most likely, you will not use WebDriver directly. Instead, you'll use libraries that integrate with WebDriver to control a page and perform assertions against that page's content and behavior. This gives you the ability to write full-featured browser tests in your favorite language. We'll be writing our tests in Elixir, of course, but a QA engineer could just as easily write these tests in a

---

3. https://www.w3.org/TR/webdriver/

different, more familiar language. It's important to write tests that both a core engineering team and QA engineering team can maintain, because acceptance tests will often be updated by members of each team.

Hound[4] is an Elixir library to write WebDriver-powered tests. Writing Hound tests is very similar to writing a normal ExUnit test—you are just controlling a real browser rather than an Elixir application. An advantage to writing automation tests in the same place that we have written other tests is that we will use the same factories and helpers we built previously.

Hound is a bit trickier to setup than other libraries we've used, so we'll walk through all of the setup steps next.

Configure Hound

The first step to get Hound set up is to download and set up ChromeDriver. Hound will be configured to use ChromeDriver, so it's important that it's running properly. You can obtain the latest stable release of ChromeDriver on the project's homepage.[5] Download the appropriate version for your system and unzip it onto your computer somewhere. It's easy to get ChromeDriver running once it's downloaded, just start it like a normal executable:

```
$ cd location/of/chromedriver
$ ./chromedriver
Starting ChromeDriver 76.0.3809.126 on port 9515...
```

You may have to start ChromeDriver differently depending on your operating system. Once ChromeDriver is configured, you can download and set up Hound. We'll start by adding the package to our mix.exs file.

sneakers_23/mix.exs
```
{:plug_cowboy, "~> 2.0"},
{:hound, "~> 1.0"}
```

Type mix deps.get after adding Hound to your mix.exs file. Next, we're going to change our Endpoint so that it can make use of our testing database connection. This step comes from the documentation of Phoenix.Ecto.SQL.Sandbox.[6] Place the following code as the final plug definition in the Endpoint module.

sneakers_23/lib/sneakers_23_web/endpoint.ex
```
if Application.get_env(:sneakers_23, :sql_sandbox) do
  plug Phoenix.Ecto.SQL.Sandbox
end
```

---

4. https://hex.pm/packages/hound
5. https://chromedriver.chromium.org/
6. https://hexdocs.pm/phoenix_ecto/Phoenix.Ecto.SQL.Sandbox.html

Next, we'll set up our test config for Hound and SQL sandbox. We'll start by allowing our application's HTTP server to run in test mode. You wouldn't do this for normal tests, but it's necessary because our acceptance tests will be executing against the running server. It is also possible to create a separate Mix environment for your acceptance tests, but we won't do that in this book.

sneakers_23/config/test.exs
```
config :sneakers_23, Sneakers23Web.Endpoint,
  http: [port: 4002],
  server: true
```

We must instruct Hound to use ChromeDriver with a headless version of Chrome. Headless Chrome is a version of the Chrome browser that runs without a visual interface—our tests will execute without a browser continuously opening and closing.

sneakers_23/config/test.exs
```
config :hound, driver: "chrome_driver", browser: "chrome_headless"
```

Finally, we can tell our application to use the SQL sandbox during tests.

sneakers_23/config/test.exs
```
config :sneakers_23, sql_sandbox: true
```

We're almost ready to write our first test, but we need to start Hound in our test_helper.exs:

sneakers_23/test/test_helper.exs
```
Application.ensure_all_started(:hound)
ExUnit.start()
```

Let's write a simple test to see everything working together. Create a new HomePageTest module in the test/acceptance folder. Type in the following code:

sneakers_23/test/acceptance/home_page_test.exs
```
Line 1  defmodule Acceptance.HomePageTest do
   -      use ExUnit.Case, async: false
   -      use Hound.Helpers
   -
   5      setup do
   -        Hound.start_session()
   -        :ok
   -      end
   -
  10      test "the page loads" do
   -        navigate_to("http://localhost:4002")
   -        assert page_title() == "Sneakers23"
   -      end
   -    end
```

This test looks like most of the other tests you've written so far in this book. We do have to bring in the Hound.Helpers on line 3—this provides the functions to control the browser. We are also starting a Hound session on line 6. This step will become important in the next section.

Our actual test is straightforward. We instruct ChromeDriver to navigate to our test application URL and then assert that the page title matches what we expect. You can use all of the standard ExUnit assertions in Hound tests.

Run mix test to verify that everything is working. If you see an error about not connecting to ChromeDriver, make sure that the ChromeDriver executable is still running by following the example at the top of this section.

Next, we're going to write tests for all of our Channel and JavaScript powered features.

Write Automated Acceptance Tests

The Sneakers23 store has two main real-time components: live sneaker drops and stock-level updates. We will write acceptance tests for each of these features to ensure our application works end-to-end.

We need to make a small change to our Inventory.Server module before we can write our tests. The application uses a single Inventory.Server process that holds the current inventory and stock levels. Our Hound tests will execute in the same environment as our tests and will pull the inventory from the global inventory process. Currently, this process loads its state at startup, and we do not have a way to change the loaded inventory. We will need to add a function—so add the following function to the bottom of the Inventory.Server module.

```
sneakers_23/lib/sneakers_23/inventory/server.ex
if Mix.env() == :test do
  def handle_call({:test_set_inventory, inventory}, _from, _old) do
    {:reply, {:ok, inventory}, inventory}
  end
end
```

This code is using a compile time check to guarantee that the message will only be handled in the test environment. This type of check lets us add convenience functions without worrying that they'll be used in the final application. We won't add a module function definition for this message, further indicating that it shouldn't be used outside of our tests.

Let's set up our ProductPageTest now.

sneakers_23/test/acceptance/product_page_test.exs

```
Line 1   defmodule Acceptance.ProductPageTest do
    -      use Sneakers23.DataCase, async: false
    -      use Hound.Helpers

    5      alias Sneakers23.{Inventory, Repo}

    -      setup do
    -        metadata = Phoenix.Ecto.SQL.Sandbox.metadata_for(Repo, self())
    -        Hound.start_session(metadata: metadata)
   10
    -        {inventory, _data} = Test.Factory.InventoryFactory.complete_products()
    -        {:ok, _} = GenServer.call(Inventory, {:test_set_inventory, inventory})

    -        :ok
   15      end
    -    end
```

Line 8 in our setup function is very important. This allows the requests that
are executed by the browser to use the test database without errors appearing.
The test's inventory is created on line 11. We are using the :test_set_inventory
message to set this in our Inventory.Server process.

It's possible to not use a global process in our tests by creating a Plug similar
to the SQL Sandbox that we set up previously. This is very powerful for
writing parallel tests, but it is not necessary for our small test suite. All of
our integration tests are marked async: false due to the global process. Tests
with async: false will run one at a time, which is useful when there is shared
global state.

Now that our database and inventory are set up, let's write an integration
test. We'll start by testing that a shoe's "coming soon" content is changed
when that shoe is released. This test will only work if our application's
Channels are properly working.

sneakers_23/test/acceptance/product_page_test.exs

```
Line 1   test "the page updates when a product is released" do
    -      navigate_to("http://localhost:4002")

    -      [coming_soon, available] = find_all_elements(:css, ".product-listing")
    5
    -      assert inner_text(coming_soon) =~ "coming soon..."
    -      assert inner_text(available) =~ "coming soon..."

    -      # Release the shoe
   10      {:ok, [_, product]} = Inventory.get_complete_products()
    -      Inventory.mark_product_released!(product.id)
    -
```

```
        # The second shoe will have a size-container and no coming soon text
        assert inner_text(coming_soon) =~ "coming soon..."
15      refute inner_text(available) =~ "coming soon..."

        refute inner_html(coming_soon) =~ "size-container"
        assert inner_html(available) =~ "size-container"
     end
```

We start by navigating to the main page. This is the only time that we use navigation in this test, so any content changes are from live updates and not from a page load. We grab the product-listing elements on line 4. There are many different ways that we can find elements on the page, but the CSS selector approach will be familiar to many people. Our first set of assertions ensures that each of the products on the page starts in a "coming soon..." state.

We release the second sneaker on line 11, exactly like we would in a normal test. After this, our UI will update due to the real-time message. You can see that the first product remains in a "coming soon" state, but the second product changes to displaying a size container.

Make sure to run mix test before moving on—everything should go green. Next, we'll ensure that an item going through a stock-level change updates the UI correctly. Type in the following test:

sneakers_23/test/acceptance/product_page_test.exs
```
Line 1  test "the page updates when a product reduces inventory" do
          {:ok, [_, product]} = Inventory.get_complete_products()
          Inventory.mark_product_released!(product.id)

5         navigate_to("http://localhost:4002")

          [item_1, _item_2] = product.items

          assert [item_1_button] =
10          find_all_elements(:css, ".size-container__entry[value='#{item_1.id}']")

          assert outer_html(item_1_button) =~ "size-container__entry--level-low"
          refute outer_html(item_1_button) =~ "size-container__entry--level-out"

15        # Make the item be out of stock
          new_item_1 = Map.put(item_1, :available_count, 0)
          opts = [previous_item: item_1, current_item: new_item_1]
          Sneakers23Web.notify_item_stock_change(opts)

20        refute outer_html(item_1_button) =~ "size-container__entry--level-low"
          assert outer_html(item_1_button) =~ "size-container__entry--level-out"
     end
```

The CSS selector on line 10 is incredibly powerful when combined with attribute selectors. We are pinpointing the specific element we care about with high precision. The assertion changes between lines 12 and 20, proving that our item has had its stock level change in the UI.

The two tests we've written are extremely powerful because they are flexing the entire application stack. The server is starting, the web page connects to it, the application's JavaScript runs, the front end connects to our Channel over WebSockets, and the front end updates in real time as changes occur. Automated acceptance tests are not perfect, however. They have a few challenges that can make their adoption difficult.

Acceptance Test Limitations

Acceptance tests are very powerful when used properly, but they can also lead to a variety of problems. These problems are manageable, but they could end up taking more of your time than desired in a large test suite. The end result is worth it, however, because you can be more confident that your application works properly end-to-end. The two major problems that affect acceptance tests are related to speed and maintainability.

Acceptance tests flex the entire application stack—a browser starts up, executes tasks, navigates to one or more pages, and then shuts down. This process is more expensive than a traditional test that doesn't leverage a browser. A large acceptance test suite could take many times longer to run than a large unit/integration test suite, so you may want to run your acceptance tests nightly or on-demand rather than with every single build of your application. It might appear that this problem would only affect large applications, but the performance cost of tests can quickly add up in smaller applications as well.

Maintainability of an acceptance test suite can be difficult to achieve due to the brittleness of front end interfaces. It's common for a design to evolve, for CSS classes to change, and for the order of elements to shift. Any of these occurrences will most likely cause tests to break in the suite. If the suite takes a while to run and is not run on every change, the breakages can add up. A large front end redesign might involve changing all the existing acceptance tests. There are strategies to deal with the inherent maintenance issues of an acceptance suite, but the problems will always exist in some form. It's outside of the scope of this book to cover maintainable acceptance test strategies, but you can find resources online that can help you with this.

Despite the challenge of a building and maintaining a robust acceptance test suite, the end result can be worth it. It's often the goal of QA teams to have a full acceptance test suite, but it can be difficult if the application didn't start out with acceptance tests. You'll need to weigh the costs and benefits to decide if it's the right choice and right time to build an acceptance suite for your application.

Wrapping Up

Software systems are difficult to write correctly, and real-time systems are even more difficult to write correctly. The challenge of persistent connections that must run for a long time without failure adds to the difficulty of developing a real-time application. Acceptance tests help ensure that applications you develop are deployed with minimal bugs.

There are multiple approaches you can take in the quality assurance process. The most accessible approach is to behave like a user would while checking that the application works as expected. Simple things like going forward/backward in the browser history, putting a computer to sleep, or experiencing an internet disconnection could cause problems in an application. A different approach to QA testing is to force issues to occur that might be very rare, such as a database going down or random Elixir processes crashing. When testing an application, follow a simple framework to keep yourself honest and focused in the test: define the test, write steps for the test, write expectations for the test, then execute the test.

Manual acceptance testing is extremely valuable, but it can also be tedious and time-consuming. You can use WebDriver based automation tests via the Hound library to write automated and repeatable end-to-end tests. These tests can be difficult to write and maintain, but they are the strongest way to repeatedly guarantee that your application works as expected in different scenarios. In practice, you are likely to use a mixture of both testing strategies to fully cover an application.

Now that you're thinking like a user, and trying to break your applications before your users do, we're going to build a more advanced real-time feature into our application. In the next chapter, we'll be adding a shopping cart so that a single user can purchase shoes. We'll consider the different techniques learned in this chapter as we implement this more advanced feature.

## CHAPTER 9

Build a Real-Time Shopping Cart

In the last chapter, we performed acceptance tests on our application to verify that our store works in a variety of scenarios. This type of testing forces us to consider both the behavior of our users and different failure scenarios, as we build our application. In this chapter, we'll build a shopping cart for our store. This will be one of the most advanced features we've built in this book, but we're well-equipped to deal with the challenges that will come up.

Shopping carts are an e-commerce feature that pretty much everyone uses. However, there are many different ways that a shopping cart can be built. We'll start this chapter by laying out exactly what our cart needs to do, along with details on how we'll go about building it. We'll go step-by-step throughout the development process and end up with a working shopping cart powered by Channels.

You'll see almost every concept that we've discussed in the book so far throughout this chapter—we'll be using Channels, PubSub, Channel state, JavaScript, and session state. We'll consider many different types of failure in our design, such as server crashes, user internet disconnections, and multi-tab support. At the end of this chapter, we'll perform manual acceptance tests against our shopping cart.

It's important to write unit tests for code you write, but it takes many pages to include and explain unit tests in a book. Instead, unit tests are provided in the source code that ships with this book. Tests are included for all of the major modules that you'll build in this chapter. Key modules that we build will have an information section telling you where to find the relevant tests.

Let's jump in and plan our shopping cart.

Plan Your Shopping Cart

Our store currently lacks any form of checkout process, so we'll be starting from scratch as we build our shopping cart. Shopping carts are conceptually very simple—put items in, take items out, and purchase the cart. However, Sneaker23's sneaker launch process means that we'll need our shopping cart to go beyond the basics. We need a shopping cart that tells a shopper when an item becomes out-of-stock, so they have a chance to select a different size very quickly.

First, we'll walk through the requirements of our shopping cart. This will help us stay focused on building the minimal working feature set, and these requirements will drive our acceptance tests. After that, you'll see our approach for the implementation of our shopping cart. Finally, you'll set up your local environment so you can build the feature.

Shopping Cart Needs

Due to the limited nature of a Sneakers23 release, our shopping cart will be fairly simple. The real-time nature of the sneaker launch process will throw a few curveballs into the requirements, though. Here is a list of the features that our final cart will need:

- Add and remove multiple items to the shopping cart.
- Only one of each shoe size can be added.
- Shoppers know when an item in their cart is out-of-stock.
- The cart persists between page reloads.
- A shopper has a single cart across multiple tabs.
- A shopper cannot checkout without using the cart.
- Admins can see what items are in different shopping carts (next chapter).

We could build our shopping cart many different ways, but we'll keep it fairly simple—we won't try to build the perfect shopping cart with a bunch of features.

Next, we'll cover our cart's architecture, and you'll see how Channels fit into our design.

Design an Application Architecture

We must turn our list of requirements into a concrete plan. We'll do this by thinking about how to implement each feature using the tools at our disposal. We'll need to consider different user behaviors and clean application design throughout our planning.

The most advanced requirement in our shopping cart is out-of-stock notifications. We want shoppers to see that their selected shoe isn't available, so they can remove the shoe from their cart and add a different size or model. We will leverage Phoenix PubSub to notify the Channel listeners from our Inventory context. Each Channel will send updated data to its connected client when it receives an out-of-stock message. The following figure captures this flow:

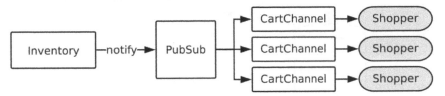

We'll make use of a PubSub feature that we haven't talked about yet—dynamic subscriptions. A process can subscribe or unsubscribe to a given topic using PubSub. A Channel process can listen to any PubSub topic, even ones that are different than that Channel's connected topic. We will dynamically add and remove PubSub subscriptions as items are added to the cart. This keeps our PubSub messages small—a Channel will not receive messages for items not in its cart.

We will build a CartChannel to power our shopping cart. A Channel can handle events from shoppers, such as adding or removing items, and it gives us a way to send data to our connected clients. A Channel can also store the current cart in the process state. When we're done, our CartChannel flow will look like the following figure:

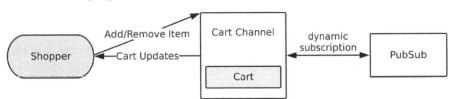

Our shopping cart needs to persist between page reloads and between multiple tabs, so that a shopper's cart doesn't disappear. There are a variety of ways to approach this problem, such as using a database or Elixir process to store a shopper's cart. Our requirements don't list the need to have persistence of a cart over a long period of time, so we will take a simpler approach.

A shopper's cart will be stored in the user's browser's localStorage. This makes the cart persist between page reloads, without needing a storage mechanism on the server. The biggest benefit of this approach is that it will lead to a good user experience without much code. As the figure on page 164 implies, our storage solution will be straightforward.

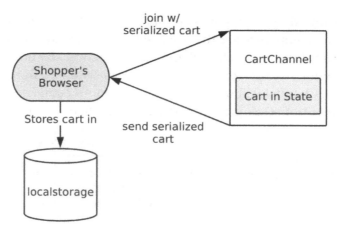

If we ever needed to move to a centralized storage mechanism, such as a database, then we'd be able to easily change how carts are stored and interacted with. We won't need to worry about that in our application, though.

A high-level architecture for our application has mostly come together. The one feature we haven't yet covered is multi-tab support. In order to handle a shopper with multiple tabs open, a Channel will broadcast a message anytime its cart changes. Other Channels that are open for that same shopper will receive the message and update themselves accordingly.

In order to support this flow with Channels, we need to have a static ID that we can broadcast to. We'll give each shopper a unique ID that is provided in the cart's topic, like cart:123abc. This will allow us to broadcast synchronization messages between multiple instances of a shopper's cart. We will leverage the HTTP session to store the ID between visits.

We now have a path forward for a shopping cart that meets all of our requirements. Our high-level application architecture looks like this:

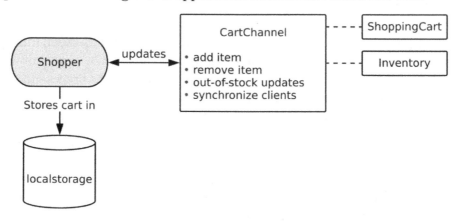

Set Up Your Project

If you've been following along in part II, you have a working Sneakers23 application. For this chapter, you can either start with a completely fresh application base, or you can use your existing project with a few files copied in. Let's go over the instructions for each option.

Set Up a Clean Project

If you want to start with a completely fresh application base, follow these steps. Make sure that you have a copy of the code, using the instructions found in Online Resources, on page xiii.

```
$ cp -R code/location/sneakers_23_cart_base ~/sneakers_23_cart
$ cd ~/sneakers_23_cart
$ git init && git add . && git commit -m "initial commit (from base)"
$ mix deps.get && mix ecto.setup && npm --prefix assets install
```

At this point, you have a clean codebase ready for this chapter's shopping cart. You can skip to the next major heading to start building our shopping cart.

Set Up Your Existing Project

If you want to use your existing repo, you simply need to copy a few files in—these files would be tedious to type otherwise.

```
$ cp code/location/sneakers_23_cart_base/assets/css/app.css \
    your/project/sneakers_23/assets/css/app.css
```

```
$ cp code/location/sneakers_23_cart_base/assets/js/cartRenderer.js \
    your/project/sneakers_23/assets/js/cartRenderer.js
```

You're now ready to build this chapter's shopping cart. We'll start with the development of our ShoppingCartChannel.

Scaffold Your Shopping Cart Channel

We'll start developing our shopping cart by writing some code that the Channel will use—our functional core. After we build our functional core, we'll use it to develop a ShoppingCartChannel. We'll start small and work our way up to a complete cart by the end of this chapter.

It's important to build a functional core that contains logic, data structures, or other parts of a program that are independent of the user interface. This helps increase the maintainability of your code, because the separation between interface and logic means that either can be changed without a complete rewrite of the application. You'll have an easier time adapting to change and adding new features when your application is split into separate parts this way.

Earlier in part II, our ProductChannel accessed inventory data through an Inventory context—this was our functional core. We're going to build something very similar in this chapter—we'll write a ShoppingCart data structure that holds cart data. We'll add this code to a Checkout context, so that our ShoppingCartChannel can use it without reaching into the context.

Let's jump into the Checkout context, followed by our ProductController. We'll build the ShoppingCartChannel in the next section.

Build a Functional Core

When I start coding a new feature, I find it helpful to start with the most central part. For us, our entire feature revolves around the concept of a shopping cart, so this is a great place to start writing code. According to our requirements, a shopping cart is a collection of items that can be added to and removed from. Let's represent this as an Elixir struct.

Create the Checkout.ShoppingCart module and add the following code:

```
sneakers_23_cart/lib/sneakers_23/checkout/shopping_cart.ex
defmodule Sneakers23.Checkout.ShoppingCart do
  defstruct items: []

  def new(), do: %__MODULE__{}
end
```

This struct provides a name and very simple shape for our shopping cart. We could represent our cart items in many ways, but we'll go with the simplest approach possible—our cart will store the id of an item only. This makes adding an item to a cart very simple. Let's write a function that adds an integer to our list.

```
sneakers_23_cart/lib/sneakers_23/checkout/shopping_cart.ex
def add_item(cart = %{items: items}, id) when is_integer(id) do
  if id in items do
    {:error, :duplicate_item}
  else
    {:ok, %{cart | items: [id | items]}}
  end
end
```

One of our requirements is that a single shoe/size combination can be added to the cart, so we're preventing duplicate items from being inserted into a cart.

It's just as easy to remove an item—add the remove_item function next.

```
sneakers_23_cart/lib/sneakers_23/checkout/shopping_cart.ex
def remove_item(cart = %{items: items}, id) when is_integer(id) do
  if id in items do
    {:ok, %{cart | items: List.delete(items, id)}}
  else
    {:error, :not_found}
  end
end
```

We need to add one more helper function for our cart—a function to extract the cart item IDs. This isn't apparent yet, but we'll use this function in our Channel. Add this function to the end of the ShoppingCart module:

```
sneakers_23_cart/lib/sneakers_23/checkout/shopping_cart.ex
def item_ids(%{items: items}), do: items
```

Our code is straightforward so far. There is one final feature that our Shopping-Cart needs to support. We must be able to serialize and deserialize a cart, so it can be stored in a browser's localStorage as a string. Phoenix.Token, which we previously used for authentication, is perfect for this task. When we sign our ShoppingCart into a token, the cart data can't be tampered with and can be passed to clients.

Add the following code to the end of the ShoppingCart module:

```
sneakers_23_cart/lib/sneakers_23/checkout/shopping_cart.ex
@base Sneakers23Web.Endpoint
@salt "shopping cart serialization"
@max_age 86400 * 7

def serialize(cart = %__MODULE__{}) do
  {:ok, Phoenix.Token.sign(@base, @salt, cart, max_age: @max_age)}
end

def deserialize(serialized) do
  case Phoenix.Token.verify(@base, @salt, serialized, max_age: @max_age) do
    {:ok, data} ->
      items = Map.get(data, :items, [])
      {:ok, %__MODULE__{items: items}}

    e = {:error, _reason} ->
      e
  end
end
```

This code should feel very similar to our usage of Phoenix.Token back in Chapter 4, Restrict Socket and Channel Access, on page 53. Upon deserialization, we extract items out of the verified map, rather than putting the data directly into a ShoppingCart struct. This technique gives us more flexibility in the deserialization process, although our use case is very simple right now.

Before we can move onto our Channel, we need to expose our ShoppingCart as context functions. Create a Checkout module and add the following function delegates.

sneakers_23_cart/lib/sneakers_23/checkout.ex
```elixir
defmodule Sneakers23.Checkout do
  alias __MODULE__.{ShoppingCart}

  defdelegate add_item_to_cart(cart, item),
    to: ShoppingCart, as: :add_item

  defdelegate cart_item_ids(cart),
    to: ShoppingCart, as: :item_ids

  defdelegate export_cart(cart),
    to: ShoppingCart, as: :serialize

  defdelegate remove_item_from_cart(cart, item),
    to: ShoppingCart, as: :remove_item
end
```

All of our logic lives in the underlying ShoppingCart module, so our context is very simple. We need to add a function to restore a cart from a serialized value, while also handling errors gracefully. A shopper who somehow gets into an invalid state shouldn't be unable to shop—they should just get a new cart. Our restore_cart/1 function reflects this:

sneakers_23_cart/lib/sneakers_23/checkout.ex
```elixir
def restore_cart(nil), do: ShoppingCart.new()
def restore_cart(serialized) do
  case ShoppingCart.deserialize(serialized) do
    {:ok, cart} -> cart
    {:error, _} -> restore_cart(nil)
  end
end
```

We now have a working functional core that can represent a shopping cart. We'll leverage this when we build our Channel. Before we can do that, we need to prepare our HTML to work with our new Channel.

Unit Tests for the Functional Core

 You'll find unit tests for the functional core in the sneakers_23_cart/test/sneakers_23 folder. There are tests for the Checkout context and the ShoppingCart. These tests aren't present in the sneakers_23_cart_base project.

Prepare the HTML

One important aspect of our application design is that a user's tabs all stay in sync. Because each tab is a different Channel instance, we need some way to link the Channels to each other. The simplest way to do this is via the

Channel topic. Two Channels with the topic "cart:123" should be linked together. They should be separate from a Channel with the topic "cart:345".

Browser cookies are a great place to store semi-permanent data. We will generate and store a random identifier in the cookie session, so that multiple tabs share the same identifier. First, we need a way to generate a random cart ID. It is best to use :crypto.strong_rand_bytes/1 for this purpose. Add the following function to the Checkout module:

```
sneakers_23_cart/lib/sneakers_23/checkout.ex
@cart_id_length 64
def generate_cart_id() do
  :crypto.strong_rand_bytes(@cart_id_length)
  |> Base.encode64()
  |> binary_part(0, @cart_id_length)
end
```

This function generates a random 64-length string when called. We need to use this, along with the cookie-based session, in order to persist a cart ID.

We want our shopping cart to be on every page, including new pages that don't yet exist. We could copy and paste the same snippet in all our controllers, but there's an easier way. The Plug[1] library allows us to easily create modules that'll execute on all page loads. First, we need to create our Sneakers23Web.CartIdPlug module.

```
sneakers_23_cart/lib/sneakers_23_web/plugs/cart_id_plug.ex
Line 1  defmodule Sneakers23Web.CartIdPlug do
          import Plug.Conn

          def init(_), do: []
   5
          def call(conn, _) do
            {:ok, conn, cart_id} = get_cart_id(conn)
            assign(conn, :cart_id, cart_id)
          end
  10
          defp get_cart_id(conn) do
            case get_session(conn, :cart_id) do
              nil ->
                cart_id = Sneakers23.Checkout.generate_cart_id()
  15            {:ok, put_session(conn, :cart_id, cart_id), cart_id}

              cart_id ->
                {:ok, conn, cart_id}
            end
  20      end
        end
```

---

1. https://hexdocs.pm/plug/readme.html

The get_session/2 function returns whatever data was previously stored in Phoenix's session management. On line 14, we generate a new cart ID if one doesn't already exist. It's important to use put_session, like we do on line 15, in order to save the cart ID in the shopper's session. Without this, every refresh would give a new cart ID. We assign the cart ID, on line 8, so that we can access it in our HTML template.

Add the following JavaScript snippet in the middle of the layout/app template to scaffold the shopping cart. We are adding this to the layout file so every page can inject a shopping cart.

```
sneakers_23_cart/lib/sneakers_23_web/templates/layout/app.html.eex
<%= render @view_module, @view_template, assigns %>

<%= if assigns[:cart_id] do %>
  <div id="cart-container"></div>

  <script type="text/javascript">
    window.cartId = "<%= @cart_id %>"
  </script>
<% end %>
```

Finally, we need to add our new Plug to our application Router module. Add a plug/1 function call in the Sneakers23Web.Router module, like so:

```
sneakers_23_cart/lib/sneakers_23_web/router.ex
pipeline :browser do
  plug :accepts, ["html"]
  plug :fetch_session
  plug :fetch_flash
  plug :protect_from_forgery
  plug :put_secure_browser_headers
  plug Sneakers23Web.CartIdPlug
end
```

Let's confirm that this is working as expected. Start your server with mix phx.server and visit http://localhost:4000. When you open your JavaScript console, you can retrieve your cart ID.

```
> window.cartId
"or513rppnugfnHJHBS l564hvd/ke7yrz0BrD+NzPXF07bTOgwxvazV3WptL1Xjlz"
```

If you refresh or open multiple tabs, you will always see the same ID. If you open your browser incognito, you'll see a different ID. Take a moment to git commit your work, since we've completed a working chunk of code.

Now that our Controller is configured with a cart ID, we're ready to build our ShoppingCartChannel.

Build Your Shopping Cart Channel

A Channel is the perfect place to store our shopping cart state and to handle user input on the cart. We'll write a ShoppingCartChannel module that handles adding items, removing items, and synchronizing clients. We'll also add real-time stock updates in the next section.

Remember that Channels are just processes—we'll use this to our advantage here. Each ShoppingCartChannel represents one open instance of Sneakers23, and the state of the Channel at any time will match what the shopper sees on their page. The Channel is in charge of sending its client the different item details, such as name and availability, for each shoe in the cart.

Let's start by writing the basic ShoppingCartChannel—we'll incrementally add more complex features to it throughout this section.

Create the Channel

We'll use the topic "cart:*" to connect to our Channel. This topic allows us to identify each connected cart by its ID, which will be useful when we need to synchronize the carts. Let's start our Channel implementation by adding this definition to the ProductSocket module.

sneakers_23_cart/lib/sneakers_23_web/channels/product_socket.ex
```
channel "product:*", Sneakers23Web.ProductChannel
➤ channel "cart:*", Sneakers23Web.ShoppingCartChannel
```

We will now start writing the ShoppingCartChannel module. Create the Shopping-CartChannel module and add the following code to it.

sneakers_23_cart/lib/sneakers_23_web/channels/shopping_cart_channel.ex
```
defmodule Sneakers23Web.ShoppingCartChannel do
  use Phoenix.Channel

  alias Sneakers23.Checkout

  def join("cart:" <> _id, _params, socket) do
    {:ok, socket}
  end
end
```

The first feature we will implement is the restoration of a cart from a serialized string. The client will provide a serialized cart string in the parameters of its join, and that will be stored in the Channel state. Modify the join function to include the cart restoration.

sneakers_23_cart/lib/sneakers_23_web/channels/shopping_cart_channel.ex

```
def join("cart:" <> id, params, socket) when byte_size(id) == 64 do
  cart = get_cart(params)
  socket = assign(socket, :cart, cart)

  {:ok, socket}
end

defp get_cart(params) do
  params
  |> Map.get("serialized", nil)
  |> Checkout.restore_cart()
end
```

Next, we need to render the cart to a map that can be sent to the client. We must return a detailed list of items in the cart as well as the serialized string that represents that cart.

Rendering a cart is not directly related to the Channel operation, so we'll add it to a new module. Create the CartView module with this code:

sneakers_23_cart/lib/sneakers_23_web/views/cart_view.ex

```
Line 1  defmodule Sneakers23Web.CartView do
   -      def cart_to_map(cart) do
   -        {:ok, serialized} = Sneakers23.Checkout.export_cart(cart)

   5        {:ok, products} = Sneakers23.Inventory.get_complete_products()
   -        item_ids = Sneakers23.Checkout.cart_item_ids(cart)
   -        items = render_items(products, item_ids)

   -        %{items: items, serialized: serialized}
  10      end

   -      defp render_items(_, []), do: []

   -      defp render_items(products, item_ids) do
  15        for product <- products,
   -            item <- product.items,
   -            item.id in item_ids do
   -          render_item(product, item)
   -        end
  20        |> Enum.sort_by(& &1.id)
   -      end

   -      @product_attrs [
   -        :brand, :color, :name, :price_usd, :main_image_url, :released
  25      ]

   -      @item_attrs [:id, :size, :sku]

   -      defp render_item(product, item) do
  30        product_attributes = Map.take(product, @product_attrs)
```

```
-      item_attributes = Map.take(item, @item_attrs)
-      product_attributes
-      |> Map.merge(item_attributes)
-      |> Map.put(:out_of_stock, item.available_count == 0)
35   end
-  end
```

This is a long code snippet, so we'll break down each function. cart_to_map/1 will be called by our Channel and, on line 9, returns a map containing the items in the cart as well as the serialized cart string. The render_items/2 function iterates over each product and looks for items that are in the cart—these items are then rendered. The render_item/2 function extracts all of the important attributes and produces a final map of the item.

The products are fetched from the Inventory.Server state, which keeps the item availability up to date. On line 34, we use this to send the client the most up-to-date version of that item's availability. Anytime that we render the shopping cart, it will have the most up-to-date availability information.

Next, let's change the ShoppingCartChannel to use the cart_to_map/1 function. We'll push the cart to the client when a client joins.

sneakers_23_cart/lib/sneakers_23_web/channels/shopping_cart_channel.ex
```
import Sneakers23Web.CartView, only: [cart_to_map: 1]

def join("cart:" <> id, params, socket) when byte_size(id) == 64 do
  cart = get_cart(params)
  socket = assign(socket, :cart, cart)
  send(self(), :send_cart)

  {:ok, socket}
end

def handle_info(:send_cart, socket = %{assigns: %{cart: cart}}) do
  push(socket, "cart", cart_to_map(cart))
  {:noreply, socket}
end
```

The Channel sends itself a message when join/3 executes. This message is processed and triggers a rendered cart to be pushed to the client. It is good to have the server send the data to the client, rather than having the client request it, because it ensures that the client is up-to-date. If a client disconnects and reconnects, it will have the most up-to-date version of its items.

Next, we'll connect the front end to the Channel. We'll start by editing app.js to connect a cart. At this point, you should have imported cartRenderer.js from the setup section earlier in this chapter. The code above setupProductChannel should be replaced with the following snippet.

Unit Tests for the Channel

You will find unit tests for the functional core in the sneakers_23_cart/test/sneakers_23_web/channels folder. The ShoppingCartChannel tests cover the code added in this section. These tests are not present in the sneakers_23_cart_base project.

sneakers_23_cart/assets/js/app.js

```
Line 1  import css from "../css/app.css"
        import { productSocket } from "./socket"
        import dom from './dom'
        import Cart from './cart'
     5
        productSocket.connect()

        const productIds = dom.getProductIds()

    10  productIds.forEach((id) => setupProductChannel(productSocket, id))

        const cartChannel = Cart.setupCartChannel(productSocket, window.cartId, {
          onCartChange: (newCart) => {
            dom.renderCartHtml(newCart)
    15    }
        })
```

We start by adding a soon-to-be-created Cart to our existing import statements. On line 6, we have set up our productSocket to always connect—the cart could be on pages that don't have product listings, so we want to make sure that the Socket is always connected. We could have created a new ProductSocket to connect to, but it wouldn't serve much purpose because our authentication requirements haven't changed.

The cart Channel setup happens on line 12. The cartId is passed from window, which we previously set up in our layout. We re-render the cart template when the cart changes, so the user sees the most up-to-date cart.

We still need to write cart.js and update dom.js. We'll start with dom.js.

sneakers_23_cart/assets/js/dom.js

```
import { getCartHtml } from './cartRenderer'

dom.renderCartHtml = (cart) => {
  const cartContainer = document.getElementById("cart-container")
  cartContainer.innerHTML = getCartHtml(cart)
}
```

This function turns the cart into HTML and replaces the content of #cart-container with the new HTML. The cartRenderer we provided for you contains the HTML for the cart.

We're almost able to test that everything is working. We'll write cart.js and then test that it all works.

sneakers_23_cart/assets/js/cart.js

```
const Cart = {}
export default Cart

Cart.setupCartChannel = (socket, cartId, { onCartChange }) => {
  const cartChannel = socket.channel(`cart:${cartId}`, channelParams)
  const onCartChangeFn = (cart) => {
    console.debug("Cart received", cart)
    localStorage.storedCart = cart.serialized
    onCartChange(cart)
  }

  cartChannel.on("cart", onCartChangeFn)
  cartChannel.join().receive("error", () => {
    console.error("Cart join failed")
  })

  return {
    cartChannel,
    onCartChange: onCartChangeFn
  }
}

function channelParams() {
  return {
    serialized: localStorage.storedCart
  }
}
```

We first create our Channel instance on line 5. It's important to note that we're providing a function for channelParams—we'll come back to it shortly. When the ShoppingCartChannel pushes a rendered cart to our JavaScript, we store that cart in localStorage and trigger the DOM update. The onCartChangeFn is set up to do both of these things when the cart changes. A console.debug statement has also been added so you can see the changes to the cart.

The channelParams function, on line 25, passes the current stored cart from local-Storage. It's crucial that these parameters are calculated each time the Channel tries to reconnect. If we used a static channelParams value, then we'd find ourselves in a situation where a cart resets each time the Channel reconnects.

Let's check our progress. Start the server with mix phx.server and then visit http://localhost:4000. Open the JavaScript console and refresh to see the cart in your console. You will see an empty cart, like this:

```
> Cart received {items: Array(0), serialized: "SFMyNTY.g3Q...0"}
```

Each time you refresh, you will see a different serialized value. This is due to how a Phoenix.Token is generated and is completely okay for our store.

Take a moment to git commit your work. Next, we'll handle adding and removing items.

Add and Remove Items to Your Cart

We have a front end that connects to our ShoppingCartChannel with an empty shopping cart—this is not very exciting. In order for you to see the cart on-screen, you have to place an item in it. Let's set up the front end to add an item to our cart when we click on it. We'll start with what we want our app.js to look like, then we'll implement the functions we need.

Add this function after the call to Cart.setupCartChannel.

```
sneakers_23_cart/assets/js/app.js
dom.onItemClick((itemId) => {
  Cart.addCartItem(cartChannel, itemId)
})
```

These functions don't exist yet, but our code's intent is clear. Next, we will implement onItemClick in dom.js.

```
sneakers_23_cart/assets/js/dom.js
dom.onItemClick = (fn) => {
  document.addEventListener('click', (event) => {
    if (!event.target.matches('.size-container__entry')) { return }
    event.preventDefault()

    fn(event.target.value)
  })
}
```

We bind an event handler on the document. This allows our click handler to trigger, even if the element wasn't on the page when the page first loaded. The button to add an item is a button element with a value set to the item ID. We'll pass the item ID through our system and into the ShoppingCartChannel.

Next, let's configure cart.js to add the item. While we're here, we'll also add the function to remove an item—it's almost exactly the same. Add this code to the end of cart.js.

```
sneakers_23_cart/assets/js/cart.js
Cart.addCartItem = ({ cartChannel, onCartChange }, itemId) => {
  cartRequest(cartChannel, "add_item", { item_id: itemId }, (resp) => {
    onCartChange(resp)
  })
}

Cart.removeCartItem = ({ cartChannel, onCartChange }, itemId) => {
  cartRequest(cartChannel, "remove_item", { item_id: itemId }, (resp) => {
    onCartChange(resp)
  })
}

function cartRequest(cartChannel, event, payload, onSuccess) {
  cartChannel.push(event, payload)
    .receive("ok", onSuccess)
    .receive("error", (resp) => console.error("Cart error", event, resp))
    .receive("timeout", () => console.error("Cart timeout", event))
}
```

Our "add_item" message is very simple; it just contains the item ID. We have some simple error handlers for timeouts and errors, although a more advanced implementation might have a different handler that alerts the shopper to the issue.

If you were to refresh your local application and click a size button, you'll see an error that "add_item" could not be handled. We need to add a handle_in callback function to the ShoppingCartChannel. Let's do that now.

```
sneakers_23_cart/lib/sneakers_23_web/channels/shopping_cart_channel.ex
def handle_in(
  "add_item", %{"item_id" => id}, socket = %{assigns: %{cart: cart}}) do
  case Checkout.add_item_to_cart(cart, String.to_integer(id)) do
    {:ok, new_cart} ->
      socket = assign(socket, :cart, new_cart)
      {:reply, {:ok, cart_to_map(new_cart)}, socket}

    {:error, :duplicate_item} ->
      {:reply, {:error, %{error: "duplicate_item"}}, socket}
  end
end
```

The core of this function is fairly short, before we add error handling. We use add_item_to_cart/2 to modify our cart, which came from our Channel state, and then we assign the new cart into the Channel's state.

Let's try out our add to cart feature. Follow these steps to start your store with a freshly seeded set of shoes:

```
$ mix ecto.reset && mix run -e "Sneakers23Mock.Seeds.seed!()"
$ iex -S mix phx.server
iex(1)> Enum.each([1, 2], &Sneakers23.Inventory.mark_product_released!/1)
:ok
```

Open http://localhost:4000 and open your JavaScript console. Click on one of the available shoe sizes. You will see a new "Cart received" message with an item count of 1. You will also see the shopping cart UI appear—it looks like the following image.

Neat! Open a second tab and navigate to http://localhost:4000. You will see the same exact cart with one item in it. If you add another item, however, you'll see that the two tabs are out of sync. They'll become in sync again if you refresh, but this isn't what we want. We need to synchronize clients across multiple instances of the cart. Take a moment to git commit before moving on.

Synchronize Multiple Channel Clients

Each shopper that joins our ShoppingCartChannel does so on a private topic, like "cart:123abc". This cart ID is random and long, so we can use it as a way to uniquely identify a cart. In order to synchronize our cart across multiple tabs, we will use this topic. We'll send the serialized version of our cart using Phoenix.PubSub and intercept it in the ShoppingCartChannel. It will only be received by Channel processes that are running with that same cart ID.

Add the following code to the ShoppingCartChannel module—we'll walk through the key parts of it.

sneakers_23_cart/lib/sneakers_23_web/channels/shopping_cart_channel.ex
```
intercept ["cart_updated"]

def handle_in(
  "add_item", %{"item_id" => id}, socket = %{assigns: %{cart: cart}}) do
  case Checkout.add_item_to_cart(cart, String.to_integer(id)) do
```

```
    {:ok, new_cart} ->
      broadcast_cart(new_cart, socket, added: [id])
      socket = assign(socket, :cart, new_cart)
      {:reply, {:ok, cart_to_map(new_cart)}, socket}

    {:error, :duplicate_item} ->
      {:reply, {:error, %{error: "duplicate_item"}}, socket}
  end
end

def handle_out("cart_updated", params, socket) do
  cart = get_cart(params)
  socket = assign(socket, :cart, cart)
  push(socket, "cart", cart_to_map(cart))

  {:noreply, socket}
end

defp broadcast_cart(cart, socket, opts) do
  {:ok, serialized} = Checkout.export_cart(cart)

  broadcast_from(socket, "cart_updated", %{
    "serialized" => serialized,
    "added" => Keyword.get(opts, :added, []),
    "removed" => Keyword.get(opts, :removed, [])
  })
end
```

The only change to the handle_in function is the addition of a call to broadcast_cart/2. This function leverages broadcast_from/3, a function provided by Phoenix.Channel. This type of broadcast differs from a standard broadcast/3 function because the calling process will not receive the message. Only other processes—other ShoppingCartChannels with the same cart ID—will receive the message. We aren't using the added and removed keys yet, but we will be shortly.

Other Channels need to both push a message to their client and update their internal state. If we only needed to push a message, we would be able to directly broadcast the "cart" message. However, we need to intercept the message and update each Channel's state. We intercept "cart_updated", so handle_out will be called with this event type. The handle_out function turns the serialized cart into a real cart, sends it to the connected client, and updates the Channel's assigned state.

Try out the demo from the previous section. When you add a shoe in a tab, all other tabs will immediately reflect the shoe in the cart.

Before we can finish the basics of our cart, we need to implement removing an item. This code will very closely resemble the code for adding an item. Let's start with the ShoppingCartChannel and work out to the front end. Add this code after the existing handle_in function:

sneakers_23_cart/lib/sneakers_23_web/channels/shopping_cart_channel.ex
```
def handle_in(
  "remove_item", %{"item_id" => id}, socket = %{assigns: %{cart: cart}}) do
  case Checkout.remove_item_from_cart(cart, String.to_integer(id)) do
    {:ok, new_cart} ->
      broadcast_cart(new_cart, socket, removed: [id])
      socket = assign(socket, :cart, new_cart)
      {:reply, {:ok, cart_to_map(new_cart)}, socket}

    {:error, :not_found} ->
      {:reply, {:error, %{error: "not_found"}}, socket}
  end
end
```

This function mirrors our add item code almost perfectly, so there's nothing new here.

Let's add item removal code to app.js that mirrors how items are added.

sneakers_23_cart/assets/js/app.js
```
dom.onItemRemoveClick((itemId) => {
  Cart.removeCartItem(cartChannel, itemId)
})
```

We've already written the Cart.removeCartItem/2 function, but we need to implement dom.onItemRemoveClick. Let's do that now.

sneakers_23_cart/assets/js/dom.js
```
dom.onItemRemoveClick = (fn) => {
  document.addEventListener('click', (event) => {
    if (!event.target.matches('.cart-item__remove')) { return }
    event.preventDefault()
    fn(event.target.dataset.itemId)
  })
}
```

Let's try out item removal now. Start your server with mix phx.server and load http://localhost:4000. You can add an item, as you could previously, but now the "×" symbol next to each shopping cart item removes the item from the cart. Try this feature with multiple tabs to make sure that everything works correctly. Take a moment to git commit your changes.

We have a shopping cart that works for many of our requirements. We can add a single size of a shoe, remove shoes, display the cart on the front end, use the same cart across multiple tabs, and persist the cart between page loads. The feature that we'll implement next is real-time updates when an item goes out-of-stock.

Add Real-Time Out-Of-Stock Alerts

The last feature that we will add to our shopping cart is out-of-stock alerts. A shopping cart consists of a set of items that have been added by a shopper. The shopping cart will notify the shopper when any of these items goes out-of-stock. If you remember from the CartView module, an item will be determined to be available (or not) each time that the cart is rendered—all that we need to do is trigger the cart to be rendered and sent to the connected client.

We'll leverage PubSub to know when the ShoppingCartChannel needs to send a message to the client. Our PubSub usage so far in this book has been tied to Channels—we've always pushed directly to a Channel topic. We can take a different approach, though. We'll walk through how to subscribe to a PubSub topic that is not the same as a Channel topic.

Using Dynamic PubSub Subscriptions

Processes can subscribe and unsubscribe to messages for any PubSub topic. A process can subscribe to as many topics as it wants to. We will use this to build out-of-stock notifications. Each item will have a topic in the format "item_out:{id}" and will broadcast messages in the format {:item_out, id}.

The ShoppingCartChannel needs to subscribe to the correct items so it gets alerted regarding only the items it cares about, which helps improve the performance of live updates. It also needs to unsubscribe to items that are removed from the cart, so that it stops getting notified about them. The following figure shows the steps that our Channel will follow:

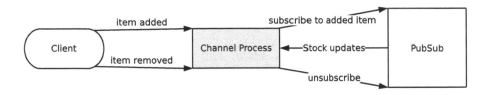

Next, we'll modify the ShoppingCartChannel module to use this approach.

PubSub in the Shopping Cart Channel

A client sends its cart in the join parameters of ShoppingCartChannel. Once the Channel has the cart, it needs to subscribe to any existing items. Without this, the cart would not receive updates for previously added items.

Let's modify the ShoppingCartChannel to add PubSub subscriptions when the Channel joins.

sneakers_23_cart/lib/sneakers_23_web/channels/shopping_cart_channel.ex

```elixir
def join("cart:" <> id, params, socket) when byte_size(id) == 64 do
  cart = get_cart(params)
  socket = assign(socket, :cart, cart)
  send(self(), :send_cart)
  enqueue_cart_subscriptions(cart)

  {:ok, socket}
end

def handle_info({:subscribe, item_id}, socket) do
  Phoenix.PubSub.subscribe(Sneakers23.PubSub, "item_out:#{item_id}")
  {:noreply, socket}
end

defp enqueue_cart_subscriptions(cart) do
  cart
  |> Checkout.cart_item_ids()
  |> Enum.each(fn id ->
    send(self(), {:subscribe, id})
  end)
end
```

The enqueue_cart_subscriptions/1 function iterates over each item in the cart and sends a message to correspond to the PubSub topic. We could subscribe to the PubSub directly, without sending a message, but the current approach will ensure that add_item and remove_item handlers don't get slowed down by the PubSub subscription.

Next, let's change the add item handle_in function to subscribe to the topic.

sneakers_23_cart/lib/sneakers_23_web/channels/shopping_cart_channel.ex

```elixir
{:ok, new_cart} ->
  send(self(), {:subscribe, id})
  broadcast_cart(new_cart, socket, added: [id])
```

We need to follow this same exact process for item removal, but we'll unsubscribe to the topic. Make the following changes to the ShoppingCartChannel.

sneakers_23_cart/lib/sneakers_23_web/channels/shopping_cart_channel.ex

```elixir
def handle_info({:unsubscribe, item_id}, socket) do
  Phoenix.PubSub.unsubscribe(Sneakers23.PubSub, "item_out:#{item_id}")
  {:noreply, socket}
end

def handle_in(
  "remove_item", %{"item_id" => id}, socket = %{assigns: %{cart: cart}}) do
  case Checkout.remove_item_from_cart(cart, String.to_integer(id)) do
    {:ok, new_cart} ->
```

```
➤      send(self(), {:unsubscribe, id})
       broadcast_cart(new_cart, socket, removed: [id])
       socket = assign(socket, :cart, new_cart)
       {:reply, {:ok, cart_to_map(new_cart)}, socket}

    {:error, :not_found} ->
       {:reply, {:error, %{error: "not_found"}}, socket}
  end
end
```

The remove_item handler mirrors the add_item handler but uses the unsubscribe
function to remove all of the active subscriptions for the current process and
topic pair.

When the PubSub dispatches a message over the "item_out:{id}" topic, all subscribed processes will receive the message.

Let's write a handler for what we want our message to look like. Add the following handle_info handler after the other handle_info functions.

sneakers_23_cart/lib/sneakers_23_web/channels/shopping_cart_channel.ex
```
def handle_info({:item_out, _id}, socket = %{assigns: %{cart: cart}}) do
  push(socket, "cart", cart_to_map(cart))
  {:noreply, socket}
end
```

Our CartView fetches the current state of an item's availability, so all that we
need to do is send the rendered cart to the connected client. If we needed to
know what items are out-of-stock in the Channel, we could save those items
at this point.

We also need to subscribe and unsubscribe from PubSub messages when a
cart is updated—that is why we included the removed and added values in our
"cart_updated" message. Let's add that now.

sneakers_23_cart/lib/sneakers_23_web/channels/shopping_cart_channel.ex
```
def handle_out("cart_updated", params, socket) do
➤   modify_subscriptions(params)
    cart = get_cart(params)
    socket = assign(socket, :cart, cart)
    push(socket, "cart", cart_to_map(cart))

    {:noreply, socket}
end

defp modify_subscriptions(%{"added" => add, "removed" => remove}) do
  Enum.each(add, & send(self(), {:subscribe, &1}))
  Enum.each(remove, & send(self(), {:unsubscribe, &1}))
end
```

Before we can test this feature out, we need to broadcast the "item_out:id" message. We'll hook into the code that runs when an Inventory item is sold—if the item is out-of-stock we'll broadcast the message.

Let's start by adding a broadcast function to the Sneakers23Web context module. This will look like a strange use of PubSub, but we'll walk through what it's doing.

Add the following function underneath the existing defdelegate calls:

```
sneakers_23_cart/lib/sneakers_23_web.ex
def notify_local_item_stock_change(%{available_count: 0, id: id}) do
  Sneakers23.PubSub
  |> Phoenix.PubSub.node_name()
  |> Phoenix.PubSub.direct_broadcast(
    Sneakers23.PubSub, "item_out:#{id}", {:item_out, id}
  )
end

def notify_local_item_stock_change(_), do: false
```

When PubSub version 2.0 is released, it will come with a local_broadcast function that works almost this same way, but is more performant.

This function will only perform a broadcast when the available count of an item is 0. We use direct_broadcast/4 to send out a broadcast. The broadcast will only be run on the specified node, which is the same one that called the initial function. Doing this ensures that the Inventory.Server process is up-to-date when the CartView renders the cart. If we broadcast the message to all nodes, then we would have a race condition and the CartView could potentially render an out-of-stock item as available.

Due to the use of direct_broadcast, the notify_local_item_stock_change/1 function must run on every node in the cluster. Luckily, we already have a place to hook this in—the Inventory.item_sold!/2 function.

item_sold!/2 is called on all servers, due to the replication code that we added previously.

Let's add the notification to this function.

```
sneakers_23_cart/lib/sneakers_23/inventory.ex
def item_sold!(id), do: item_sold!(id, [])
def item_sold!(item_id, opts) do
  pid = Keyword.get(opts, :pid, __MODULE__)
  being_replicated? = Keyword.get(opts, :being_replicated?, false)

  avail = Store.fetch_availability_for_item(item_id)
  {:ok, old_inv, inv} = Server.set_item_availability(pid, avail)
  {:ok, item} = CompleteProduct.get_item_by_id(inv, item_id)
```

```
  unless being_replicated? do
    Replication.item_sold!(item_id)
➤   {:ok, old_item} = CompleteProduct.get_item_by_id(old_inv, item_id)
    Sneakers23Web.notify_item_stock_change(
      previous_item: old_item, current_item: item
    )
  end

➤ Sneakers23Web.notify_local_item_stock_change(item)

  :ok
end
```

This function has not changed much—we now call Sneakers23Web.notify_local_item_stock_change/1 and we extract the get_item_by_id/2 function up to a higher scope. It's important that this code is run outside of the being_replaced? conditional statement, because we want it to run on each node and not just on the original node.

Our shopping experience is almost complete. There's one final bit of code to include to finish it off—the checkout process.

Complete the Checkout Process

We're not going to walk through the checkout process for our store due to limited time. However, I think it's important for you to see the complete shopping experience. You will find a simple checkout process included in the code that ships with this book. You can copy the following files and snippets into your project to finish the checkout process.

```
$ cp sneakers_23_cart/lib/sneakers_23_web/controllers/checkout_controller.ex \
    your_project/lib/sneakers_23_web/controllers/checkout_controller.ex

$ cp -R sneakers_23_cart/lib/sneakers_23_web/templates/checkout \
      your_project/lib/sneakers_23_web/templates/checkout

$ cp sneakers_23_cart/lib/sneakers_23_web/views/checkout_view.ex \
    your_project/lib/sneakers_23_web/views/checkout_view.ex
```

Next, add the router entries to your Router module.

```
sneakers_23_cart/lib/sneakers_23_web/router.ex
  get "/", ProductController, :index
➤ get "/checkout", CheckoutController, :show
➤ post "/checkout", CheckoutController, :purchase
➤ get "/checkout/complete", CheckoutController, :success
```

Finally, you'll need an additional function added to the Checkout context, inside of the existing scope.

sneakers_23_cart/lib/sneakers_23/checkout.ex
```elixir
def purchase_cart(cart, opts \\ []) do
  Sneakers23.Repo.transaction(fn ->
    Enum.each(cart_item_ids(cart), fn id ->
      case Sneakers23.Checkout.SingleItem.sell_item(id, opts) do
        :ok ->
          :ok

        _ ->
          Sneakers23.Repo.rollback(:purchase_failed)
      end
    end)

    :purchase_complete
  end)
end
```

This code sells all of the items in the shopping cart. The entire order is can-
celled if any item is unavailable, so the system remains in the right state. All
of this code runs inside of a transaction thanks to the Repo.transaction/1 function.
You could also use Ecto.Multi[2] to write database transactions.

We're ready to test that our cart works as expected. Next, we'll walk through
each feature built in this chapter to make sure that it works as expected. This
will also give you a demo of the complete cart. Take a moment to git commit
your changes before moving on.

Acceptance Test the Shopping Cart

All the code for our shopping cart is in place. We're going to walk through a
few different scenarios and ensure the cart works as expected in each. You
would be performing these types of tests incrementally as you build the system, but it's important to run through all of the scenarios again when the
code is complete.

Our test scenarios revolve around the requirements—we'll combine multiple
requirements into a single scenario, so that we can quickly work through our
acceptance tests. To keep things concise, we won't test what happens after
clicking the purchase button.

Our first scenario will be a test of the add and remove item features.

First Scenario

We'll follow the same pattern as outlined in Chapter 8, Break Your Application
with Acceptance Tests, on page 141: define the test, write steps for the test,

---

2.   https://hexdocs.pm/ecto/Ecto.Multi.html

write expectations for the test, and execute the test. Our first test will hit on most requirements except for out-of-stock notifications.

Define the test

A shopper is connected to the store, waiting for the shoes to be released. The shoes are released and the shopper adds one of each shoe to their cart. The shopper removes one of the shoes from their cart. The shopper closes the page and re-opens it. The shopper opens a second tab. The shopper removes all items from their cart and then adds two sizes of each shoe. The shopper clicks the "checkout" button.

Write steps for the test

1. Start the server in a freshly seeded state.

2. Load http://localhost:4000.

3. Release both shoes.

4. Add size 6 of the top shoe and size 10 of the bottom shoe.

5. Remove the size 10 shoe.

6. Navigate away from current page, to any other website.

7. Navigate back to http://localhost:4000.

8. Open a second tab of http://localhost:4000.

9. Remove all items in the cart by clicking on the "×" symbol, from the second tab.

10. Switch to the first tab.

11. Add any two sizes from each shoe—four total.

12. Click the checkout button.

Write expectations for the test

- The shopper sees "coming soon" and no cart after step 2.

- The shopper sees the size selectors after step 3.

- The shopper sees two items in their cart after step 4.

- The shopper sees one item in their cart, size 6, after step 5.

- The shopper sees each cart matches the other after step 8.

- The shopper sees that each tab has an empty cart (it disappears) after step 10.

- The shopper sees four shoes in their cart after step 11.

- The shopper sees the shoes they selected on the checkout page after step 12.

Acceptance tests can get lengthy, like this one. It's important to ensure that all behavior works as expected, even if an area of the application wasn't affected by the current changes.

Use the following instructions to execute the test. If one of the shoes you're supposed to add is sold out, which can happen due to the random seed, then simply select a different available size.

```
$ mix ecto.reset && mix run -e "Sneakers23Mock.Seeds.seed!()" # (step 1)
$ iex -S mix phx.server
# (step 3)
iex(1)> Enum.each([1, 2], &Sneakers23.Inventory.mark_product_released!/1)
:ok
# Follow steps 4 through 12 using the above instructions
```

If you've followed each step, you will see that all of our expectations pass! Next, we'll execute a scenario for out-of-stock updates.

Second Scenario

This scenario will ensure that some of the more complex features of our shopping cart work as expected. We haven't yet tested how our cart works in a multi-server setup, so we'll perform this scenario across two servers to ensure that it does work.

Define the test

A shopper is connected to the store and sees that the shoes have already been released. The shopper adds a shoe to their cart, removes it, and adds it again. The shopper opens a second tab and adds another shoe to their cart from the second tab. The shoes sell out, from a second server. The shopper sees that their items are sold out, and they remove the items from their cart.

Write steps for the test

1. Start two servers (app and backend) in a freshly seeded state.
2. Release both shoes (from the backend server).
3. Load http://localhost:4000.
4. Add size 6 of the top shoe, remove it, and add it again.
5. Open a second tab of http://localhost:4000.
6. Add a second shoe to the cart from the second tab.
7. Run the inventory reducer script (from the backend server).

8. Check both tabs' cart displays once the items are sold out.
9. Remove all shoes from your cart.
10. Try to add a sold-out shoe to your cart.

Write expectations for the test
- The shopper sees the size selectors after step 3.
- The shopper sees one item in their cart after step 4.
- The shopper sees that both tabs show one shoe in the cart after step 5.
- The shopper sees that both tabs show two shoes in the cart after step 6.
- The inventory reducer script runs without error.
- The shopper sees that all items in their cart are grayed out.
- The shopper can remove all items from their cart.
- The shopper cannot add sold-out shoes to their cart.

Use the following instructions to execute the test. We'll start multiple servers and you will run Elixir functions only on the "backend" server.

```
$ mix ecto.reset && mix run -e "Sneakers23Mock.Seeds.seed!()" # (step 1)
$ iex --name app@127.0.0.1 -S mix phx.server
# Do not run commands from the "app" server

$ iex --name backend@127.0.0.1 -S mix
iex(1)> Node.connect(:"app@127.0.0.1")
:ok
# (step 2)
iex(2)> Enum.each([1, 2], &Sneakers23.Inventory.mark_product_released!/1)
:ok
# Follow steps 4-6
iex(3)> Sneakers23Mock.InventoryReducer.sell_random_until_gone!() # (step 7)
:ok
# Follow steps 8+
```

Walk through the steps and ensure that each expectation passes—everything should work for you. Our test shows that our shopping cart works when the store runs on multiple servers, and that the out-of-stock update works as expected. This test saved me, as I initially put the notify_local_item_stock_change/1 before the replication conditional. This resulted in a final state where one cart showed as fully out-of-stock but another appeared as still having a shoe in-stock, until I refreshed the page.

There are, of course, many more acceptance tests we could perform against our shopping cart. A professional QA tester will flex the edge cases of the system even further to find out if it breaks in different circumstances. You could add additional features if you are looking to challenge yourself. Try to make it so that only a single size of each shoe can be added to the cart. Think about what acceptance tests you would run against this new requirement, and then automate the tests with Hound. We won't cover those tasks in this book, but they would be excellent practice.

Our shopping cart is now finished, at least from a shopper perspective. We'll be coming back to our cart in the next chapter, by adding admin-specific features to it.

Wrapping Up

We've built a fully functioning shopping cart, using the tools we've covered throughout this book. We had to flex all of our Channel and real-time system skills to build this relatively complex feature. We used the basic handle_in and handle_out features in Phoenix Channels to take client commands and send data to the clients. We leveraged PubSub with dynamic subscriptions to keep track of when an item goes out-of-stock. We made our system work across distributed servers by using an order of operations in our inventory updates that provides our shoppers with a consistent view of their cart.

Acceptance tests, whether manual or automated, are extremely useful in finding bugs in the code that we write. We performed two complex acceptance tests that showed our cart works in a variety of situations. We did all of this while writing clean code that respects the contextual boundaries of our application.

We're going to take the momentum from this chapter and run with it in the next one. We'll be looking at how to use Phoenix Tracker and Presence to build an admin portal that shows how many carts are connected and shows the breakdown of connected shoppers carts at the present moment.

## CHAPTER 10

Track Connected Carts with Presence

In the last chapter, we built a shopping cart with real-time out-of-stock alerts. That feature completed the shopper-facing section of our Sneakers23 application. In this chapter, we'll build an admin-facing dashboard that will show real-time information about all the current shoppers on the website. You'll learn about and use Phoenix Tracker and Presence along the way.

Distributed state is a hard problem. Variations in time and network partitions are just some of the challenges you'll face when writing a distributed system. Phoenix Tracker makes distributing a list of processes and metadata about each process an easy endeavor. Tracker uses an advanced data structure to distribute state across a cluster in an efficient and accurate way, which allows us to know how many Channels are connected currently. This is a hard problem to tackle properly, but Tracker handles it for us!

We'll start this chapter by going over the plan for our admin dashboard. The most important feature that we'll implement in this chapter is the active shopper list. This will show a store admin the number of connected shopping carts and which shoes are most popular. We'll also restrict access to the dashboard so that only admins can access it. Of course, we'll use Phoenix Channels and Tracker to power our dashboard. We'll compare the base Phoenix.Tracker module to a version with additional features—Phoenix.Presence—before we start building our dashboard.

After we cover what Tracker is, we'll scaffold the admin dashboard, build a Presence that can track carts, and then wire all of these pieces together in an interface build for admins. We'll do this all in a modest amount of code, due to the powerful abstractions provided by Tracker and Presence. You'll then load test the dashboard using an Elixir application that simulates many shoppers connected to Sneakers23.

Let's get started by looking at what we're going to build.

Plan Your Admin Dashboard

Shoppers are able to use our store right now, but we don't know how many shoppers are online, what they have in their cart, or where they are in the checkout process. With this information, we will be able to know how well a launch is performing—maybe the demand is more or less than expected and the launch needs to be adjusted.

In this chapter, we'll build a dashboard for Sneaker23 admins that provides live store analytics. Our dashboard will have the following features:

- Show the count of unique shoppers.
- Show the count of shoppers based on the page they're on.
- Show the count of shoes that are in an active cart, by size.
- Restrict access to admins only.

We'll start, in this section, with a plan for how we'll go about building our admin dashboard. Let's jump in.

Turn Requirements into a Plan

We'll use the access restriction techniques covered in Chapter 4, Restrict Socket and Channel Access, on page 53 to restrict access to our dashboard. Our admin dashboard needs a higher level of restriction than the previous chapters' features, so we will create a dedicated Socket for it. The following figure shows our Socket and Channel structure:

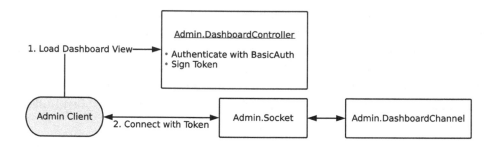

The Admin.DashboardController is in charge of authentication and Phoenix.Token creation. We will use HTTP basic authentication for our project, but a real-world application could easily use a different type of authentication. The client will use its provided token to connect to the Admin.Socket. The Admin.Socket only allows admins to connect, so we do not need to add topic authorization to the Admin.DashboardChannel.

The other requirements will prove more complex to build. We'll leverage a Tracker to know how many shopping carts are connected. Each ShoppingCartChannel will track itself in the CartTracker when the Channel connects, and this data will be read by the Admin.DashboardChannel to build the user interface. The tracker setup will look like the following figure:

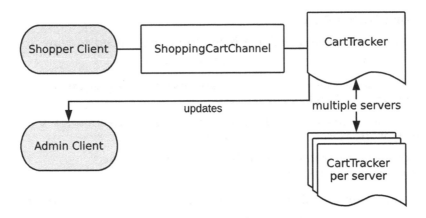

We'll cover what Phoenix Tracker is and how it keeps data in sync across a cluster. Before we can do that, you will need to set up your project so that you can easily add this chapter's features to it.

Set Up Your Project

If you've been following along in part II, you have a shopping cart in your Sneakers23 application that satisfies the acceptance tests from the last chapter. For this chapter, you can either start with a completely fresh application base, or you can use your existing project. Choose the next section based on what you'd like to do.

Set Up a Clean Project

Make sure that you have a copy of this book's code, using the instructions found in Online Resources, on page xiii. Next, copy the base application into a development location.

```
$ cp -R code/location/sneakers_23_admin_base ~/sneakers_23_admin
$ cd ~/sneakers_23_admin
$ git init && git add . && git commit -m "initial commit (from base)"
$ mix deps.get && mix ecto.setup && npm --prefix assets install
```

If you don't have the hello_sockets project, copy the following folder for the Tracker example that we will write shortly.

```
$ cp -R code/location/hello_sockets_without_tracker ~/hello_sockets
$ cd ~/hello_sockets
$ mix deps.get && npm --prefix assets install
```

At this point, you have a clean codebase ready for this chapter's admin dashboard. You can skip to the next major heading now—we'll go over what Phoenix Tracker is.

Set Up Your Existing Project

If you want to use your existing repo, you simply need to copy a few files in—these files would be tedious to type otherwise.

```
$ cp code/location/sneakers_23_admin_base/assets/css/admin.css \
    your_project/assets/css/admin.css
```

```
$ cp code/location/sneakers_23_admin_base/assets/js/admin/dom.js \
    your_project/assets/js/admin/dom.js
```

```
$ cp code/location/sneakers_23_admin_base/index.html.eex \
    your_project/index.html.eex
```

You're now ready to build this chapter's admin dashboard. Before we do that, let's go over what Phoenix Tracker is.

On Track with Phoenix Tracker

Phoenix Tracker solves the problem of tracking processes and metadata about those processes across a cluster of servers. This sounds like an easy problem, but it's challenging due to the types of conflicts that occur when replicating information between servers. We'll use Tracker in our application to track each connected ShoppingCartChannel process, along with metadata for each cart. Before we add Tracker to our application, let's go over what it is and how to use it.

Tracker uses a special type of data structure to replicate its information across a cluster. We'll go over this data structure and look at what guarantees it provides. We'll then cover different use cases for Tracker. Finally, we'll set up a basic Tracker to demo how it works.

Let's get started by looking at how Tracker works.

Phoenix Tracker's Design

Phoenix Tracker maintains accurate and timely presence lists across a cluster of servers. It does so without having a single authoritative source (like a database)—each server contributes to the known state. Time is not our friend when it comes to distributed state, and it makes this problem challenging. A first pass at this problem—dispatching changes to a set—would quickly run into many edge cases. There would be conflicts in data, lost updates, and inefficient performance. Phoenix Tracker uses a data structure called a conflict-free replicated data type (CRDT) to implement its state tracking.

A CRDT provides replicated state across multiple servers with independent and concurrent updates to the underlying data—each data structure can be updated without asking other copies for permission. There are many different types, but Phoenix Tracker uses an ORSWOT (Observe-Remove-Set-Without-Tombstones) to manage its state. It's outside of this book to go over exactly how the ORSWOT works, as it's a fairly advanced data structure. The important thing to know is that it's designed to efficiently use memory and it handles conflicts by preferring adds over removes. You don't have to worry about the implementation of the ORSWOT to use Tracker—it just works.

The OTP process structure of Tracker is more relevant to us. The following figure shows the multi-shard process structure that Tracker uses:

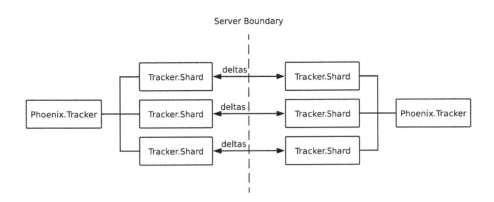

The Phoenix.Tracker module is a facade over a number of Tracker.Shard processes. You invoke functions from the Phoenix.Tracker module, but the actual data is provided by the underlying shard processes. This design removes a single process bottleneck that can make Elixir systems sometimes perform poorly. Tracker performs sharding based on the tracked topic string, so a single topic with many tracked processes will still go through a single process bottleneck.

Each Tracker.Shard process collects changes in its state and broadcasts the changes over Phoenix PubSub to all other nodes in the cluster. The state distribution broadcast has a configurable delay in it, less than two seconds, that batches messages together. This makes Tracker eventually consistent—writes will not immediately be reflected across the entire cluster.

Tracker is an advanced tool that gives us a small but powerful set of features. Let's look at a few ways that it can be used.

Phoenix Tracker in Our Dashboard

Tracker was built for a particular use case, but it can be of value for many problems. Originally, Tracker was built to answer "who's online?" in a chat app. In this use case, each user's Channel is tracked when they connect, along with metadata such as their name and user ID. Each client that is listening to the chat room topic receives updates to the online status list in real-time. Later in this chapter we'll see how Presence, a special type of Tracker, makes this particular problem easy to solve.

We'll be using Tracker for a similar but slightly different use case. Each ShoppingCartChannel will become tracked when it connects, and admins will be able to access the data showing who is online. We'll attach metadata to the tracker to know what is in each of the shopping carts. The admin dashboard will read and aggregate this information in real-time.

Tracker in a Pipeline

Not all use cases for Tracker are user facing—a great place to use Tracker is in a data pipeline. A data pipeline that has a costly enrichment process, such as accessing a database or third-party API, will end up doing work for users that aren't online. We can use Tracker to answer the question "is this user online?" before performing the expensive enrichment operation. This is recommended only if your enrichment process has a high cost, as there is a slight performance cost when you use Tracker.

Before we continue with the Sneakers23 application that we've been building in Part II, we're going to take a little detour to see how to use Tracker by adding it to our sample application from Part I.

Use Tracker in an Application

The HelloSocket application from Part I serves as a reference project that provides contained examples of how to use different Phoenix features. We'll add our Phoenix.Tracker code to this application, so that you have an example to revisit if needed. We'll continue with our Sneakers23 application shortly.

If you have completed Part I of this book, then your hello_sockets project will serve as the starting code for this Tracker project. If you do not have this project, then you can find the hello_sockets_without_tracker folder in the code that ships with this book. Follow the instructions in the "Set Up Your Project" section from earlier in this chapter.

It's easy to get started with Tracker in an application. We will first define a module that implements the Phoenix.Tracker behaviour. This module hides the Tracker function calls and provide a simple interface for our Channels to use. We'll then track our desired Channel processes when they join. Finally, we'll use the Phoenix.Tracker.list/2 function to get all of the tracked data.

We'll revisit the HelloSockets application from Part I for this example. First, create a new module at the path lib/hello_sockets_web/channels/user_tracker.ex.

```
hello_sockets/lib/hello_sockets_web/channels/user_tracker.ex
defmodule HelloSocketsWeb.UserTracker do
  @behaviour Phoenix.Tracker

  def child_spec(opts) do
    %{
      id: __MODULE__,
      start: {__MODULE__, :start_link, [opts]},
      type: :supervisor
    }
  end

  def start_link(opts) do
    opts =
      opts
      |> Keyword.put(:name, __MODULE__)
      |> Keyword.put(:pubsub_server, HelloSockets.PubSub)

    Phoenix.Tracker.start_link(__MODULE__, opts, opts)
  end

  def init(opts) do
    server = Keyword.fetch!(opts, :pubsub_server)

    {:ok, %{pubsub_server: server}}
  end
end
```

This module is mostly boilerplate that can be reused in other projects. The start_link/1 function sets up default options that are then passed into Phoenix.Tracker.start_link/3. The Tracker process is then started—it supervises a collection of Phoenix.Tracker.Shard processes. The init/1 function is called for each Shard that is created. We must provide the pubsub_server key in the init/1 function, or the Tracker will crash.

Tracker requires that a handle_diff/2 function is implemented. This is where you perform logic based on the changes in state. Let's implement a handle_diff/2 function that prints out the changes.

hello_sockets/lib/hello_sockets_web/channels/user_tracker.ex
```
require Logger

def handle_diff(changes, state) do
  Logger.info inspect({"tracked changes", changes})
  {:ok, state}
end
```

This will allow us to inspect the changes as Channels are joined and closed. Next, we'll define the public interface for our module. We'll provide a way to track a Channel, as well as a function to get the current Tracker state.

hello_sockets/lib/hello_sockets_web/channels/user_tracker.ex
```
def track(%{channel_pid: pid, topic: topic, assigns: %{user_id: user_id}}) do
  metadata = %{
    online_at: DateTime.utc_now(),
    user_id: user_id
  }

  Phoenix.Tracker.track(__MODULE__, pid, topic, user_id, metadata)
end

def list(topic \\ "tracked") do
  Phoenix.Tracker.list(__MODULE__, topic)
end
```

Phoenix.Tracker.track/5 is the most important call for our Tracker. This will take a pid and track it for a given topic. Any metadata can be provided here, which is useful for knowing who is connected and when they joined.

We need to add our UserTracker module to our application's supervision tree. Add it after the Endpoint.

hello_sockets/lib/hello_sockets/application.ex
```
HelloSocketsWeb.Endpoint,
{HelloSocketsWeb.UserTracker,
  [pool_size: :erlang.system_info(:schedulers_online)]}
```

We pass in the pool_size option to our Tracker. Generally, you should set this to the number of schedulers that you have available. This maximizes the parallel throughput of your application. There are other configuration options[1] available as well. It's worth saying again: Tracker shards based on the topic, so all changes for a single large topic will end up going through the same Shard GenServer.

---

1.   https://hexdocs.pm/phoenix_pubsub/Phoenix.Tracker.html#module-optional-pool_opts

Next, we'll create a new Channel for our demo. Let's first add it to our existing AuthSocket module.

hello_sockets/lib/hello_sockets_web/channels/auth_socket.ex
```
channel "ping", HelloSocketsWeb.PingChannel
channel "tracked", HelloSocketsWeb.TrackedChannel
```

Next, create the TrackedChannel module.

hello_sockets/lib/hello_sockets_web/channels/tracked_channel.ex
```
defmodule HelloSocketsWeb.TrackedChannel do
  use Phoenix.Channel

  alias HelloSocketsWeb.UserTracker

  def join("tracked", _payload, socket) do
    send(self(), :after_join)
    {:ok, socket}
  end

  def handle_info(:after_join, socket) do
    {:ok, _} = UserTracker.track(socket)
    {:noreply, socket}
  end
end
```

We invoke UserTracker.track/1 in a message after the Channel has connected. This allows our Channel to quickly respond back to the client before tracking itself.

In order to illustrate different user_id combinations, we'll make our user ID dynamic in the PageController. Create a function to handle the /tracked endpoint.

hello_sockets/lib/hello_sockets_web/controllers/page_controller.ex
```
def tracked(conn, params) do
  fake_user_id = Map.get(params, "user_id", "1")

  conn
  |> assign(:auth_token, generate_auth_token(conn, fake_user_id))
  |> assign(:user_id, fake_user_id)
  |> render("index.html")
end
```

You also need to add the new route to your Router file.

hello_sockets/lib/hello_sockets_web/router.ex
```
  get "/", PageController, :index
➤ get "/tracked", PageController, :tracked
```

Our last step is to update our socket.js file with our new Channel. I recommend temporarily commenting out all the existing content after export default socket, so that your console remains clean for our demo.

```
hello_sockets/assets/js/socket.js
const trackedSocket = new Socket("/auth_socket", {
  params: { token: window.authToken }
})

trackedSocket.connect()

const trackerChannel = trackedSocket.channel("tracked")
trackerChannel.join()
```

We're ready to see our Tracker in action. Start two servers as follows.

```
$ iex --name app@127.0.0.1 -S mix phx.server
# Do not run commands from the "app" server
```

```
$ iex --name backend@127.0.0.1 -S mix
iex(1)> Node.connect(:"app@127.0.0.1")
:ok
```

Next, load http://localhost:4000/tracked?user_id=1 and http://localhost:4000/tracked?user_id=other
in two different tabs. Run UserTracker.list/0 on both the app and back-end nodes
to see Tracker in action.

```
iex(1)> HelloSocketsWeb.UserTracker.list()
[
  {"1",
   %{
     online_at: ~U[2019-10-14 01:26:54.061366Z],
     phx_ref: "h/NBlMJyHw0=",
     user_id: "1"
   }},
  {"other",
   %{
     online_at: ~U[2019-10-14 01:27:41.230174Z],
     phx_ref: "eLJJLlfJvmQ=",
     user_id: "other"
   }}
]
```

The Tracker has distributed its state across the cluster. Try to create more tabs,
close the tabs, and turn servers on and off to observe what happens in each
of these scenarios. The end result is that Tracker will right itself in whatever
scenario that you throw at it, but it might take some time (up to 30 seconds)
depending on what you do. However, most changes will feel immediate.

You will also notice that the handle_diff/2 function was called on both the app
and back-end servers with a list of the changes—a map of topics with added
and removed lists. You can do whatever you want with the changes, but it is
important to remember that the handle_diff function is called on each node.

Presence is a type of Tracker that provides some additional useful features for Channel-based applications. We'll go over Presence and how it differs from Tracker next.

Phoenix Tracker Versus Presence

Phoenix Presence is an implementation of Tracker that provides helper functions for working with Channels. Its implementation of handle_diff/2 broadcasts changes locally using PubSub when a process joins or leaves the Tracker. Clients listen for change messages and process them to keep a client-side version of the Tracker state. The official Phoenix JavaScript library includes a Presence class that handles the messages automatically for us. The following figure shows the flow of Presence updates:

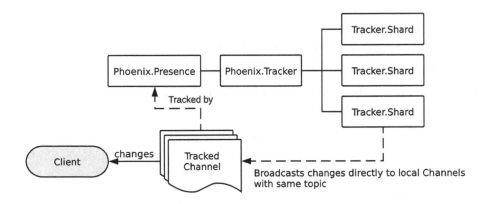

Due to the similarity between the two libraries, it can be confusing to decide which one to use. If you want to have every change broadcast to clients on a given topic, then use Presence. If you want to be in control of how diffs are handled, or if you don't want to broadcast changes to clients, use Tracker.

For example, you would use Presence to maintain a user list that updates on a client in real-time, but you would use Tracker if you are optimizing your data pipeline based on whether clients are connected. If you find yourself intercepting and discarding handle_out("presence_diff") in your Channel, then Tracker is better for you.

Even if your clients are not processing Presence messages, you may be sending data to them with Presence. You should always confirm that your Presence implementation is working as expected to avoid sending data to an incorrect client. You can do this by inspecting the WebSocket messages in your browser's developer tools and verifying that Presence updates are not incorrectly sent to clients.

We'll be using Presence in our admin dashboard because we want to update the admins in real-time. We do not want shoppers to receive updates, though, so we'll be careful with the topic that our Presence tracks. Let's start building the foundation for the Sneakers23 admin dashboard.

Scaffold the Admin Dashboard

There are a lot of moving parts in setting up a brand new section of an application. We'll tackle this together so you can see how you'd go about it in other projects. Our scaffolding will consist of these steps:

1. Define our new Router entries.
2. Setup an admin layout.
3. Create the Admin.DashboardController.
4. Create the Admin.Socket and Admin.DashboardChannel.
5. Create admin JS and CSS.

We'll move quickly through these steps. Once this is done, we'll have the right foundation to build our admin dashboard.

Unit Tests for the Dashboard

 You will find unit tests for most of the modules we create in the sneakers_23_admin/test/ folder. For brevity, these tests are not included in the book text.

We'll start with our route definition. Our admin dashboard will be behind an HTTP Basic Auth screen, and luckily there is a library to help with this. Add the basic_auth library to your mix file.

sneakers_23_admin/mix.exs
```
{:hound, "~> 1.0"},
{:basic_auth, "~> 2.2.2"}
```

Run mix deps.get after you add it. Next, we'll configure our local login to be admin/password. Add this snippet to the end of your dev config file:

sneakers_23_admin/config/dev.exs
```
config :sneakers_23, admin_auth: [
  username: "admin",
  password: "password"
]
```

You will enter these credentials when the HTTP Basic Auth screen appears.

Now we are ready to add our routes. We'll create a new pipeline and scope for our admin dashboard. Add these at the end of the Router module:

```
sneakers_23_admin/lib/sneakers_23_web/router.ex
pipeline :admin do
  plug BasicAuth, use_config: {:sneakers_23, :admin_auth}
  plug :put_layout, {Sneakers23Web.LayoutView, :admin}
end

scope "/admin", Sneakers23Web.Admin do
  pipe_through [:browser, :admin]

  get "/", DashboardController, :index
end
```

We could change our Router to not perform the CartIdPlug in the :browser pipeline, but it won't affect our final product to leave it as it is.

We just completed step 1 of our scaffold. Next, we'll complete step 2 by adding an admin layout. Rather than typing this file in, we'll simply copy from the existing app.html.eex file. You can type this on a single line.

```
$ cp lib/sneakers_23_web/templates/layout/app.html.eex \
      lib/sneakers_23_web/templates/layout/admin.html.eex
```

Delete the block of code that checks if the cart_id is present. We don't need this in our admin dashboard because we won't show admins a shopping cart.

Next, change "app.css" to "admin.css". Also, change "app.js" to "admin.js".

```
sneakers_23_admin/lib/sneakers_23_web/templates/layout/admin.html.eex
<link
  rel="stylesheet"
  href="<%= Routes.static_path(@conn, "/css/admin.css") %>" />
```

```
sneakers_23_admin/lib/sneakers_23_web/templates/layout/admin.html.eex
<script
  type="text/javascript"
  src="<%= Routes.static_path(@conn, "/js/admin.js") %>"></script>
```

This layout file will show a different shell for the admin dashboard, with different assets loaded. This will allow us to separate our user-facing code from our admin-facing code, which helps reduce the risk of errors.

We're ready to move onto the Admin.DashboardController. This will feel very familiar to our past controllers because it's a combination of the ProductController and the HelloSocket PageController.

```
sneakers_23_admin/lib/sneakers_23_web/controllers/admin/dashboard_controller.ex
defmodule Sneakers23Web.Admin.DashboardController do
  use Sneakers23Web, :controller

  def index(conn, _params) do
    {:ok, products} = Sneakers23.Inventory.get_complete_products()

    conn
    |> assign(:products, products)
    |> assign(:admin_token, sign_admin_token(conn))
    |> render("index.html")
  end

  defp sign_admin_token(conn) do
    Phoenix.Token.sign(conn, "admin socket", "admin")
  end
end
```

We've included the products so we can use them in our interface later. We
need to define the template for this controller. Add the following shell of a
template—we'll fill it out soon.

```
sneakers_23_admin/lib/sneakers_23_web/templates/admin/dashboard/index.html.eex
<div class="admin-container">
  <h1>Admin Dashboard</h1>
</div>

<script type="text/javascript">
  window.adminToken = "<%= @admin_token %>"
</script>
```

Each template needs a View to be rendered with. We'll create an empty view
for this.

```
sneakers_23_admin/lib/sneakers_23_web/views/admin/dashboard_view.ex
defmodule Sneakers23Web.Admin.DashboardView do
  use Sneakers23Web, :view
end
```

Start your server with mix phx.server and visit http://localhost:4000/admin to verify
that the endpoint loads. You'll need to enter admin/password when prompted.

We can now set up our Socket, so that we can use Presence. We'll start by
adding a socket definition in our Endpoint module. Add this after the existing
/product_socket definition.

```
sneakers_23_admin/lib/sneakers_23_web/endpoint.ex
socket "/admin_socket", Sneakers23Web.Admin.Socket,
  websocket: true,
  longpoll: false
```

Our Admin.Socket is going to mirror the AuthSocket that we wrote in Part I. Nothing is new here—we're defining a Socket that validates a token upon connection.

```elixir
sneakers_23_admin/lib/sneakers_23_web/channels/admin/socket.ex
defmodule Sneakers23Web.Admin.Socket do
  use Phoenix.Socket
  require Logger

  ## Channels
  channel "admin:cart_tracker", Sneakers23Web.Admin.DashboardChannel

  def connect(%{"token" => token}, socket) do
    case verify(socket, token) do
      {:ok, _} ->
        {:ok, socket}

      {:error, err} ->
        Logger.error("#{__MODULE__} connect error #{inspect(err)}")
        :error
    end
  end

  def connect(_, _) do
    Logger.error("#{__MODULE__} connect error missing params")
    :error
  end

  def id(_socket), do: nil

  @one_day 86400

  defp verify(socket, token),
    do:
      Phoenix.Token.verify(
        socket,
        "admin socket",
        token,
        max_age: @one_day
      )
end
```

The "admin:cart_tracker" topic is very important. We'll use this topic in the next section when we configure our Phoenix Presence module.

We'll use a basic Admin.DashboardChannel for now. Let's set that up next.

```elixir
sneakers_23_admin/lib/sneakers_23_web/channels/admin/dashboard_channel.ex
defmodule Sneakers23Web.Admin.DashboardChannel do
  use Phoenix.Channel

  def join("admin:cart_tracker", _payload, socket) do
    {:ok, socket}
  end
end
```

Our final step is to configure our admin JavaScript and CSS files. We could tie this into the existing app.js file, but it's better to keep these files separated. In order to get multiple files, we'll need to modify our webpack.config.js file, which is something we haven't yet covered. Make the following changes to the file but keep everything else in the file as it is.

sneakers_23_admin/assets/webpack.config.js

```
entry: {
  './app': glob.sync('./vendor/**/*.js').concat(['./js/app.js']),
  './admin': glob.sync('./vendor/**/*.js').concat(['./js/admin.js'])
},
output: {
  filename: '[name].js',
  path: path.resolve(__dirname, '../priv/static/js')
},
plugins: [
  new MiniCssExtractPlugin({ filename: '../css/[name].css' }),
  new CopyWebpackPlugin([{ from: 'static/', to: '../' }])
]
```

These changes create multiple entry points—admin and app—that output JavaScript and CSS files. This provides us with the separation between the two scripts. Let's create the admin.js file now.

sneakers_23_admin/assets/js/admin.js

```
import { Presence } from 'phoenix'
import adminCss from '../css/admin.css'
import css from "../css/app.css"
import { adminSocket } from "./admin/socket"
import dom from './admin/dom'

adminSocket.connect()

const cartTracker = adminSocket.channel("admin:cart_tracker")
const presence = new Presence(cartTracker)
window.presence = presence // This is a helper for us

cartTracker.join().receive("error", () => {
  console.error("Channel join failed")
})
```

This loads in the adminSocket and connects to it. The Presence wrapper isn't doing anything yet, but we'll be using it in the next section. Our final step is to define the admin/socket.js file.

sneakers_23_admin/assets/js/admin/socket.js

```
import { Socket } from "phoenix"

export const adminSocket = new Socket("/admin_socket", {
  params: { token: window.adminToken }
})
```

That completes the final step of our scaffolding. You can test that everything works by starting your server with mix phx.server and loading http://localhost:4000/admin. If you previously entered a password, you won't need to again. Use your browser's Dev Tools to verify that /admin_socket/websocket is running and that the "admin:cart_tracker" topic has been joined.

We're finally ready to use Phoenix Presence to implement our CartTracker. Let's jump in.

Track Shopping Carts in Real-Time

We'll use Presence to track each ShoppingCartChannel and the shopper's cart item IDs. Each change to a cart will dispatch an update to the CartTracker, and the admin client will automatically receive the changes. Our process for this task will break down into these steps:

1. Create a CartTracker module using Phoenix.Presence.
2. Connect ShoppingCartChannel to the CartTracker.
3. Send cart updates to the CartTracker.
4. Configure admin.js to receive Presence updates.
5. Aggregate and display the information in the dashboard.

First, create the CartTracker module under the sneakers_23_web/channels directory.

sneakers_23_admin/lib/sneakers_23_web/channels/cart_tracker.ex
```
defmodule Sneakers23Web.CartTracker do
  use Phoenix.Presence, otp_app: :sneakers_23,
                        pubsub_server: Sneakers23.PubSub
end
```

We get all the functions that Presence provides when we use Phoenix.Presence. This gives us a fairly wide-open public interface. We'll create a smaller interface that is specifically for our application. Let's start with the most important function of our Tracker, the ability to track a cart. Add each of the following functions to the end of the CartTracker module.

sneakers_23_admin/lib/sneakers_23_web/channels/cart_tracker.ex
```
@topic "admin:cart_tracker"

def track_cart(socket, %{cart: cart, id: id, page: page}) do
  track(socket.channel_pid, @topic, id, %{
    page_loaded_at: System.system_time(:millisecond),
    page: page,
    items: Sneakers23.Checkout.cart_item_ids(cart)
  })
end
```

We use track/4, which allows us to specify the topic that we're going to track on. It's important that this topic is different than the ShoppingCartChannel topics, because we don't want our shoppers to get Presence updates. The metadata that is passed into track/4 gives our admin dashboard the information that it needs.

If we track a cart's items, we need to make sure that the metadata stays up to date as the cart changes. Presence provides an update/4 function for this purpose. Add the update_cart/2 function now.

sneakers_23_admin/lib/sneakers_23_web/channels/cart_tracker.ex
```
def update_cart(socket, %{cart: cart, id: id}) do
  update(socket.channel_pid, @topic, id, fn existing_meta ->
    Map.put(existing_meta, :items, Sneakers23.Checkout.cart_item_ids(cart))
  end)
end
```

The final argument of update/4 can take either a map of metadata, or a function that returns the new metadata. The function form is useful to us, because we only want to change the items in the cart.

The next function we'll add returns all data currently tracked.

sneakers_23_admin/lib/sneakers_23_web/channels/cart_tracker.ex
```
def all_carts(), do: list(@topic)
```

This is a basic proxy function, but it gives us the ability to change how the cart is stored if needed. The list/1 function is provided to CartTracker by Phoenix.Presence.

That wraps up our CartTracker—I still get surprised at how little code is needed. In order to use CartTracker, we need to start the Presence process when our application boots. Put the definition for CartTracker after the existing Endpoint definition in the Application.

sneakers_23_admin/lib/sneakers_23/application.ex
```
Sneakers23Web.Endpoint,
{Sneakers23Web.CartTracker,
  [pool_size: :erlang.system_info(:schedulers_online)]},
```

In most applications, it's important to pass the pool_size argument. If you don't, then a single Tracker shard will be used for all Tracker changes. Sharding won't impact our application, because we're using a single large topic.

We're ready to use our CartTracker in the ShoppingCartChannel. We will need to track the Channel when it joins, and then update using update_cart/2 when the cart changes. We'll track the Channel in an :after_join message.

```
sneakers_23_admin/lib/sneakers_23_web/channels/shopping_cart_channel.ex
def join("cart:" <> id, params, socket) when byte_size(id) == 64 do
  cart = get_cart(params)
  socket = assign(socket, :cart, cart)
  send(self(), :send_cart)
  enqueue_cart_subscriptions(cart)

  socket = socket
    |> assign(:cart_id, id)
    |> assign(:page, Map.get(params, "page", nil))

  send(self(), :after_join)

  {:ok, socket}
end

def handle_info(:after_join, socket = %{
  assigns: %{cart: cart, cart_id: id, page: page}
}) do
  {:ok, _} = Sneakers23Web.CartTracker.track_cart(
    socket, %{cart: cart, id: id, page: page}
  )
  {:noreply, socket}
end
```

We'll hook into two different functions to update the tracked cart: when the Channel broadcasts its cart, and when it receives a broadcast that the cart contents have changed. Add the highlighted send/2 function calls in the existing ShoppingCartChannel functions.

```
sneakers_23_admin/lib/sneakers_23_web/channels/shopping_cart_channel.ex
def handle_info(:update_tracked_cart, socket = %{
  assigns: %{cart: cart, cart_id: id}
}) do
  {:ok, _} = Sneakers23Web.CartTracker.update_cart(
    socket, %{cart: cart, id: id}
  )
  {:noreply, socket}
end

def handle_out("cart_updated", params, socket) do
  modify_subscriptions(params)
  cart = get_cart(params)
  socket = assign(socket, :cart, cart)
  push(socket, "cart", cart_to_map(cart))
  send(self(), :update_tracked_cart)

  {:noreply, socket}
end

defp broadcast_cart(cart, socket, opts) do
  send(self(), :update_tracked_cart)
  {:ok, serialized} = Checkout.export_cart(cart)
```

```
  broadcast_from(socket, "cart_updated", %{
    "serialized" => serialized,
    "added" => Keyword.get(opts, :added, []),
    "removed" => Keyword.get(opts, :removed, [])
  })
end
```

Presence works by sending an initial state to a client and keeping that state up to date by pushing changes. We need to send the initial state ourselves in the Admin.DashboardChannel. Add the following after_join message to the existing join function.

sneakers_23_admin/lib/sneakers_23_web/channels/admin/dashboard_channel.ex
```
def join("admin:cart_tracker", _payload, socket) do
  send(self(), :after_join)
  {:ok, socket}
end

def handle_info(:after_join, socket) do
  push(socket, "presence_state", Sneakers23Web.CartTracker.all_carts())
  {:noreply, socket}
end
```

The "presence_state" message is automatically picked up by the Presence class on the front end, which causes the initial state to be set.

One of our requirements is to know how many users are on each page of the site. We can get this by tracking the pathname when the productChannel is joined. Our cart.js file has the params extracted in a helper function, so this is a quick change.

sneakers_23_admin/assets/js/cart.js
```
function channelParams() {
  return {
    serialized: localStorage.storedCart,
    page: window.location.pathname
  }
}
```

Let's do a quick test of our Presence integration before we assemble all of the pieces for our admin dashboard.

```
$ mix ecto.reset && mix run -e "Sneakers23Mock.Seeds.seed!()"
$ iex -S mix phx.server
iex(1)> Enum.each([1, 2], &Sneakers23.Inventory.mark_product_released!/1)
:ok
```

Open two browser tabs to http://localhost:4000 and another tab to http://localhost:4000/admin, which requires admin/password to login. If your browser has an "incognito" mode, open a tab using it to http://localhost:4000—this will simulate multiple shopping carts with different cookies. Add and remove several items to each cart. Visit the checkout page from one of these tabs as well.

Without closing the tabs, go to the admin dashboard and open your JavaScript console. Enter window.presence.state and look at the output. You will see the up-to-date Presence data, complete with all our important metadata. The Presence state looks like this:

```
> window.presence.state
<· ▼ {WvmZN3TK3cdrD5wemJIKx9W1NaO5tO75qzlx//c3DZjeHPRUetlW0SzSE1pKKtOc: {…}, 2
    ▼ 2x6rsLbRfBGV3ata74g0abhZjQcY/zzLZRoO+B7zRejtAARBubBMSzuTNOk9opQY:
      ▼ metas: Array(2)
        ▼ 0:
          ▶ items: (4) [16, 12, 15, 2]
            page: "/"
            page_loaded_at: 1571188853586
            phx_ref: "LZ2Nutz13+0="
            phx_ref_prev: "nZMlxNp8B/4="
          ▶ __proto__: Object
        ▼ 1:
          ▶ items: (4) [16, 12, 15, 2]
            page: "/checkout"
            page_loaded_at: 1571189138014
            phx_ref: "Sg4PvDwH4Dc="
          ▶ __proto__: Object
          length: 2
        ▶ __proto__: Array(0)
      ▶ __proto__: Object
    ▼ WvmZN3TK3cdrD5wemJIKx9W1NaO5tO75qzlx//c3DZjeHPRUetlW0SzSE1pKKtOc:
      ▼ metas: Array(1)
        ▼ 0:
          ▶ items: (5) [17, 16, 15, 14, 1]
            page: "/"
            page_loaded_at: 1571188816525
            phx_ref: "jT296jfG26o="
            phx_ref_prev: "li1uvwlSXFo="
          ▶ __proto__: Object
          length: 1
        ▶ __proto__: Array(0)
      ▶ __proto__: Object
    ▶ __proto__: Object
```

Close the tabs to see the Presence state update immediately. We'll leverage the real-time updating of the Presence and Tracker when we assemble our dashboard.

Assemble the Admin Dashboard

At this point in the project, our CartTracker is working from end-to-end. The Presence updates are flowing through our application and making their way to the admin dashboard. The final step in this chapter is to piece together the Presence state into a format that completes our requirements.

In order to make a visually appealing dashboard, we need to do some work with our CSS and HTML. You grabbed the admin.css file earlier in the setup instructions, but there's a few more files you will need to copy from the book's source code. If you don't have the source code, instructions can be found in Online Resources, on page xiii. Copy the completed index template, like so:

```
$ cp ./index.html.eex \
    lib/sneakers_23_web/templates/admin/dashboard/index.html.eex
```

To check that everything is set up correctly, start your server with mix phx.server and visit http://localhost:4000/admin. You will see a page that looks like the following image.

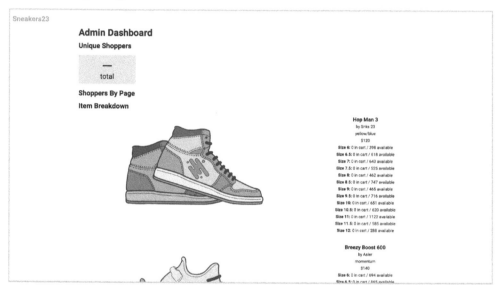

The first feature that we'll tackle is the shopper count. In our Presence state, we have a list of cart ID to metadata mappings. A cart ID represents a unique shopper, so we only need to count the size of the presence.state. The dom.js file that you imported previously has a function that will update the DOM correctly based on the count. Add the following snippet to the end of admin.js.

```
sneakers_23_admin/assets/js/admin.js
presence.onSync(() => {
  dom.setShopperCount(getShopperCount(presence))
})

function getShopperCount(presence) {
  return Object.keys(presence.state).length
}
```

The next feature we'll tackle is the list of page counts. This is more advanced because we'll need to parse through the Presence metadata. Each tab that a shopper has loaded increases the page count, so a single shopper could be shown on two pages at the same time.

```
sneakers_23_admin/assets/js/admin.js
presence.onSync(() => {
  dom.setShopperCount(getShopperCount(presence))
  dom.assemblePageCounts(getPageCounts(presence))
})

function getPageCounts(presence) {
  const pageCounts = {}
  Object.values(presence.state).forEach(({ metas }) => {
    metas.forEach(({ page }) => {
      pageCounts[page] = pageCounts[page] || 0
      pageCounts[page] += 1
    })
  })
  return pageCounts
}
```

In this snippet, we iterate over the presence.state values to get all of the metadata for our carts. We extract the page out of each and increment a counter. The dom.js file has a function that will turn this into a list for the user interface.

The final feature of our dashboard is to update the count of each shoe in a cart. The "items" property of the Presence metadata has this information. We only need to worry about the first metadata for each shopper, because a shopper's cart synchronizes across tabs.

```
sneakers_23_admin/assets/js/admin.js
presence.onSync(() => {
  dom.setShopperCount(getShopperCount(presence))
  dom.assemblePageCounts(getPageCounts(presence))

  const itemCounts = getItemCounts(presence)
  dom.resetItemCounts()
  Object.keys(itemCounts).forEach((itemId) => {
    dom.setItemCount(itemId, itemCounts[itemId])
  })
})

function getItemCounts(presence) {
  const itemCounts = {}
  Object.values(presence.state).forEach(({ metas }) => {
    metas[0].items.forEach((itemId) => {
      itemCounts[itemId] = itemCounts[itemId] || 0
      itemCounts[itemId] += 1
    })
  })
  return itemCounts
}
```

Our interface will now properly display all three sections and will update in real-time. The only thing left to do is test to make sure it works. We won't walk through a full acceptance test for our dashboard, but we'll still throw a scenario at it. Follow the same steps, repeated below, as you did at the end of the previous section.

```
$ mix ecto.reset && mix run -e "Sneakers23Mock.Seeds.seed!()"
$ iex -S mix phx.server
iex(1)> Enum.each([1, 2], &Sneakers23.Inventory.mark_product_released!/1)
:ok
```

Open two browser tabs to http://localhost:4000 and another tab to http://localhost:4000/admin. If your browser has an "incognito" mode, open a tab there to http://localhost:4000—this will simulate multiple shopping carts with different cookies. Add and remove several items to each cart. Visit the checkout page from one of these tabs as well.

Watch the admin dashboard as you navigate between pages, add shoes, remove shoes, or close tabs. The interface will update in real-time for all of the different actions you take. You can even try tests with multiple servers running like we performed in previous chapters.

Our final task is a small load test against the admin dashboard.

Load Test the Admin Dashboard

Our admin dashboard seems like it will work well for us, but we've only tested it with two shoppers connected. We need to test it with many more connected clients in order to know if it will work properly when a launch happens. This would be an impossible task to do ourselves. However, we can use Elixir to help us out.

A load test is a type of test where you send many connections, messages, or whatever else you want to test to your back-end server. You can write these tests in any language, but we'll use Elixir for our tests. The basic flow of our load test will be to open many ProductSocket connections and then join a unique CartChannel. We'll leverage Elixir's process model to spawn many instances of a Shopper process that performs these steps.

We won't walk through the entire load test application, although you should feel free to read and modify it. Make sure that you have the code that distributes with this book and then copy the project using the following commands.

```
$ cp -R code/location/sneaker_admin_bench ~/sneaker_admin_bench
$ cd ~/sneaker_admin_bench
$ mix deps.get
```

The load testing application uses the open-source PhoenixClient[2] library to connect to our Socket and Channel. This library mimics the Phoenix.Socket and Phoenix.Channel APIs to provide a simple way to connect to Channels and then exchange data with them.

Take a look at the following code, extracted from the SneakerAdminBench.Shopper module. You don't need to enter it anywhere, since this code was provided when you copied the sneaker_admin_bench source code. The purpose of this code is to demonstrate how easy PhoenixClient is to use. You can use it to build load-testing applications completely in Elixir, or to consume your Phoenix Channel applications from other Elixir applications.

sneaker_admin_bench/lib/sneaker_admin_bench/shopper.ex
```elixir
def handle_continue([], state) do
  {:ok, socket} = PhoenixClient.Socket.start_link(@socket_opts)
  send(self(), :connect_channel)
  {:noreply, Map.put(state, :socket, socket)}
end
```

PhoenixClient.Socket.start_link/1 opens a WebSocket to the Sneakers23 ProductSocket. Once the WebSocket connects, we can join the Channel.

sneaker_admin_bench/lib/sneaker_admin_bench/shopper.ex
```elixir
{:ok, _response, channel} = PhoenixClient.Channel.join(
  socket,
  "cart:#{generate_cart_id()}",
  %{page: "/bench/#{:rand.uniform(4)}"}
)

state = Map.put(state, :channel, channel)

{:ok, _message} = PhoenixClient.Channel.push(
  channel, "add_item", %{item_id: random_item_id()}
)
```

PhoenixClient.Channel.join/3 joins the ShoppingCartChannel and returns when the join is successful. We then add a random item to the connected cart with Phoenix-Client.Channel.push/3. This load test is a happy-path test—we're not performing any error handling or recovery in it.

Let's use the load-testing application now. Start the Sneakers23 admin application from the main project folder.

```
$ mix ecto.reset && mix run -e "Sneakers23Mock.Seeds.seed!()"
$ iex -S mix phx.server
iex(1)> Enum.each([1, 2], &Sneakers23.Inventory.mark_product_released!/1)
:ok
```

---

2. https://github.com/mobileoverlord/phoenix_client

Open the admin dashboard at http://localhost:4000/admin. Next, open an iex session in the sneaker_admin_bench folder and run the start_connections/0 function.

```
$ cd ~/sneaker_admin_bench
$ iex -S mix
iex(1)> SneakerAdminBench.start_connections()
```

You will see the dashboard update immediately. You will end up with 1000 active connections that are equally distributed on all of the different shoes. Your dashboard will look something like the following.

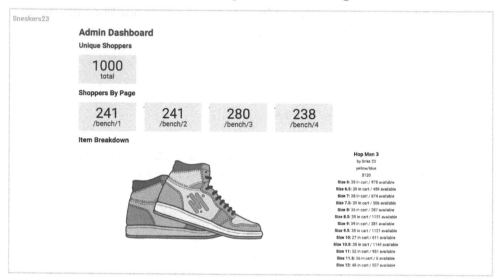

Feel free to play around with more or fewer connections to see what happens. My computer does act flaky at a certain point, around 6000 connections, but that is due to the operating system's connection handling and is not related to the application itself.

Wrapping Up

Phoenix Tracker takes a hard problem—distributed process state—and makes it easy for you. Tracker uses a conflict-free replicated data type to provide correct distributed state that is eventually consistent. Tracker is commonly used to maintain real-time user presence lists, or to optimize a data pipeline that pushes data to users.

Phoenix Presence is a special type of Tracker that is optimized for Channel use cases. It provides a convenient set of functions on top of Tracker, but more importantly it dispatches Presence changes to a particular topic. Presence, combined with its JavaScript client, allows us to quickly build real-time lists in our user interface.

We used Presence to build an admin dashboard for Sneakers23. You set up a new section of an application from start to end, and then used Presence to create a shopping cart tracker. The CartTracker we built allows us to answer questions like "how many shoppers are online?" and "how many of each shoe are in a cart?" You used a load-testing tool to verify that the admin dashboard works with many shoppers connected, which provides confidence for a launch.

This wraps up Part II of this book. Next up, in Part III, we'll be looking at how to deploy Channel-based applications and what type of challenges can occur in production.

Part III

Bringing Real-Time Applications to Production

We've written an application, but the fun is only beginning. We'll go over different tools for deploying Elixir applications and the specific challenges that real-time applications face.

## CHAPTER 11

Deploy Your Application to Production

In part II, we built a complete real-time application using Phoenix Channels. Throughout the development process, we used many of the tools that we covered in part I. In part III, we'll discuss the deployment and observability of real-time apps in production. We'll first cover the current landscape of Elixir application deployment and the specific challenges that real-time applications will encounter.

Your (or your company's) specific needs will dictate how you deploy and run your application—there isn't a silver bullet for all situations. Deployment techniques also change over time as new libraries, tools, and platforms emerge. This chapter is not a guide to deploying Elixir applications, and we won't code a deployment in it. Instead, you'll receive an overview of current deployment options before we cover more specific real-time problems: load balancing WebSockets, deployment strategies, and BEAM Node clustering options.

Deployment can be daunting—there's a lot of things to consider when you first set up an application. However, you'll gain a reusable set of deployment strategies after you complete your first real-world deployment. It may be frustrating at first, but the reward of a running application is worth it.

We'll start this chapter with today's lay of the land for deploying Elixir applications. We'll cover topics such as Mix releases versus Distillery and what services can run your application. After that, we'll discuss load balancing WebSockets and the challenges that happen with persistent connections during deployment. Finally, you'll see what tools can help you cluster your production BEAM nodes together.

Let's start with the current landscape for deploying Elixir applications.

The Lay of the Land

Deploying an app for the first time is a great feeling—it's one of the final steps to bringing your application to users. However, it's also daunting. There are many different techniques, platforms, and technologies to deploy with, so you'll need to find what works for you and then implement it. Much of this may already be decided for you based on your company's decisions, but you may be in a position of greenfield development, with many available options.

The two common ways to run an Elixir application are directly with Mix or with releases. We'll cover each of these options so you can decide what is best for you. Releases are produced with one of two tools—Mix or Distillery. We'll go over each before covering some of the available platform options you can use to deploy your app.

We'll start with different ways to run and package your application.

Mix, Releases, Distillery, Oh My!

You have already used one of the ways to run an application many times throughout this book. You used mix phx.server to start a local web server for the examples in this book, and you can use this command when running your application in production. This is the simplest way to get an application running in production, but you will be missing out on a few features that releases provide. If you want to go this route, *Adopting Elixir [Tat18]* has detailed steps on how to use mix to run your application.

An alternative to using the mix command is to package your application into a release. There are two tools to do this in Elixir: Mix Release[1] and Distillery.[2] If you're starting with a new project, then you will likely get all the features you need from Mix Release. It was designed with a similar approach to Distillery, and the setup is close enough to be swapped out if needed. Distillery has been around longer and has some additional features that Mix does not have, but you may not need them.

The Elixir community has rallied around releases for deployment, so you should use releases to deploy your applications unless you have a reason not to. There are several benefits that releases provide that you do not get for free with mix phx.server or mix run. A few of the benefits are:

---

1. https://hexdocs.pm/mix/Mix.Tasks.Release.html
2. https://github.com/bitwalker/distillery

Self-contained packages

> Your application can be bundled with the BEAM and Erlang Run-Time System, so you do not need any special software installed on your deployment machine. You also ship compiled files as your application, instead of raw source code.

Management scripts

> You get a set of scripts, for free, that allow you to do things such as connect an interactive session to the running server, execute remote calls, and run your application as a daemon.

Start-up customization

> You can easily customize how the BEAM starts up. This allows you to set flags that control how the BEAM behaves. We'll cover a flag in the next chapter that changes how garbage collection works.

Code preloading

> It's very important that a server can quickly serve its traffic. Releases load all code at the time of start up to decrease initial latency—this is called embedded mode. If you don't use a release, modules will be loaded the first time that they're used.

You get all of these benefits with both Mix Release and Distillery, so you can use either one. Some of these features, such as management scripts, are critical for operating production applications. You'll see an example of inspecting an application via the shell in the next chapter, which is extremely useful when you debug a running application in production. We won't cover how to set up a release in this chapter, because both tools have thorough documentation available online.

No matter how you decide to package your application, you'll need a place to run it. We'll cover popular options next.

Platforms and Tools for Deployment

There are many different options for where you can run your application, and what tools you use to run it. There are dedicated Platform as a service (PaaS) products that will manage everything for you. You can also use virtual private servers if you want to manage the operating system and application yourself. Either approach will work great for Elixir applications and is largely a matter of preference and system administration experience.

Many cloud providers support Elixir applications—most of them will work without much trouble. However, there are a few things to look out for when

How I Deploy Applications at Work

At SalesLoft, we've been running Elixir applications roughly the same way for the past couple of years—so you could say that we're happy with our approach. We use Kubernetes[a] to run all of our various applications. We use Docker to build and run each application. Our Dockerfile uses Distillery to create a release of our application, then uses Docker's multi-stage build pipeline to create a clean Docker image containing just an operating system and the compiled release.

Our applications are able to start up quickly because they are already compiled and ready to go. We also get the benefit of being able to start a remote interactive shell to any running pod—an instance of an application in Kubernetes—so we can easily troubleshoot problems that occur.

Tools like Docker and Kubernetes are not replacements for the BEAM, or vice versa—they exist in a way that compliments one another. You don't have to use these tools to deploy your applications, but you can build a solid foundation with them.

---

a.   https://kubernetes.io

deploying real-time Elixir apps. It is important that the provider supports many concurrent connections to your application. WebSockets are long-lived connections, and some providers do not support a large number at the same time. The second thing to look out for is whether the provider supports BEAM clustering, which we'll cover later in this chapter.

There are two prominent PaaS used in the Elixir community that support these needs: Gigalixir[3] and Render.[4] I don't hold a preference of one over the other and have seen good reviews from users of each. Both platforms have thorough documentation on how to deploy an Elixir application, as well as how to do tasks like configure BEAM clustering. The availability of documentation is important when you set up your first deployment.

Elixir applications can also be deployed to virtual private servers or bare-metal servers. These options are great if you're looking to keep monetary costs low, and if you have the experience to set up and manage this type of server. The time that you or your teammates will spend on system administration should be considered when going down this route.

Your deployment choices are important for your application, but deployment isn't the most important topic in this chapter. We'll cover load balancing your WebSocket connections next.

---

3.   https://gigalixir.com/
4.   https://render.com/

Achieve Scalability with Load Balancing

You should always load balance your production application with at least two servers available to serve requests, so your application can stay online when a server restarts. At its simplest, load balancing is the act of making sure that all servers receive roughly the same number of requests over a given time period. A well-balanced application will be less likely to develop hot nodes that have stressed resource usage compared to other nodes. You can also add new servers to a well-balanced application to help reduce the load on all other servers in the cluster.

We'll discuss the basics of load balancing before looking at how WebSockets can make achieving a well-balanced system more difficult than a traditional HTTP-powered application.

The Basics of Load Balancing

A load balancer is specialized software that acts as a proxy between a client and servers that respond to requests. Requests are sent fairly to back-end servers in round-robin, least connections, or based on the criteria that you define. Load balancers provide many benefits such as the ability to quickly add or remove back-end servers, create fair distribution of work, and increase redundancy.

Here's an example of a load that is not properly balanced. The top application server has received many more requests than the other servers in the application.

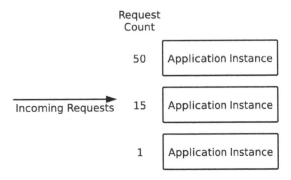

In a well-balanced application, each server in this figure would have roughly 22 requests. A better balance allows for a more predictable usage of system resources.

As with all software, there are free open-source and commercial closed-source load balancers you can use with your application. Most cloud service providers, such as Amazon Web Services, Google Cloud, and Digital Ocean, provide their own load balancers that work out-of-the-box. You may also opt for an open-source load balancer such as HAProxy[5] or nginx.[6]

You will need to pick a load balancer that supports WebSockets—most now support it in some way, so that's less of a problem than in previous years. Still, some load balancers will require running in a mode such as "TCP only" to route WebSocket requests, which causes the load balancer to not try to interpret a request or change the headers in any way. The specific WebSocket-safe setup will depend on the particular load balancer that you use.

Load balancers rely on the fact that web requests are stateless and short-lived to provide an even distribution. A user can make a request to a URL and be sent to server A, and then immediately make another request and be sent to server B. The process is seamless and the user has no idea that this occurred. Load balancers get a bit trickier when persistent connections, such as WebSockets, are involved.

WebSockets and Load Balancers

In order to illustrate the challenge with persistent connections and load balancers, let's run through a practical scenario. Imagine that your application has two servers. Each server has been running for some time and has 1000 active WebSocket connections each, because they're evenly balanced.

Your site reliability alarms are going off because your servers are stressed out, so you add a third server. This server comes online, but it has no Web-Socket connections.

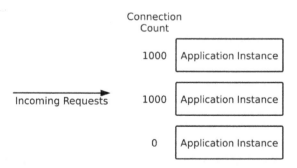

5.   https://www.haproxy.org/
6.   https://nginx.org/en/docs/http/load_balancing.html

In this case, the added capacity has no effect on the existing servers. They have persistent connections that do not reconnect unless a network failure or application restart occurs. A load balancer could add all new connections to the new server, using a least connections approach, but the existing servers would remain at high utilization until connections are closed.

Unfortunately, there's not an elegant solution to this problem. The added server would need to cause the other server's clients to disconnect their WebSocket connection and connect directly to the new server. A load balancer could handle this scenario, but it would involve custom configuration and knowledge of your application.

There are application-level solutions to this problem. One simple solution is to disconnect certain clients on the old servers so that the new server picks up the connection. This gets more difficult with many servers, because the chance of a new server being selected in the load balancing process is usually random. Here's a figure of the three servers undergoing this type of load balance.

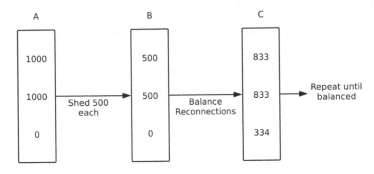

The problem here is that 1000 connections were shed from the two servers, but only about 334 would make it to the new server. This means that the process would nccd to bc repeated until it becomes balanced. In addition, there are 1000 disconnected clients at point B in the process. Ideally the clients reconnect very quickly, but this is a place where bugs are likely to appear.

Another option is to shed connections from an application server only when a critical resource (like CPU or memory) has been out of an acceptable range for a period of time. In this case, the two servers may shed load based on the alarm criteria but would quickly reach a healthy state.

One last, very simple, approach to load balancing is to disconnect WebSocket connections after a period of time. This would cause your system to be unbalanced only for brief durations. There are trade-offs to everything, though.

This approach would not balance the system very quickly, and clients would be reconnected throughout their time on the application.

You may not see load-balance issues as a problem until a certain scale or threshold is reached. Always load balance your production applications with at least two servers, but solve the problem of unbalanced servers only when you start dynamically changing the number of servers that back your application. You can use the techniques discussed in this section to perform load balancing, or you may think of creative ways based on your specific use case.

Next, we'll look at a few different ways to perform a deployment.

Push New Code Safely

The initial deployment of your application is only the first hurdle to overcome. Your code will evolve and needs to be redeployed over time. This presents its own set of challenges, because you want your application updates to be invisible to users. Some teams may solve this by only deploying off-hours, but we'll look at strategies that allow you to deploy your code at any time.

We'll discuss two different strategies for doing deployments. The first type that we'll cover is rolling deployment. We'll then look at an alternative called blue-green deployment. You'll see how the deploy method you choose can influence your load balance and uptime. Before we get into the types of deploys, let's look at the impact that deployment will have on your application.

The Reality of Deployment

We need to start with an important disclaimer about deployments—your servers will restart and any active connections will disconnect. Clients may remain disconnected for a few seconds, unable to receive new messages from your application.

Connections will quickly reconnect, but any data that was in-memory, such as in processes or ETS tables, will be gone. You can design applications that are resilient to restarting by ensuring that all data is kept in a less ephemeral place, such as on the front end or in a database.

Elixir supports hot code reloading—this allows you to change the code while the system is still running. However, it's something that you should use very sparingly, if at all. There is a lot of complexity involved in making sure that your data structures and GenServers are able to migrate while remaining online. This complexity puts you in a situation where an erroneous deployment forces you to restart all servers, which may be a problem if it's not something you do often.

With that out of the way, let's look at a basic deployment tactic—rolling deployments.

Rolling Deployments

Rolling deployments work very well for many applications. A server comes offline and then one comes online (or vice versa) so the application remains stable throughout. This works for short-lived requests, but a problem occurs when we do rolling deployments with WebSockets. The first server that restarts will receive a majority of the traffic after the deployment is finished. Here's a figure demonstrating how this happens.

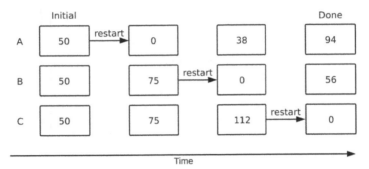

When a server goes offline, all of its connected clients immediately try to reconnect. The server is still restarting, so it is not yet available to handle requests. This causes all of the new connections to be balanced to the existing servers. This continues for each server in the cluster until the end state is reached. Throughout the process, some servers will receive a spike in connections before being restarted.

This problem is less severe in applications where clients reconnect often, because the connections will balance over a short period of time. Your applications may work great even with the spread in WebSocket connections that rolling deployments can cause. Also, your load balancer may support the least connections balance mode, which would help alleviate the issue during rolling deployments. Alternatively, you could implement an application-level load balancing scheme—like you saw in the previous section—or you could change to a different model of deployment.

We'll cover an alternative to rolling deployments, blue-green deployments, next.

Blue-Green Deployments

A rolling deployment is one of the simplest ways to deploy an application. This type of deployment will probably work well for you, but there are other options as well. A more advanced type of deployment is called blue-green. In this strategy, your application cluster remains online while a second cluster is deployed. Once the second cluster is healthy and ready to serve traffic, the load balancer cuts over to it. This can happen either immediately or slowly over time. The following figure shows how this works:

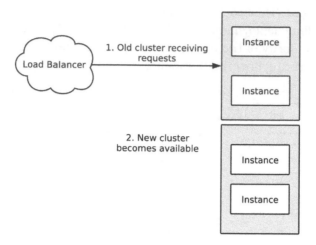

Once the new cluster is available, the load balancer switches which cluster it connects to:

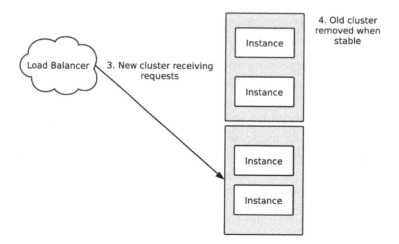

This approach causes all existing connections to disconnect and reconnect. They will connect in a balanced fashion, but they could all connect at roughly the same time, depending on how the existing connections are closed.

This is the opposite of rolling deployments, where the connections will establish throughout the time that it takes to deploy but will end in an unbalanced state.

The approach you take largely depends on your application's and users' needs. Both deployment strategies are established ways of deploying code and are used successfully by companies in the Elixir community. There is a lot of nuance in how these deployments can be set up—you may be able to avoid certain problems by crafting your deployments carefully.

An important aspect of Elixir application deployment is node clustering. Next, we'll discuss clustering your BEAM nodes in production, and why this is critical for real-time applications.

Cluster Your BEAM Nodes Together

You must connect your BEAM nodes together when deploying a real-time application to production. We covered in previous chapters that a WebSocket-based application broadcasts outbound messages to all nodes in the cluster, using PubSub, so that connections on other nodes receive the message for connections that they own. If your nodes can not talk to each other, some messages will be missed and not sent to clients.

There are two ways to implement clustering in your application. The first way, that comes out-of-the-box with OTP, is to connect nodes together with distributed Erlang. This creates a direct peer-to-peer connection between all nodes in the cluster. However, some deployment environments may not be able to network nodes this way due to connectivity restrictions. In these cases, it's possible to use Redis as an alternative to clustering.

We'll cover libraries that help you with clustering, and we'll cover what to do if native clustering isn't available to you.

Ready Your Application for Clustering

One of my favorite things about Elixir/Erlang is that it comes with support for node-to-node connectivity out-of-the-box. In addition to being provided as a standard in the language, it works really well.

The :net_kernel.connect_node/1 function connects the node that invoked it to a specified remote node. Once the TCP connection is established, the connection is kept fresh with a heartbeat and will automatically become disconnected if the nodes can no longer talk to each other. This comes out-of-the-box, but there are a few things that you must set up in order to use it.

The first requirement of connecting nodes together is to have a way for your BEAM nodes to talk over a given port and IP. You can hard-code the port that BEAM uses for distribution, or you can have the Erlang Port Mapper Daemon[7] running and available between the remote nodes. epmd maps symbolic node names to machine addresses, so your application can use an atom like :my_app@my_host and be mapped to the right port and IP address. epmd should never be exposed to the public internet, only between the nodes in the cluster. This isolation is possible to set up using a virtual private cloud.

The second requirement is a shared cookie between all nodes in the cluster. The cookie is an atom that is compared between two nodes when they try to connect to each other. If the cookie doesn't match, the connection is not allowed. Tools like Mix Release and Distillery will automatically set this up for you, although you can change it to be longer or a different value.

Adopting Elixir [Tat18] goes into more detail on how to configure distributed Erlang, epmd, SSL, and cookies. Many of these things are handled for you automatically if you deploy your application using a release.

Let's look at what libraries are used for clustering next.

Libraries for Clustering

Elixir makes it very easy to cluster two nodes together. Earlier in the book, you ran the code Node.connect(:"server@127.0.0.1") to connect two local nodes to each other. A bigger challenge is identifying which nodes need to be connected to each other and where they're located. Discovery is an easy task locally, because you know exactly where the node is running and you know the node's name. In production, however, your nodes will be separated across physical servers and IP addresses. They may even be in completely different data centers.

There are two libraries that solve the problem of node discovery very well. Peerage[8] and libcluster[9] both provide a few different ways to perform node discovery. The simplest approach you can take is to hard-code your node names in a configuration. You can utilize more powerful features like DNS-based discovery, Kubernetes API discovery, or even write your own strategy for discovery.

libcluster is a powerful tool to have at your disposal, but you may not be able to set up distributed Erlang due to networking restrictions. Next, we'll cover an alternative way of communicating using Redis-based PubSub.

---

7.   https://erlang.org/doc/man/epmd.html
8.   https://github.com/mrluc/peerage
9.   https://github.com/bitwalker/libcluster

Redis-based PubSub—A Clustering Alternative

You may be in a situation where distributed Erlang is simply not possible. Some cloud providers lock down their networking, or maybe a corporate policy prevents it. Phoenix Channels are built on top of Phoenix PubSub, which abstracts away the actual communication in a way that can be swapped out. One of the libraries that is available to use with Phoenix PubSub is phoenix_pubsub_redis.[10]

With phoenix_pubsub_redis, all messages are sent through Redis's native PubSub commands. Your application subscribes to specific topics that allow the application to listen to events from other servers. This is a powerful library to have in your back pocket, just in case you find yourself in this situation. It's straightforward to set up by following the Phoenix.PubSub.Redis documentation,[11] so we won't set it up in this chapter.

One caveat of using the Redis PubSub adapter is that all messages will be sent through a single Redis server. This can cause spikes in utilized network bandwidth if your application sends many messages at once—each server receives a copy of the message, just like in distributed Erlang. This is not going to be an issue for most applications, but you should monitor your Redis server's statistics if you go down this path.

Redis-based PubSub is not a complete alternative to distributed Erlang. An application that uses it will not be able to use native distribution functions, and you will not have a direct connection to any other node. However, Phoenix Channels will work out-of-the-box with Redis-based PubSub, and many other features that you may need can be implemented with it.

Next, we'll look at different configuration options that you'll need to set when you deploy a Phoenix application.

Advanced Phoenix Channel Configuration

You will need to make a few small changes to your Phoenix application configuration when you deploy to production, although most things will work out-of-the-box. Phoenix provides a guide[12] on how to deploy with releases. This guide helps you configure your application secrets, runtime configuration, and asset bundling.

There is one configuration that is specific for Channel-based applications—origin checking. Let's look at that now.

---

10. https://hex.pm/packages/phoenix_pubsub_redis
11. https://hexdocs.pm/phoenix_pubsub_redis/Phoenix.PubSub.Redis.html
12. https://hexdocs.pm/phoenix/releases.html

Origin Checking

Origin checking is a security measure to restrict which websites can connect to your application. By default, incoming connections to a Channel transport inspect the Origin HTTP header and ensure that it matches an allowed list. The only allowed origin, by default, is the host config that is set in your application config. For example, the following config only allows connections that originate from the origin "app.sneakers23.com".

```
config :sneakers_23, Sneakers23Web.Endpoint,
  url: [host: "app.sneakers23.com", port: 80]
```

You should set the host field for your application, so that connections will work when you deploy your application to production. If you are deploying an application that serves connections from multiple hosts, or from clients like browser extensions, you can change which origins are allowed. You can configure your Socket to use a list of origins, a custom origin-checking function, or disable it completely by setting the check_origin option to false.

It's easy to change the check_origin configuration for all Sockets in your application, like so:

```
config :sneakers_23, Sneakers23Web.Endpoint,
  check_origin: [
    "//app.sneakers23.com",
    "chrome://extension-id",
    "https://sneakers23.com"
  ]
```

Alternatively, you can set the check_origin configuration on a per-socket basis in the Endpoint definition. This is done by passing check_origin as an argument to socket/3.

```
socket "/socket", MyStoreWeb.ProductSocket,
  websocket: [
    check_origin: {MyStoreWeb.Origin, :allowed?, []}
  ]
```

This configuration will invoke MyStoreWeb.Origin.allowed?(uri) to check the URI's origin. The specified function should return true or false depending on whether the origin is allowed. Any of the available formats can be used in either configuration.

Other configuration options are available for Phoenix Sockets. Let's look at these other options.

Other Configuration Options

There is documentation[13] available that lists all the options you can use to configure Phoenix Sockets and Channels. We won't cover all the available options in detail, because many applications will not need to use them. However, it's important you know that additional options exist and know where to find more information about them.

We've already covered the check_origin option, which is one of the more common options to change. The connect_info option is also useful for some applications. This allows your Phoenix.Socket.connect/3 callback to receive additional information that you can use to decide if a connection should be allowed. Of note, you can configure your Socket to receive additional headers or even the user's session information. (You must include a CSRF token in the connection request to get session information, due to WebSocket security.)

Other options are available to change how a WebSocket behaves. You can compress WebSocket frames by setting the compress: true option when you call socket/3 in your Endpoint. This option decreases the size of data payloads but comes at the cost of additional CPU on the server and client. You can also configure the maximum size of each WebSocket frame, which is useful if you have dynamic payloads coming from clients. You may not need to use these options for your application, but it's good to know they're available if needed.

Wrapping Up

There are many different ways to deploy an Elixir application. You can customize the deployment process to you or your company's specific needs and still be successful. One constant in the deployment process is that code needs to be packaged and executed. You can start simple with mix commands to run your application, but you get more features by using releases. Releases now come out-of-the-box with Elixir 1.9 and are widely accepted in the community.

Production applications should use multiple servers to handle requests. This increases redundancy and allows for additional scalability when needed. A load balancer is used to ensure that multiple back-end servers receive a fair number of requests. WebSockets cause problems with load balancers because WebSocket connections stay open for long periods of time, so they do not readily become balanced. You can solve this problem both at the application level by reconnecting active WebSockets, or at the load-balancer level.

---

13. https://hexdocs.pm/phoenix/Phoenix.Endpoint.html#socket/2

There are two primary ways to restart servers with new code. The first, and most simple, approach is to do a rolling deploy. This causes nodes to go offline and come back online before continuing with more nodes—the maximum number of disconnected nodes is capped out. Rolling deploys can cause an imbalance of WebSocket connections during the deployment process. An alternative that can help reduce this problem is blue-green deployment. Hot code deployment is also possible on the BEAM, but it is not recommended for most applications.

Nodes in a production cluster must be able to communicate with each other. Erlang/OTP ships with distribution mechanisms out-of-the-box, and it's usually as simple as configuring a library to enable node-to-node communication. Sometimes this isn't available though, for reasons outside of your control. In these situations, Redis PubSub can be used to communicate between nodes.

We covered the aspects of deploying a real-time Elixir application, but the actual runtime execution of an application is just as important. In the next chapter, we'll look at how to manage different system resources like CPU and memory. We'll also look at tools that can help diagnose performance problems in deployed real-time applications.

## CHAPTER 12

Manage Real-Time Resources

In the last chapter, we covered different things for you to consider when deploying your applications to production. In this chapter, we'll look at how different system resources are managed by the BEAM, and we'll discuss the needs of real-time applications versus more traditional applications.

There are two main resources that are required to run applications: CPU and memory. You'll see how the BEAM uses these resources and how you can build your application to best utilize your system's available resources. The BEAM is a solid virtual machine to run applications on top of, but you do need to be mindful of how it schedules work and uses memory when you deploy high-volume applications.

We'll start by looking at how the BEAM performs work. You'll see how the scheduler works and we'll look at how applications can effectively utilize a system's CPU. After that, we'll go over how the BEAM allocates and garbage collects memory. Finally, you'll see a tool that allows you to inspect how a production system is using its resources.

Let's jump in—we'll start with how an Elixir process performs work.

Getting Comfortable with Elixir's Scheduler

The most important role of any software is getting work done. It's easy to take this for granted—we just write code and it runs on a CPU. However, the way that work gets done can make or break your experience with a language. Some languages require you to be very explicit about everything—you get full control, but you can easily encounter problems. Other languages take away some control in order to provide you with ease of use and stability. Elixir falls into the camp of ease and stability, but its virtual machine has a scheduler with properties that are well-suited for soft real-time applications.

Scheduling is the method that assigns work to be performed by some resource, like the CPU. We'll first look at Elixir's scheduler design and what properties this design provides for your applications. After this, we'll consider how real-time applications are affected by the scheduler and what you can do to make sure that your applications remain performant.

Elixir's Scheduler Design

It may seem daunting to understand how a virtual machine's scheduler works, but you only need to know a few key concepts. The first concept we'll cover is how work is sliced up and executed on a CPU. The second concept is how work is executed so your system does not completely freeze when running CPU-bound code.

Let's define a few terms that are important to know for this section.

Scheduler

> A scheduler picks a process and executes the code for that process.

Run Queue

> A list of processes that have work to be performed. A single process only exists in a single run queue.

Let's jump into how work is sliced up and executed on a CPU.

How Work is Scheduled

There are a variety of ways to schedule work to run on the CPU. Let's look at the simplest case first: a single scheduler with a single run queue of work to execute.

This is a simple model to understand. The virtual machine has a single queue of work so that the oldest scheduled work is up next, and work executes on a single CPU core. We don't need to worry about software locks or hard distribution problems in this design, but there are problems with this approach. The biggest problem is that your application can not take advantage of a multi-core CPU. The design on page 239—multiple schedulers with a single run queue—allows an application to perform work on multiple CPU cores.

This design is able to take advantage of all available cores, but it comes with a cost of needing lockable data structures for the run queue. The necessary locking becomes a large bottleneck as more schedulers are introduced.

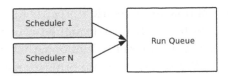

The following figure shows what the BEAM uses today: multiple schedulers, each with their own run queue.

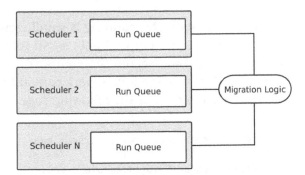

The BEAM also has migration logic to allow for better load balancing of work across available cores—this is known as work stealing. The end result of this design is that each core can be efficiently used, and locking is decreased. Elixir is often touted as magically scaling across a CPU—this design is how that happens.

Let's look at how CPU-heavy work is executed without freezing your entire application.

How Work is Executed

It's easy in some languages to get stuck in an infinite loop—no matter how long you wait, the system will not exit the loop and must be killed via some external signal. The BEAM can max out a CPU, but it will still be able to execute new work when this happens—it doesn't get stuck in an infinite loop. Let's look at how that's possible.

The BEAM has a preemptive scheduler that can stop work that is being executed and swap it out for another unit of work that needs to be executed. This is different than a cooperative scheduler, where the code must explicitly release control flow back to the scheduler.

Preemptive scheduling isn't magic; there has to be a clean break where work can be stopped. In the case of the BEAM, the clean break is after a function runs. This works well in practice because functions generally do not execute a large amount of CPU-bound work without invoking other functions.

The BEAM keeps track of how much work a process has performed by incrementing a reduction counter each time (roughly) a function is invoked for that process. After a certain number of reductions, that process is preempted and placed at the end of the run queue and other processes are executed. It is this preemption process that prevents a single process from taking over an entire CPU core, which would starve other processes from executing. If you want to know how much work a process has done, it's important to track the number of reductions.

Let's see how this works in practice by running a small example in an iex session. We'll define a recursive function that acts as an infinite loop. We'll spin up a number of processes that execute the recursive function, so that each scheduler is busy. We'll then see that new work can still be executed by the BEAM. Start an iex session and enter the following code.

```
$ iex
iex(1)> defmodule Test do def recurse(), do: recurse() end
iex(2)> :observer.start
iex(3)> schedulers = :erlang.system_info(:schedulers_online)
iex(4)> Enum.each((1..schedulers), fn _ -> Task.async(&Test.recurse/0) end)
iex(5)> Enum.map((1..10000), & &1 + &1) |> Enum.sum()
```

If you watch the scheduler load chart and process list provided by :observer, you will see that all of your schedulers are completely maxed out. The process list shows that the number of reductions is very high for these recursive processes—this is an indication that they are doing a lot of work. Your :observer window will look like the image on page 241.

Despite being completely maxed out, the BEAM is still able to execute our Enum.map and Enum.sum functions very quickly. This is due to the BEAM's preemptive scheduling.

There are exceptions and edge cases here, because it's possible to run native code via a NIF—Native Implemented Function. A NIF cannot be preemptively scheduled due to it running outside of Erlang's functional paradigm. This means that a scheduler can be occupied for the duration of the NIF call, which leads to VM instability. It's outside of this book to go deeper into this topic, but NIFs can be made to work well on the BEAM, and there is a new scheduler type (dirty scheduler) that slower NIFs can run on.

Let's look at how your applications are affected by the BEAM's scheduler design.

CPU in Real-Time Applications

Real-time applications are very similar to non-real-time Elixir applications when it comes to CPU usage. The most common performance problem that

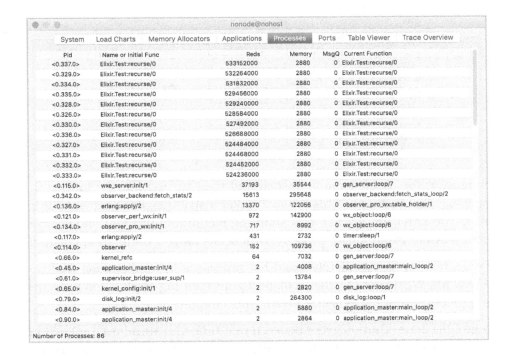

you'll run into is single-process bottlenecks. We'll look at how to avoid these in your applications.

You just saw that Elixir's scheduler distributes work across CPU cores on a per-process basis. You want to ensure that applications you write do not have single-process bottlenecks, so that work can be processed as quickly as possible. These bottlenecks occur when you have many processes, such as Channels, simultaneously making requests to a process. Processes handle a single message at a time, so all messages end up waiting for other messages to be processed—this leads to slower response times.

One way to avoid a single-process bottleneck is to shard your processes based on a key or some other criteria. For example, you could split up a process that stores data for different teams into a process per team. This produces one process per key, which looks like the figure on page 242.

With this approach, you end up with many more processes than schedulers. Elixir balances the processes across all schedulers to provide a consistent CPU throughput across all cores. If you had a single process instead, a single core would receive all of the work.

You can tweak this approach to not have as many processes. For example, Phoenix Tracker splits its CRDT processes into the number of shards you

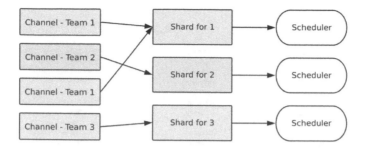

configure it for. Each topic is hashed and then turned into an integer that maps to a shard process. This is how Tracker distributes itself across multiple cores. You can't always use this sharding technique, but you should think about ways to avoid single-process bottlenecks as you build an application.

There's no way to completely avoid hot processes in applications that do a lot of work. We'll look at ways to inspect your running application to identify hot processes and bottlenecks later in this chapter.

While CPU is not that different between real-time and standard applications, memory is a different story. Next, we'll look at how Elixir manages memory and what you need to look out for when you write real-time applications.

Manage Your Application's Memory Effectively

Software depends on memory to run properly. You won't necessarily get big performance boosts by using less memory, but you'll be able to scale your application to more users while using fewer servers if you think about how memory is used by your application. You can use a few simple techniques to dramatically reduce your exposure to memory problems in Elixir applications.

The main principle that we'll cover in this section is memory allocation and garbage collection. Elixir doesn't have a radical garbage collector, but it has key differences when compared to other languages. We'll cover how garbage collection works before looking at how short-life and long-life processes differ in memory usage. You'll see two techniques for managing memory: manual garbage collection and process hibernation. Let's dive in.

Elixir's Garbage Collector Design

Garbage collection is the process of automated memory management in a program's runtime. This helps prevent your application from taking up a lot of memory by making unused memory available again or by returning it to the operating system. The BEAM will keep a bit of extra memory, rather than returning it all right away, which helps speed up future allocations. It's easy to think about garbage collection only as the freeing of memory, but a garbage collector will also allocate memory for your program. There are many different types of garbage collectors, and the BEAM has a fairly unique one.

You don't need to know all of the details of how memory allocation and garbage collection works to write effective Elixir applications, but you will get better memory utilization in your applications by knowing the basics. Let's look at a high-level overview of the BEAM garbage collector as of OTP 20,[1] which has been around for a few years. The topic of memory management is very detailed, but this overview won't go extremely deep.

Each BEAM process has its own stack and heap for small data binaries (less than 64 bytes.) Larger binaries are stored in a shared memory space with a reference-counted pointer (called ProcBin) that lives in a Process's heap. This means that there are many data stacks and heaps in our application, one per process, unlike many other languages that have a single stack and heap. A process can be visualized, like so:

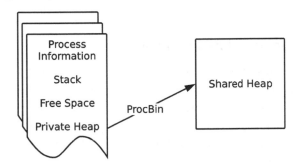

The private heap grows in size and would eventually fill up with old data. Garbage collection is performed to clean up a process's memory. The BEAM is different than many other virtual machines because garbage collection happens on a single process, not globally. Many processes can undergo garbage collection at the same time, but only if they need it.

There are two different types of garbage collection that occur in BEAM processes. The first type, which occurs frequently, is called generational garbage collection. You'll also see it called minor garbage collection. This method reclaims heap memory that is no longer referenced by the process, and that was allocated since the last generational garbage collection occurred. This relies on the idea that most memory is only used for a short period of time.

---

1.   https://www.erlang.org/downloads/20.0

This method is highly performant, but it only looks at recently allocated memory.

The second type of garbage collection is called full-sweep, also known as major garbage collection. This looks at the entire heap of a process, not just the young section, and reclaims as much memory as possible. It comes at the cost of being a bit slower to run, because it looks at all memory owned by a process. Full-sweep garbage collection happens much less frequently than generational garbage collection—it happens when the heap is close to being full, when a certain number of generational collections happens, or when manually called. Full-sweep garbage collection is fast in practice, but it can be slow if executing on a process that is actively holding a lot of data.

There is a lot of nuance in how garbage collection works. The most important thing to know is that there are two distinct forms of garbage collection that occur in a BEAM process. This works well for most processes and applications, but sometimes we have to tweak how often garbage collection is performed.

Next, we will see why real-time processes can be problematic for garbage collection.

Short-Life Versus Long-Life Processes

Real-time applications rely on long-lived processes in order to have a direct connection to clients—this allows them to send data immediately when the data is available. There is a downside to this, though. It's possible that processes get stuck in a state where garbage collection doesn't occur, but memory isn't being used. This can cause large memory bloat when amplified across thousands of processes.

If a piece of memory makes it past generational garbage collection, it lives until a full-sweep garbage collection occurs. This happens, by default, every 65535 generational passes or when the process is close to using its available memory. It's possible for a Channel, Socket, or other long-lived process to get stuck in a state where there is plenty of free memory, but not enough work to trigger a generational pass. A process in this state will live without memory being collected, and it will potentially take up more memory than necessary.

Processes that are created and terminated quickly (short-lived processes) do not get into this state because their memory is reclaimed when the process is terminated. While all applications use long-life processes to some degree, real-time apps use them in the thousands. This amplifies the impact of memory bloat.

You can fix this problem by forcing a full-sweep garbage collection to occur by using a manual garbage collection call, or with process hibernation. We'll look at process hibernation first.

Process Hibernation Helps Prevent Bloat

One of the easiest ways to trigger garbage collection is to put a long-running process into a hibernated state. Hibernation releases the call stack and immediately garbage collects the process. This is useful if you don't expect the process to receive a new message in the near future—within 10–30 seconds. If you hibernate a process after every message, but then it immediately receives another message, your application will do extra work for hibernation only to revive the process right away. However, this is often an acceptable trade-off, unless you are in an extremely high throughput environment.

In order to see how hibernation works, let's create a simple process that allocates memory and gets stuck in a spot where garbage collection is not automatically triggered. Start by creating a new mix project with mix new memory.

```
$ mix new memory
$ cd memory
```

Next, replace the lib/memory.ex file with the following code:

memory/lib/memory.ex
```
defmodule Memory do
  use GenServer

  def init([]) do
    {:ok, []}
  end

  def handle_call({:allocate, chars}, _from, state) do
    data = Enum.map((1..chars), fn _ -> "a" end)
    {:reply, :ok, [data | state]}
  end

  def handle_call(:clear, _from, _state) do
    {:reply, :ok, []}
  end

  def handle_call(:noop, _from, state) do
    {:reply, :ok, state}
  end
end
```

This GenServer responds to messages that will allocate string data or clear the allocated data. We can use this to demonstrate how memory bloat can happen in a GenServer. We could alternatively allocate binary data, which would be inspected differently, but we won't get into that. The :noop message handler allows the process to execute functions that won't increase memory usage.

Start the project using iex -S mix in the project folder.

```
iex(1)> {:ok, pid} = GenServer.start_link(Memory, [])
{:ok, #PID<0.147.0>}
iex(2)> :erlang.process_info(pid, :memory)
{:memory, 2820}

iex(3)> GenServer.call(pid, {:allocate, 4_000})
:ok
iex(4)> :erlang.process_info(pid, :memory)
{:memory, 142804}

iex(5)> GenServer.call(pid, :clear)
:ok
iex(6)> :erlang.process_info(pid, :memory)
{:memory, 142804}

iex(7)> Enum.each((1..100), fn _ -> GenServer.call(pid, :noop) end)
:ok
iex(8)> :erlang.process_info(pid, :memory)
{:memory, 142804}

iex(9)> :erlang.garbage_collect(pid)
true
iex(10)> :erlang.process_info(pid, :memory)
{:memory, 2820}
```

We first create a new process for the Memory GenServer, and we see that it starts out with 2820 bytes. We then allocate 4000 string characters, and the memory jumps to 142804 bytes. We issue the :clear call, which empties out the state, and then send it messages to handle. Throughout, the memory stays at 142804 bytes—our process's garbage is not collected. Finally, we manually issue an :erlang.garbage_collect/1 function on the pid, and the memory drops to the initial 2820 bytes.

It's okay for processes to manually issue garbage collection—often you would do this from the process itself when you know that a certain function generates a lot of memory. However, you can also put a process into hibernation by returning :hibernate at the end of the GenServer callbacks. Let's add a :clear_hibernate function to the bottom of memory.ex.

memory/lib/memory.ex
```
def handle_call(:clear_hibernate, _from, _state) do
  {:reply, :ok, [], :hibernate}
end
```

Run the following example with iex -S mix.

```
iex(1)> {:ok, pid} = GenServer.start_link(Memory, [])
{:ok, #PID<0.147.0>}
iex(2)> :erlang.process_info(pid, :memory)
{:memory, 2820}

iex(3)> GenServer.call(pid, {:allocate, 4_000})
:ok
iex(4)> :erlang.process_info(pid, :memory)
{:memory, 142804}

iex(5)> GenServer.call(pid, :clear_hibernate)
:ok
iex(6)> :erlang.process_info(pid, :memory)
{:memory, 1212}
```

This message caused our Memory GenServer to hibernate, and a major garbage collection was triggered. We can also cause hibernation to automatically occur when a process is idle for a number of milliseconds. This is done by passing the hibernate_after option to the GenServer.start/3 function.

```
iex(1)> {:ok, pid} = GenServer.start_link(Memory, [], hibernate_after: 1_000)
iex(2)> GenServer.call(pid, {:allocate, 4_000})
iex(3)> GenServer.call(pid, :clear)
iex(4)> Process.sleep(1_000)
iex(4)> :erlang.process_info(pid, :memory)
{:memory, 1212}
```

This example shows that hibernation is easy to use and is very effective at reclaiming garbage.

Phoenix Channels use the hibernate_after option to enter hibernation 15 seconds after processing their last message. This timing of Channel hibernation can be changed or hibernation can be disabled altogether. The default will work for most applications, but you may need to lower this value or manually garbage collect your Channel process if you receive messages frequently. You can force a Channel to immediately hibernate by returning the :hibernate atom in a Channel callback, like we did for the Memory GenServer.

Channels use hibernation out-of-the-box, but processes that you write need to set it up themselves. Another option for garbage collection is to manually trigger it, which we'll do next.

Manually Collect Garbage as Needed

For cases where hibernation doesn't make as much sense, like for processes that receive messages frequently, you can use manual garbage collection to clean up memory as needed. We did this in the previous example by using the function :erlang.garbage_collect/1. You can pass any process's pid into this function, or you can use :erlang.garbage_collect/0 to trigger garbage collection for the process that invoked the function.

If you are debugging a high-memory system and want to know if more strict garbage collection would help, you can easily trigger garbage collection for every process. Try the following command in an iex session.

```
$ iex
iex(1)> Process.list() |> Enum.each(&:erlang.garbage_collect/1)
:ok
```

The BEAM's utilized memory will most likely drop significantly if this is run on a long-running application. However, it may quickly stabilize to the previous value. This pattern indicates that additional hibernation or manual garbage collection may help your application memory usage.

Another option for garbage collection is also available. Next, we'll adjust the number of minor garbage collections that a process has to perform before a major garbage collection occurs.

Adjust How Often Garbage Collection Happens

You can customize the BEAM with a variety of flags that change how it operates. There are a number of flags related to memory allocation and garbage collection. One of these flags, ERL_FULLSWEEP_AFTER, changes the value of minor garbage collections necessary to do a major garbage collection from 65535 to whatever value you'd like.

The easiest way to change this value is to modify the vm.args file that comes with Distillery and Mix Release. You can set this value by using the following syntax:

```
-env ERL_FULLSWEEP_AFTER 20
```

You can replace 20 with any value that you want. I've found that 20 works well for my applications, but this can vary.

This approach can lead to a much lower memory utilization by performing major garbage collections more often, but as with anything, trade-offs exist. Garbage collection prevents a process from responding to messages, so you could end up blocking processes more often. In practice, I have not experienced process blocking or high CPU from this approach, so I continue to use it for applications that have long-running processes.

We've covered how the BEAM manages resources, but you also need to know how to know if there's a problem in a running application. Next, we'll look at how the :observer_cli tool can help you diagnose problems on a running server.

Inspect a Running Application

Consider the following scenario: you see a performance problem with your production application, but you can't quite figure out what is causing it. Your server may be having periods of slow requests, high memory usage, or failed requests. You collect metrics using StatsD or another tool, but it just doesn't seem to pinpoint the exact problem. Luckily, you can run commands against a live server to find the problem.

In this section, we're going to look at tools for inspecting running applications and how to use them. You'll need to have a way to log into a running server to use the tools listed in this section. If you are using Mix Release or Distillery to package your production application, then you can use the remote_console command to connect to your running server. If you do not have access to a running server, then you'll need to use collected metrics to debug performance problems.

First, we'll look at tools that can help you collect and inspect metrics from running processes. We'll focus heavily on a CLI-based observer tool that provides much of the same information that the GUI-based observer tool provides.

Tools for System Inspection

One of the most important tools to have available in your production environment is a way to inspect running processes to identify performance problems. We covered how to use StatsD to send metrics from your running servers to a metrics collector in Part I. A metrics collector is important, but sometimes it is necessary to see a performance problem happen live, on a running server.

Elixir ships with several functions that provide information about processes. You can use Process.info/1 to collection information about a process. Let's open an iex session to try it out.

```
$ iex
iex(1)> Process.info(self())
[
  current_function: {Process, :info, 1},
  initial_call: {:proc_lib, :init_p, 5},
  status: :running,
  message_queue_len: 0,
  ...
]
```

The Process.info/1 function provides useful information such as:

- message_queue_len—The number of messages waiting to be handled by this process

- total_heap_size—The amount of heap memory that this process is using

- reductions—Represents the amount of work this process has performed

- current_function—The function currently being executed by this process

This information can also be retrieved by passing the specific data that you're looking for to Process.info/2. This function is considered safer, because it won't return expensive data unless you ask for it by name. Due to this, only use Process.info/1 when you're actively debugging.

It is useful to have this information for a single process, but it becomes much more powerful when you have it for all processes in your application. You could write helper functions that iterate over each process, or you could use a visual interface. The observer_cli[2] library provides a visual interface to access live information about your application. We'll look at this library next.

Basics of observer_cli

observer_cli is a terminal-based library that provides important and relevant information about a running system. It is based on the recon[3] library. We won't cover how to use recon in this book, but you can learn more about it in the excellent (and free) e-book Erlang in Anger.[4] We'll look at the different views that observer_cli provides before trying it out locally.

observer_cli opens to a home screen of a paginated list of all processes. You navigate the interface with character keys that are listed at the bottom of the screen. The image on page 251 is a view of observer_cli in a stock Elixir application.

All key BEAM metrics are listed at the top. You can see memory stats, process counts, garbage collection information, and scheduler utilization—this information is all available at a quick glance.

The top right shows allocated memory and used memory stats. The BEAM holds onto some memory, even after garbage collection happens. This allows it to allocate memory faster in the future, because it doesn't need to go to the underlying operating system. You may see a discrepancy between internal

---

2. https://github.com/zhongwencool/observer_cli
3. https://ferd.github.io/recon/
4. https://www.erlang-in-anger.com/

```
|Home(H)|Network(N)|System(S)|Ets(E)|App(A)|Doc(D)|Plugin(P)recon:proc_count(memory, 19) Interval:1500ms          | 0Days 0:9:55      |
|Erlang/OTP 22 [erts-10.4.3] [source] [64-bit] [smp:12:12] [ds:12:12:10] [async-threads:1] [hipe]                                     |
|System      | Count/Limit      | System Switch      | Status      | Memory Info      | Size              |
|Proc Count  | 95/262144        | Version           | 22.0.4      | Alloced Mem      | 54.9844 MB  | 100.0% |
|Port Count  | 3/65536          | Multi Scheduling  | enabled     | Use Mem          | 38.4463 MB  | 69.92% |
|Atom Count  | 18137/1048576    | Logical Processors| 12          | Unuse Mem        | 16.5381 MB  | 30.08% |
|Mem Type    | Size             | Mem Type          | Size        | IO/GC            | Interval: 1500ms  |
|Total       | 40.8826 MB  | 100.0% | Binary     | 232.9922 KB | 00.56% | IO Output   | 5.7207 KB         |
|Process     | 15.8403 MB  | 38.75% | Code       | 9.1326 MB   | 22.34% | IO Input    | 0 B               |
|Atom        | 490.7676 KB | 01.17% | Reductions | 123895      |        | Gc Count    | 6                 |
|Ets         | 852.7188 KB | 02.04% | RunQueue   | 2           |        | Gc Words Reclaimed | 213271     |
|I1              00.36% I7         00.02% I13          00.00% I19          00.00% |
|I2              00.02% I8         00.02% I14          00.00% I20          00.00% |
|I3              00.02% I9         00.02% I15          00.00% I21          00.00% |
|I4              00.02% I10        00.02% I16          00.00% I22          00.00% |
|I5              00.02% I11        00.02% I17          00.00% I23          00.00% |
|I6              00.02% I12        00.01% I18          00.00% I24          00.00% |
|No | Pid       |       Memory |Name or Initial Call          |         Reductions| MsgQueue |Current Function       |
|1  |<0.64.0>   |    7.2838 MB |group:server/3                |          12165693| 0        |group:more_data/6      |
|2  |<0.43.0>   |  726.7070 KB |application_controller        |           1474405| 0        |gen_server:loop/7      |
|3  |<0.49.0>   |  416.5117 KB |code_server                   |           2374040| 0        |code_server:loop/1     |
|4  |<0.9.0>    |  416.5117 KB |erl_prim_loader               |           7639000| 0        |erl_prim_loader:loop/3 |
|5  |<0.78.0>   |  139.7148 KB |disk_log:init/2               |             18415| 0        |disk_log:loop/1        |
|6  |<0.48.0>   |   90.0391 KB |kernel_sup                    |              3104| 0        |gen_server:loop/7      |
|7  |<0.151.0>  |   41.5547 KB |Elixir.Hex.Supervisor         |              3997| 0        |gen_server:loop/7      |
|8  |<0.1.0>    |   27.4141 KB |erts_code_purger              |            235570| 0        |erts_code_purger:wait_for_request|
|9  |<0.0.0>    |   25.9023 KB |init                          |              3955| 0        |init:loop/1            |
|10 |<0.116.0>  |   21.1289 KB |Elixir.Mix.ProjectStack       |              3515| 0        |gen_server:loop/7      |
|11 |<0.180.0>  |   21.0430 KB |erlang:apply/2                |              2949| 0        |observer_cli_store:loop/1|
|12 |<0.57.0>   |   18.2695 KB |file_server_2                 |              3788| 0        |gen_server:loop/7      |
|13 |<0.178.0>  |   16.5898 KB |Elixir.IEx.Evaluator:init/4   |              2932| 0        |io:execute_request/2   |
|14 |<0.41.0>   |   16.4414 KB |logger                        |              2177| 0        |gen_server:loop/7      |
|15 |<0.61.0>   |   13.4609 KB |supervisor_bridge:user_sup/1  |              1131| 0        |gen_server:loop/7      |
|16 |<0.153.0>  |   13.4102 KB |Elixir.Hex.State              |              5879| 0        |gen_server:loop/7      |
|17 |<0.68.0>   |   11.7656 KB |logger_sup                    |              1241| 0        |gen_server:loop/7      |
|18 |<0.114.0>  |   11.5820 KB |Elixir.Mix.State              |              1953| 0        |gen_server:loop/7      |
|19 |<0.127.0>  |   10.6523 KB |logger_std_h_ssl_handler      |               590| 0        |gen_server:loop/7      |
|q(quit) p(pause) r/rr(reduction) m/mm(mem) b/bb(binary mem) t/tt(total heap size) mq/mmq(msg queue) 9(proc 9 info) F/B(page forward/back)|
```

tools like observer_cli and external tools like top due to this. Metrics taken from inside of the BEAM VM will provide you with the most accurate information.

The power of the observer_cli list view comes in the sortable options that are provided. You can sort by memory usage, reduction amount, and message queue length. This allows you to quickly identify heavily utilized processes in your running system.

There are additional views available as well. You can see network utilization for your application, detailed system utilization, and an ETS table listing. You can also view detailed information about a single process. These views help you piece together the full picture of your application, which allows you to hunt down problems faster.

Next, we'll walk through how to use observer_cli.

Local Demo of observer_cli

We'll install the observer_cli library into a new Elixir application, then we'll explore some of the different options that are available. It might feel overwhelming at first, but the interface is labeled to help you more easily navigate it. First, create a new project and add the observer_cli dependency to it.

```
$ mix new observer
$ cd observer
```

Now add the observer_cli dependency to the mix.exs file.

```
observer/mix.exs
defp deps do
  [
    {:observer_cli, "~> 1.5"}
  ]
end
```

Run mix deps.get and then start a session with iex -S mix. For this example, we'll start two looping processes, then we'll locate these processes using the observer_cli library.

```
$ iex -S mix
iex(1)> defmodule Test do def recurse(), do: recurse() end
iex(2)> Enum.each((1..2), fn _ -> Task.async(&Test.recurse/0) end)
iex(3)> :observer_cli.start
```

You'll see the observer_cli home screen once you run the observer_cli.start/0 function. You will see that schedulers 1 and 2 are close to full utilization all of the time, because we started two looping processes.

```
|Home(H)|Network(N)|System(S)|Ets(E)|App(A)|Doc(D)|Plugin(P)|recon:proc_count(memory, 19) Interval:1500ms          | 0Days 0:12:44          |
|Erlang/OTP 22 [erts-10.4.3] [source] [64-bit] [smp:12:12] [ds:12:12:10] [async-threads:1] [hipe]                    |
|System     | Count/Limit     | System Switch      | Status   | Memory Info        | Size                |
|Proc Count | 97/262144       | Version            | 22.0.4   | Alloced Mem        | 56.9844 MB | 100.0% |
|Port Count | 3/65536         | Multi Scheduling   | enabled  | Use Mem            | 39.6988 MB | 69.67% |
|Atom Count | 18522/1048576   | Logical Processors | 12       | Unuse Mem          | 17.2856 MB | 30.33% |
|Mem Type   | Size            | Mem Type           | Size            | IO/GC               | Interval: 1500ms    |
|Total      | 41.4345 MB | 100.0% | Binary        | 167.1484 KB | 00.39% | IO Output         | 5.7217 KB           |
|Process    | 16.1039 MB | 38.87% | Code          | 9.3384 MB   | 22.54% | IO Input          | 0 B                 |
|Atom       | 504.0000 KB | 01.19% | Reductions    | 1266466434         | Gc Count          | 5                   |
|Ets        | 879.6719 KB | 02.07% | RunQueue      | 3                  | Gc Words Reclaimed | 219278             |
|11 |||||||||||||||||||||| 98.32% |7                   00.01% |13              00.00% |19                  00.00% |
|12 ||||||||||||||||||||| 99.96% |8                    00.01% |14              00.00% |20                  00.00% |
|13                       01.91% |9                    00.01% |15              00.00% |21                  00.00% |
|14                       00.01% |10                   00.01% |16              00.00% |22                  00.00% |
|15                       00.01% |11                   00.01% |17              00.00% |23                  00.00% |
|16                       00.01% |12                   00.01% |18              00.00% |24                  00.00% |
|No | Pid         |        Memory | Name or Initial Call          |  Reductions| MsgQueue |Current Function          |
|1  |<0.64.0>   |    7.2838 MB |group:server/3                  |   151117293| 0        |group:more_data/6          |
|2  |<0.43.0>   |  726.7070 KB |application_controller          |     147568| 0        |gen_server:loop/7          |
|3  |<0.49.0>   |  416.5117 KB |code_server                     |     242744| 0        |code_server:loop/1         |
|4  |<0.9.0>    |  416.5117 KB |erl_prim_loader                 |    7971136| 0        |erl_prim_loader:loop/3     |
|5  |<0.78.0>   |  139.8555 KB |disk_log:init/2                 |      19264| 0        |disk_log:loop/1            |
|6  |<0.178.0>  |  107.3281 KB |Elixir.IEx.Evaluator:init/4     |     494802| 0        |io:execute_request/2       |
|7  |<0.48.0>   |   90.0391 KB |kernel_sup                      |       3248| 0        |gen_server:loop/7          |
|8  |<0.151.0>  |   41.5547 KB |Elixir.Hex.Supervisor           |       4141| 0        |gen_server:loop/7          |
|9  |<0.62.0>   |   34.0664 KB |user_drv                        |     338632| 0        |user_drv:server_loop/6     |
|10 |<0.57.0>   |   25.9883 KB |file_server_2                   |       4159| 0        |gen_server:loop/7          |
|11 |<0.0.0>    |   25.9023 KB |init                            |       4099| 0        |init:loop/1                |
|12 |<0.116.0>  |   21.1289 KB |Elixir.Mix.ProjectStack         |       3659| 0        |gen_server:loop/7          |
|13 |<0.41.0>   |   16.4414 KB |logger                          |       2321| 0        |gen_server:loop/7          |
|14 |<0.61.0>   |   13.4609 KB |supervisor_bridge:user_sup/1    |       1280| 0        |gen_server:loop/7          |
|15 |<0.153.0>  |   13.4102 KB |Elixir.Hex.State                |       6023| 0        |gen_server:loop/7          |
|16 |<0.68.0>   |   11.7656 KB |logger_sup                      |       1386| 0        |gen_server:loop/7          |
|17 |<0.114.0>  |   11.5820 KB |Elixir.Mix.State                |       2097| 0        |gen_server:loop/7          |
|18 |<0.127.0>  |   10.6523 KB |logger_std_h_ssl_handler        |        690| 0        |gen_server:loop/7          |
|19 |<0.133.0>  |    8.8086 KB |ssl_connection_sup              |       1532| 0        |gen_server:loop/7          |
|q(quit) p(pause) r/rr(reduction) m/mm(mem) b/bb(binary mem) t/tt(total heap size) mq/mmq(msg queue) 9(proc 9 info) F/B(page forward/back)
```

If you don't see a view like this, make sure that your terminal is large enough to display the information. The interface is automatically adjusted based on terminal size, and information is truncated when the terminal is too small.

Press r + enter to sort the process list by reduction count. When you do this, the top two heavily utilized processes appear.

```
|No | Pid        |Reductions    |Name or Initial Call   ...
|1  |<0.205.0>   |60362032000   |Elixir.Test:recurse/0 ...
|2  |<0.206.0>   |60323980000   |Elixir.Test:recurse/0 ...
```

Press 1 + enter to view process details for the first process listed on the screen. You can view any process by entering its number, which is visible on the list view. The process detail view collects the amount of memory and reductions on each tick. This lets you know how CPU and memory usage change during a small window of time.

You can access a lot of information about the process from this view. You will see the message queue, process dictionary, stack, and state for the selected process.

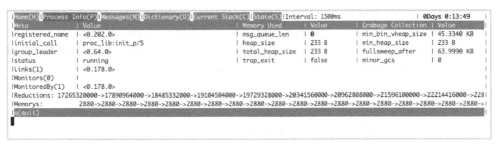

Press h + enter to navigate back to the home view. Play around with observer_cli to get more comfortable with it.

observer_cli is a useful tool to include in any Elixir application. It works great with Mix and Distillery Releases, because of the remote_console feature that releases provide. You should include a tool like observer_cli or recon early on in your project. You don't want to be in a situation where you need to use it to identify the root cause of a problem, but it's not available.

Wrapping Up

When you understand how a language's virtual machine handles memory and performs work, you will write better applications in that language. It's not a necessity when you first get started, but knowing about Elixir's scheduler and garbage collector will help your applications be more performant.

Each BEAM process is assigned to a scheduler, which is the part of the VM that gets work done. Elixir uses a multi-scheduler design with work stealing. This is what allows Elixir applications to easily scale across all cores without much effort. Elixir's scheduler is preemptive—this allows your applications to still handle requests when CPU-heavy work is performed. You can use techniques such as process sharding to avoid single-process bottlenecks from forming in your application.

Memory management is just as important as work scheduling. The BEAM runs garbage collection in each process, so stop-the-world garbage collection does not happen. Long-life processes are susceptible to memory bloat when they get stuck in a state where memory is allocated, not used, and not being garbage collected. This is amplified in real-time applications where you might have tens of thousands of long-running processes alive. You can use hibernation or manual garbage collection to trigger garbage collection for these processes.

Your application will inevitably run into problems, and viewing process information on a running server can help quickly pinpoint a culprit. The observer_cli tool provides a visual observer interface to let you safely and effectively inspect your running applications. Features such as sorted process lists, system utilization, and process details let you piece together the full picture when you're investigating a problem.

That wraps up our deployment chapters. We're going to mix things up in the next chapter by looking at Phoenix LiveView. LiveView is an exciting way to build real-time applications without writing JavaScript.

Part IV

Exploring Front-End Technologies

Front-end technologies continue to evolve, often at a breakneck pace. You can level up your skills by staying at the edge of this evolution. We'll go over two different ways of writing real-time application front ends—Phoenix LiveView and React single-page apps.

## CHAPTER 13

Hands-On with Phoenix LiveView

So far in this book, you've seen that Phoenix Channels make the server side of real-time application development a breeze, but we still ended up writing a lot of front-end client code. This is acceptable for many applications, but wouldn't it be nice if we could write real-time applications without spinning up a JavaScript front-end as well? Enter Phoenix LiveView.

LiveView[1] is an exciting library that shakes up the traditional real-time application development life cycle. In a typical web application, you integrate real-time features into an interface based on standard HTML and JavaScript. In Chapter 7, Build a Real-Time Sneaker Store, on page 121, we did this by passing HTML fragments from the server to the client, and also by passing JSON data to the client. In both solutions, the front end received the Channel's message and modified the interface based on its content.

LiveView changes this paradigm by defining your application's user interface in Elixir code. The interface is automatically kept up to date by sending content differences from server to client. A very small amount (a few lines) of JavaScript is used to initialize LiveView, but otherwise LiveView handles all updates to the DOM. With LiveView, you can build a rich real-time web application without writing any custom JavaScript.

We'll start this chapter by covering the basics of LiveView. You'll see more of what it is, the programming model it uses, and how it compares to Channels. We'll then implement the Sneakers23 product page in LiveView, instead of the Channel-based approach that we used previously. This will be a fun one—let's jump in!

---

1. https://hex.pm/packages/phoenix_live_view

Getting Started with LiveView

LiveView has scratched an itch for real-time applications that seems obvious in hindsight. Libraries like it have existed in different languages over the years, but Elixir and Phoenix are perfectly aligned to satisfy the goals that LiveView has. Developers have expressed boosts in productivity and satisfaction when coding with LiveView, which is a good indicator that it's a solid library to have in your development toolbox.

LiveView is new and innovative, but you'll be able to get started quickly because it's built on a foundation that you already know. We'll go over this strong foundation and the benefits that LiveView draws from it. We'll then look at how data flows in a LiveView application, from front end to back end and then back to the front end again. Lastly, you'll see situations where LiveView thrives, and what trade-offs you should consider when you use it.

Let's jump into an overview of LiveView before we look at a basic LiveView demo.

LiveView Overview

LiveView is based on existing technologies you're familiar with: Channels and Sockets. It takes these tools a step further by providing a rich front-end client and server-side rendering engine that work together to provide a full-stack development experience. The following figure captures the flow of LiveView:

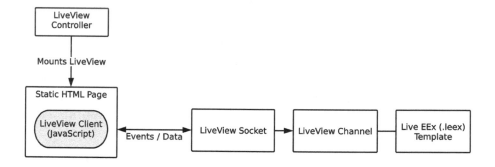

This flow is very similar to how Channels work, because LiveView is based on Channels, although there are a few extra additions.

The flow starts with a web request to a LiveView-powered route, which renders a static version of the LiveView and provides it to the front end. The front-end page has a LiveView JavaScript client running on it. This client is what connects to the back-end server and turns the static page into a real-time LiveView.

Once the front-end client connects to the back-end LiveView Socket, the back end spins up a new LiveView process and the front-end connection is established. The LiveView renders a Live EEx template based on the current state of the LiveView process. When the state of the LiveView process changes, the LiveView sends a minimal payload to the front end that contains the changes. The front end then displays the correct HTML in real-time. The front-end interface stays up to date for as long as the LiveView is connected. The front end also sends events (such as clicks, key presses, etc.) to the back-end LiveView.

The best part about LiveView is that it uses the same technologies you're already familiar with. Live EEx templates are just normal EEx templates[2] that have a special engine to efficiently track changes. The Socket that the front-end client connects to is based on the standard Phoenix.Socket module. Finally, the LiveView itself implements the Phoenix.Channel behaviour. The LiveView Channel is one of the most complex parts of the flow, but it's still familiar due to its foundation in familiar technologies.

You will see how LiveView works and accomplishes this flow throughout this chapter. Let's go over a quick LiveView example before we dive deeper into the how.

A Quick LiveView Example

We'll look at a very basic example before we dive into how LiveView works. You don't need to code this example, because we're going to build a more complete project later in this chapter. We'll look at most of the code that powers the following LiveView.

Current count: 99250   [-] [+]

The count starts as a random number up to 100,000. The plus and minus buttons increment and decrement this counter using the LiveView.

Here is the main LiveView file that powers this interface.

---

2. https://hexdocs.pm/phoenix/templates.html

```
live_view_demo/lib/live_view_demo_web/live/counter_live.ex
defmodule LiveViewDemoWeb.CounterLive do
  use Phoenix.LiveView

  def render(assigns) do
    ~L"""
    Current count: <%= @count %>
    <button phx-click="dec">-</button>
    <button phx-click="inc">+</button>
    """
  end

  def mount(%{count: initial}, socket) do
    {:ok, assign(socket, :count, initial)}
  end

  def handle_event("dec", _value, socket) do
    {:noreply, update(socket, :count, &(&1 - 1))}
  end

  def handle_event("inc", _value, socket) do
    {:noreply, update(socket, :count, &(&1 + 1))}
  end
end
```

We define our template, the initial state of the interface, and handlers for button clicks. This code feels very much like a GenServer, because that's what it is. The ~L in the render/1 function defines a Live EEx template string. There are other ways to include these templates, but this is the simplest way.

The update/3 function is a helper that LiveView provides to easily update state. Alternatively, we could read and increment the socket.assigns property, just like in a Channel.

The next file to look at is the controller.

```
live_view_demo/lib/live_view_demo_web/controllers/page_controller.ex
defmodule LiveViewDemoWeb.PageController do
  use LiveViewDemoWeb, :controller
  import Phoenix.LiveView.Controller

  def index(conn, _params) do
    live_render(conn, LiveViewDemoWeb.CounterLive, session: %{
      count: :rand.uniform(100_000)
    })
  end
end
```

The live_render/3 function provides a static HTML page, which then becomes real-time when the front-end client connects to it. We're even able to pass state from the controller all the way through to the final rendered LiveView.

LiveView provides a signed session mechanism that allows for user authentication and state passing out-of-the-box.

There is only a very small amount of front-end JavaScript code that was added for this example.

```
live_view_demo/assets/js/app.js
import css from "../css/app.css"
import "phoenix_html"
import { Socket } from "phoenix"
import LiveSocket from "phoenix_live_view"

let liveSocket = new LiveSocket("/live", Socket)
liveSocket.connect()
```

This JavaScript is generic, so it's fair to say that there's no custom JavaScript in this example.

There are a few additional files that have code in them, such as the Endpoint module, but this is the bulk of the code. This example shows how simple it is to get started with LiveView, and how we can build dynamic interfaces without any custom JavaScript. You can run this code by starting the live_view_demo project that is distributed with this book, but you'll code a different example shortly.

We'll break down how LiveView works in the rest of this section.

A Rock Solid Foundation

One of the strengths of LiveView is that it's based on technologies that you already know: Elixir, Channels, and socket transports such as WebSockets. LiveView's foundation in established technologies helps to increase its stability and scalability. You'll also feel a bit familiar with LiveView, right from the beginning, because of your understanding of Channels.

LiveView's vertical scalability is primarily due to Elixir. One of the challenges that LiveView has to face is to store state on the server, then quickly and efficiently send diffs to the front end. This is one of Elixir's sweet spots. Processes allow for in-memory state and operations on that state, and processes are seamlessly scaled vertically, across CPU cores.

Phoenix Channels and PubSub provide horizontal scalability across multiple machines already, and LiveView leverages this as well. In addition to benefitting from Phoenix Channels and PubSub, LiveView also leverages Phoenix Controllers to provide statically mounted pages out-of-the-box. Server-side rendering is a complex problem to solve, but LiveView's foundation and implementation in a single language makes it seamless for you.

The flow of data in LiveView is based on established design patterns. We'll look at this next.

LiveView's Programming Model

The way that data moves around your application can greatly impact scalability and maintenance. While programming ecosystems can be a bit divided sometimes, it is clear that two front-end patterns have emerged as popular: declarative user interfaces and unidirectional data flow.

In declarative programming, you describe what the world should look like when the state is a certain way. For example, you can write a template that declares what to do when the weather says it will rain:

```
<div>
  <%= if will_rain?(state) do %>
    <span>It's going to rain</span>
  <% else %>
    <span>It's a clear day!</span>
  <% end %>
</div>
```

This template would get rendered and used automatically when the weather is loaded into the state. An imperative programming model would involve modifying the content of the DOM when the weather is fetched, which might look like this:

```
function setWeather(weather) {
  if (weather.willRain) {
    weatherElement.setText("It's going to rain")
  } else {
    weatherElement.setText("It's a clear day!")
  }
}
```

It seems like a small difference, but this imperative programming model works against you in a large codebase. Declarative programming makes it easier to reason about, maintain, and grow a codebase. LiveView uses a declarative programming model, so your code gains these benefits.

Another important aspect of LiveView is its unidirectional data flow. LiveView's interface is based on the current state of its Channel. The interface emits events when actions happen, such as button clicks or any HTML-based event, which are then processed by the Channel and may change the state. Any update to the state causes the template to be efficiently re-rendered and the difference sent back to the user interface. This sounds like a lot, but is easy to visualize as shown in the figure on page 263.

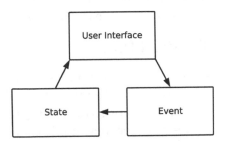

Data in this model flows in a single direction. Again, it seems like a small thing, but this adds up as a project gets larger. Unidirectional data flow is easier to understand than bidirectional flow, and is one of the reasons that LiveView is able to keep state in the Channel, away from the front end.

The data model and programming paradigm help improve performance and readability of applications, but LiveView would be difficult to use without an efficient way to change content. We'll look at how content is swapped out and modified next.

How LiveView Changes Content

LiveView has two major elements for managing content. The first is its template engine, which allows it to be efficient in how data is sent from server to client. The second is the JavaScript that runs and interprets the changes. LiveView does use JavaScript, but it's mostly hidden away from you, with only small portions exposed.

When you write a template for LiveView, it's compiled using the Live EEx[3] template engine. This engine separates the static parts of your template from the dynamic parts. When a dynamic template part changes, the engine knows how to only send the changes to the client. This allows for efficient data exchange between server and client. The content of the template is then sent to the front end for processing.

LiveView's front end uses morphdom[4] to efficiently change the DOM based on what LiveView knows the DOM should be. LiveView's JavaScript client is in charge of other things as well, such as unpacking the template data and creating a clean interface between a developer and the mechanisms that LiveView uses.

---

3. https://hexdocs.pm/phoenix_live_view/Phoenix.LiveView.Engine.html
4. https://github.com/patrick-steele-idem/morphdom

Enough waiting, it's time to build something real with LiveView. We're going to revisit Sneakers23's product page. We'll rebuild it to use LiveView.

Build a LiveView Product Page

You're going to see just how easy it is to get set up with LiveView in this example. We will revisit the product page that we built back in Chapter 7, Build a Real-Time Sneaker Store, on page 121. This product page lists out all of the different shoes, shows whether they're released or not, and shows the availability of each size. This page updates in real time when a shoe is released or when a size's availability changes. It looks like this:

We already have a working version of this page powered by Channels and JavaScript code. We're going to leave much of the Elixir code unchanged, because it's already present and working, but our LiveView implementation will have only a few lines of JavaScript in it!

This example is intentionally kept simple, for the sake of brevity. There are mechanisms that LiveView provides that allow us to implement a slightly more efficient version of this example. These are mentioned at the end of this section but won't be used in this example.

Let's start by setting up the project. You will first download the base code, and then we'll install the LiveView library.

Set Up Your Project

Make sure you have a copy of this book's code, using the instructions found in Online Resources, on page xiii. Next, copy the base application into a development location. If you already have the sneakers_23 folder from building the project in previous chapters, then there's no need to run the following block of commands.

```
$ cp -R code/location/sneakers_23_admin_base ~/sneakers_23_live_view
$ cd ~/sneakers_23_live_view
$ mix deps.get && mix ecto.setup && npm --prefix assets install
```

To set up LiveView, we'll need to include the Mix dependency and also update our front-end package file. Let's start with the mix.exs file. Add the phoenix_live_view library into the deps function. I grouped it with the other Phoenix packages.

sneakers_23_live_view/mix.exs
```
{:phoenix_ecto, "~> 4.0"},
{:phoenix_live_view, "~> 0.4.1"},
```

It will probably be okay for you to use a newer version of LiveView because we're going to use basic features only. LiveView is still a rapidly changing library, so the latest version may be different for you.

Run mix deps.get to fetch the LiveView code. Next, we need to adjust our assets/package.json file. Point the phoenix_live_view dependency to the local dependency version, like so:

sneakers_23_live_view/assets/package.json
```
"dependencies": {
  "phoenix": "file:../deps/phoenix",
  "phoenix_html": "file:../deps/phoenix_html",
  "phoenix_live_view": "file:../deps/phoenix_live_view"
},
```

There are two code items we'll add before we start building. We need to define the LiveView signing salt in our application config. You can use the salt included below, but you should always generate a distinct salt for each application you put into production. You can do this by defining the salt in your prod environment config.

sneakers_23_live_view/config/config.exs
```
config :sneakers_23, Sneakers23Web.Endpoint,
  url: [host: "localhost"],
  render_errors: [view: Sneakers23Web.ErrorView, accepts: ~w(html json)],
  pubsub: [name: Sneakers23.PubSub, adapter: Phoenix.PubSub.PG2],
  # run `mix phx.gen.secret 32` to generate a salt
  live_view: [signing_salt: "4HQtYoFXxy289OQFbZTEWLTm8NATIkay"]
```

Lastly, we need to set up our Endpoint module to know about LiveView.

```
sneakers_23_live_view/lib/sneakers_23_web/endpoint.ex
socket "/live", Phoenix.LiveView.Socket,
  websocket: true,
  longpoll: false
```

LiveView uses a Phoenix.Socket, so we use the standard socket/3 function to define our LiveView. The Phoenix.LiveView.Socket module is provided by LiveView, so you don't need to code it yourself. The Phoenix.Socket foundation helps LiveView feel familiar in our application.

We're ready to code our LiveView now.

Using LiveView

A LiveView revolves around a central module that calls use Phoenix.LiveView. This basic module provides the LiveView code, just like Channels call use Phoenix.Channel. Each LiveView must define the render/1 function, but most will also define a mount/2 function and event handlers.

We're replacing features of our ProductChannel, so we'll call our LiveView module ProductPageLive.

```
sneakers_23_live_view/lib/sneakers_23_web/live/product_page_live.ex
defmodule Sneakers23Web.ProductPageLive do
  use Phoenix.LiveView

  alias Sneakers23Web.ProductView

  def render(assigns) do
    Phoenix.View.render(ProductView, "live_index.html", assigns)
  end

  def mount(_params, socket) do
    {:ok, products} = Sneakers23.Inventory.get_complete_products()
    socket = assign(socket, :products, products)

    {:ok, socket}
  end
end
```

This LiveView fetches the complete listing of products, exactly like Sneakers23Web.ProductController does. It assigns the data into the socket state, making it usable by the render/1 function. This feels very familiar to a Channel or GenServer.

Our render function won't work because live_index.html.leex does not yet exist. Let's create that next. We actually already have a fully working product page template, but it's not a Live EEx file. Create a copy of the existing index file, but give it the .leex extension.

```
$ cp lib/sneakers_23_web/templates/product/index.html.eex \
    lib/sneakers_23_web/templates/product/live_index.html.leex
```

The index template expects to receive an assignment for products. We've already done that, so our template will just work!

We'll add our real-time features next. We already have messages being sent over PubSub when the events that we care about happen. These messages are sent over the topic matching "product:*", so we need to subscribe to the topic for each product that we care about. We do this when the LiveView mounts.

```
sneakers_23_live_view/lib/sneakers_23_web/live/product_page_live.ex
def mount(_params, socket) do
  {:ok, products} = Sneakers23.Inventory.get_complete_products()
  socket = assign(socket, :products, products)

  if connected?(socket) do
    subscribe_to_products(products)
  end

  {:ok, socket}
end

defp subscribe_to_products(products) do
  Enum.each(products, fn %{id: id} ->
    Phoenix.PubSub.subscribe(Sneakers23.PubSub, "product:#{id}")
  end)
end
```

LiveView first renders the template server-side. In this case, the web process is going to quickly complete, so we don't want to subscribe to the PubSub topics. We use connected?/1 for code that we want to run only when connected in Socket mode.

We need to change the products when our LiveView gets updates about the products. We could do this by changing only the affected product or item, but we'll take the easier route of fetching the complete product set from memory. Add the following callbacks to ProductPageLive.

```
sneakers_23_live_view/lib/sneakers_23_web/live/product_page_live.ex
def handle_info(%{event: "released"}, socket) do
  {:noreply, load_products_from_memory(socket)}
end

def handle_info(%{event: "stock_change"}, socket) do
  {:noreply, load_products_from_memory(socket)}
end

defp load_products_from_memory(socket) do
  {:ok, products} = Sneakers23.Inventory.get_complete_products()
  assign(socket, :products, products)
end
```

A LiveView is just a process, so we use handle_info/2 to process the incoming messages. We change the state by assigning the products to the socket state.

At this point, our LiveView module is finished, but we need to expose a route for our LiveView before we can use it. There are several different ways that we could mount a LiveView. We'll use the Router based approach. Add the following code to the Router module.

sneakers_23_live_view/lib/sneakers_23_web/router.ex
```
import Phoenix.LiveView.Router

scope "/", Sneakers23Web do
  pipe_through :browser

  live "/drops", ProductPageLive
end
```

There are other options for mounting the LiveView. You could render it from a controller, in a regular Phoenix template, or even in other LiveViews.

We have an application that will mount the LiveView and render our page now. It shouldn't update in real-time because we haven't set up the JavaScript yet, but our existing code is going to pick up the page content and enrich it to update in real-time. This is simply a by-product of our existing Channel-based application, so let's modify our app.js file to not join the existing ProductChannel Channels.

Modify the code above the definition of cartChannel in app.js to look like the following:

sneakers_23_live_view/assets/js/app.js
```
productSocket.connect()

if (document.querySelectorAll("[data-phx-main]").length) {
  // connectToLiveView()
} else {
  const productIds = dom.getProductIds()
  productIds.forEach((id) => setupProductChannel(productSocket, id))
}
```

This code will not set up the ProductChannel if there is an HTML element with a data-phx-main attribute. LiveView includes this attribute on the root <div>, so this change will give us the desired effect. You would not need to do this normally, but we had existing code that was interacting with our LiveView-rendered interface.

It's important to understand that LiveView separates server rendering from real-time updates. Let's demo this by seeing that our LiveView does not update in real-time yet, because we haven't connected the JavaScript LiveView client. Follow these steps to start your server:

```
$ mix ecto.reset && mix run -e "Sneakers23Mock.Seeds.seed!()"
$ iex -S mix phx.server
```

Next, load http://localhost:4000/drops to load the LiveView-powered page. You will see two shoes on the page, and each will be unreleased. Run the following command in the iex session to release the shoes.

```
iex(1)> Enum.each([1, 2], &Sneakers23.Inventory.mark_product_released!/1)
:ok
```

When you look at the web page, you'll see that nothing has changed—it's not real-time. Let's make it real-time by setting up the LiveView client. We'll create a function that connects the LiveView Socket. Add the following code to socket.js.

sneakers_23_live_view/assets/js/socket.js
```
import { Socket } from "phoenix"
import LiveSocket from "phoenix_live_view"

export const productSocket = new Socket("/product_socket")

export function connectToLiveView() {
  const liveSocket = new LiveSocket("/live", Socket)
  liveSocket.connect()
}
```

The path in the LiveSocket maps to the path that we added to the Endpoint module. We need to call the connectToLiveView function in app.js. Uncomment the connect-ToLiveView function that you added earlier, and add the function import.

sneakers_23_live_view/assets/js/app.js
```
import { productSocket, connectToLiveView } from "./socket"

if (document.querySelectorAll("[data-phx-main]").length) {
  connectToLiveView()
} else {
```

This is all the code we need to power our LiveView. Let's test out the features of our product page. We'll release the shoes and sell them out, and we should see everything update in real-time. Follow these steps to start your server:

```
$ mix ecto.reset && mix run -e "Sneakers23Mock.Seeds.seed!()"
$ iex -S mix phx.server
```

Next, load http://localhost:4000/drops to load the LiveView-powered page. You will see two shoes on the page, and each will be unreleased. Run the following command in the iex session to release the shoes and start selling them out.

```
iex(1)> Enum.each([1, 2], &Sneakers23.Inventory.mark_product_released!/1)
:ok
iex(2)> Sneakers23Mock.InventoryReducer.sell_random_until_gone!
```

Your interface will update in real-time, just like the Channel approach does. You can also add the shoes to your cart, because the existing CartChannel code is hooked into the interface with the JavaScript handlers that we wrote in previous chapters.

Try out the message inspection techniques covered all the way back in Chapter 2, Connect a Simple WebSocket, on page 15 to inspect the messages that the LiveView Channel sends to the front end. You'll see how the template is split into chunks based on static and dynamic content.

We are using if statements inside of list comprehensions in our LiveView, so most of our content is marked as dynamic. LiveView provides mechanisms such as live_component to help optimize the payload sizes in this case, although this example has purposefully been kept simple. I implemented this example using a combination of live_component and send_update, which dramatically reduced the byte size. The trade-off is that the code becomes slightly more complex to manage. You can read the engine documentation[5] to understand the optimizations that LiveView uses to get small payload sizes in most situations.

Now that we have a working ProductLiveView, let's write tests for it.

Write Tests for a LiveView

LiveView, like Channels, provides test helpers that allow you to quickly write meaningful tests for your LiveView module. The Phoenix.LiveViewTest[6] module provides all the helpers you need to get started writing tests.

Our LiveView is fairly simple because it doesn't respond to front-end events. Our tests will be basic because of this. We'll ensure that ProductLiveView mounts, renders the correct HTML, updates when shoes release, and updates when shoes sell out.

To get started, we'll need to add a test dependency to our mix.exs file. LiveViewTest uses Floki to parse HTML, so let's add that.

```
sneakers_23_live_view/mix.exs
{:hound, "~> 1.0"},
{:floki, ">= 0.0.0", only: :test}
```

As always, run mix deps.get to fetch the dependency. Next, create ProductLiveViewTest using the following skeleton code.

---

5. https://hexdocs.pm/phoenix_live_view/Phoenix.LiveView.Engine.html#content
6. https://hexdocs.pm/phoenix_live_view/Phoenix.LiveViewTest.html

sneakers_23_live_view/test/sneakers_23_web/live/product_page_live_test.exs

```
defmodule Sneakers23Web.ProductPageLiveTest do
  use Sneakers23Web.ConnCase, async: false
  import Phoenix.LiveViewTest

  alias Sneakers23.Inventory

  setup _ do
    {inventory, _data} = Test.Factory.InventoryFactory.complete_products()
    {:ok, _} = GenServer.call(Inventory, {:test_set_inventory, inventory})

    {:ok, %{inventory: inventory}}
  end

  defp release_all(%{products: products}) do
    products
    |> Map.keys()
    |> Enum.each(& Inventory.mark_product_released!(&1))
  end

  defp sell_all(%{availability: availability}) do
    availability
    |> Map.values()
    |> Enum.each(fn %{item_id: id, available_count: count} ->
      Enum.each((1..count), fn _ ->
        Sneakers23.Checkout.SingleItem.sell_item(id)
      end)
    end)
  end
end
```

Most of this code is setup functions that are specific to Sneakers23. However, all LiveView tests should use Web.ConnCase and also import Phoenix.LiveViewTest.

The first test we'll write is to ensure that the right HTML is rendered when LiveView does server rendering.

sneakers_23_live_view/test/sneakers_23_web/live/product_page_live_test.exs

```
test "the disconnected view renders the product HTML", %{conn: conn} do
  html = get(conn, "/drops") |> html_response(200)
  assert html =~ ~s(<main class="product-list">)
  assert html =~ ~s(coming soon...)
end
```

This test is exactly like you would write for a normal Plug-based route, so it might feel familiar already. It gets more interesting when we use the live/2 function to mount a connected LiveView instance.

```
sneakers_23_live_view/test/sneakers_23_web/live/product_page_live_test.exs
test "the live view connects", %{conn: conn} do
  {:ok, _view, html} = live(conn, "/drops")
  assert html =~ ~s(<main class="product-list">)
  assert html =~ ~s(coming soon...)
end
```

The tuple that is returned from live/2 will be used in future tests that we write—it is the magic that drives the LiveView tests. In this test, we're simply making sure that our view works when Socket mounted, just like it does when server-mounted.

When you test that a LiveView processes PubSub messages, you can simply send those messages to PubSub like you normally would. However, you must then call render/1 to get the updated view. The next test that we'll write uses this to ensure that released products update the interface from "coming soon..." to a size selector.

```
sneakers_23_live_view/test/sneakers_23_web/live/product_page_live_test.exs
test "product releases are picked up", %{conn: conn, inventory: inventory} do
  {:ok, view, html} = live(conn, "/drops")
  assert html =~ ~s(coming soon...)

  release_all(inventory)
  html = render(view)

  refute html =~ ~s(coming soon...)
  Enum.each(inventory.items, fn {id, _} ->
    assert html =~ ~s(name="item_id" value="#{id}")
  end)
end
```

The release_all/1 function releases the items, which emits a PubSub message. ProductLiveView picks up these messages and updates the state, which updates the interface. Our final test is very similar to this, only we sell the items after we release them.

```
sneakers_23_live_view/test/sneakers_23_web/live/product_page_live_test.exs
test "sold out items are picked up", %{conn: conn, inventory: inventory} do
  {:ok, view, _html} = live(conn, "/drops")

  release_all(inventory)
  sell_all(inventory)
  html = render(view)

  Enum.each(inventory.items, fn {id, _} ->
    assert html =~
      ~s(size-container__entry--level-out" name="item_id" value="#{id}")
  end)
end
```

You should see your tests turn green when you run mix test test/sneakers_23_web/live /product_page_live_test.exs. We are now confident that ProductLiveView works as expected!

In addition to testing LiveView with ExUnit, you can also write automated acceptance tests. I created the Acceptance.LiveProductPageTest test for you already—I just added /drops to the URL. Our existing automated acceptance tests work on our new LiveView-powered interface because we didn't change the user interface at all—we simply changed the technology that powers it. The HTML is exactly the same and behaves the same way to the user. You can run these tests yourself with mix test, but make sure that ChromeDriver is started.

Wrapping Up

LiveView allows you to write real-time interfaces with little to no JavaScript. LiveView builds on the power of Elixir, Phoenix Channels, and Phoenix PubSub to provide a stable and efficient base. With LiveView, you express your user interface and behavior in a declarative format. This would normally be difficult for real-time interactive applications that span multiple languages, but LiveView makes it feel intuitive. LiveView's unidirectional data flow, combined with its declarative model, makes your applications clearer to read, extend, and maintain.

We rewrote the real-time product page from earlier chapters using LiveView. Amazingly, we didn't change our application's business logic at all. We wrote a LiveView that renders the same template as our controller did previously and handles the same messages that we were already emitting in our application.

Our existing automated acceptance tests worked out-of-the-box with LiveView. We only had to point them at the new interface instead of the old one. We wrote new tests for our LiveView using the provided test helpers. These tests were a breeze to write and read, due to the simplicity of the LiveViewTest helpers.

As of the time of writing this book, LiveView is still rapidly evolving and becoming more polished. Features may be slightly different than what is presented in this book, but the essence is the same. There will be even more features and optimizations available in the future. Also, as Phoenix Channels and Elixir evolve, so will LiveView. Its strong technical foundations in these existing technologies provides a feedback loop where improvements in one can potentially provide improvements to the others.

We're going to look at a completely different way of writing application front ends next. You'll see how Phoenix Channels can easily be integrated into React single-page apps, or even React Native mobile apps.

## CHAPTER 14

Single-Page Apps with React

Front-end frameworks have taken over the application development space. There's a good chance you are using a library such as React,[1] Vue.js,[2] or Angular[3] to develop the front end of your application. These powerful libraries can all be used to build single-page applications. If you're using one of these libraries with a real-time Phoenix back end, then you need to have a solution in place to use Phoenix Channels. Luckily, it's easy to integrate Channels into any of these libraries. In this chapter, we'll use Phoenix Channels in a React single-page app.

In a single-page app, a user navigates forward and backward without a full-page reload. This allows the app to maintain state throughout the user's flow, as well as provide quicker page transitions in the app. The project is basic in this chapter, with much of the code already written for you. This chapter assumes some React knowledge, but not knowing React won't block you from progressing.

We'll start by covering the different ways that state can be stored in React. State is the foundation of any application. This is especially true for real-time applications, because we need a place to store and access the Phoenix Channel client and the data that is exchanged over it. This will lead us into a component-driven architecture that separates the Phoenix Socket and Channel connections from the rest of the front end. We'll then put everything into practice by finishing the code for a provided React application. Finally, we'll briefly touch on React Native and the power of real-time on mobile.

Let's jump into React state management.

---

1. https://reactjs.org/
2. https://vuejs.org/
3. https://angular.io/

Manage Channel State in React

State management is a fairly complex topic in the front-end development world. At first glance it's very easy, but state management code can quickly morph to become complex and error-prone. Despite the complexity, applications would not be very useful without state and a way to manage that state. We'll look at some of the different state-management options, then continue the chapter with the techniques the community has largely adopted.

State management is important to us because we need a place to store and work with the Phoenix Channel. We need to fully control the Channel throughout the application life cycle to reduce the risk of bugs.

React, and essentially every front-end library, has undergone an evolution in state-management technique since it was first created. You can implement the same application a dozen different ways, and all are correct. The trade-offs of different techniques may not appear until an application gets large, or a large team works on the application. Let's look at the different options available, starting with the oldest and ending with most recent.

Component State with Props

The first and most basic way of managing state is to keep the state in a component and then expose that state to child components via props. This approach is very easy to conceptualize and is easy to get started with, but it becomes difficult to manage in large applications. For example, if you have a global application state, such as a Socket, you will pass the socket throughout your entire application tree as a prop.

This approach serves as the basis for React's more recent state-management approaches. However, it's generally not recommended outside of small use cases. You can find posts online about prop drilling—the act of deeply passing props around an application—and why it's bad.

Redux-based State

Redux[4] was built to solve complex application state management. With Redux, state is kept in an isolated store, completely separate from the React application. No part of the user interface ever modifies the state directly. Instead, events are dispatched to the Redux store, and then the state is modified by dedicated functions. This is a unidirectional data flow, just like you saw with LiveView in the last chapter.

---

4. https://redux.js.org/

Redux is a library that I'm a big fan of, and it works well for Phoenix Socket state management. We won't use it in this chapter, though. Instead, we'll stick to options that React comes with out-of-the-box.

React Contexts

React introduced contexts[5] to allow applications to easily pass state to deeply nested child components, without explicitly passing the prop to every component. This approach significantly increases the ease of managing state in a component and removes the prop-drilling problem.

We'll use contexts in our sample React application to manage the Socket and Channel state.

React Hooks

React Hooks[6] are a relatively new addition to the React library. Hooks allow you to use state, contexts, and life cycle management without writing class-based components. Hooks were introduced primarily to allow for easier code re-use than class-based components allow. You'll work with hooks later in this chapter.

These are only a few of the options available for state management with React. There are many more external libraries available, although the out-of-the-box mechanisms are covered above. You may be wondering what you should use for your applications. The community has rallied heavily around state management with hooks and contexts, or alternatively with Redux. We'll be using React Hooks and Contexts for our example.

The mechanism you get started with doesn't actually matter that much, because you can build a working application with any of them. The structure of your application does matter, though. A well-structured application lets you move parts around without much hassle and is easier to maintain in the long run. In the next section, we'll look at isolating Phoenix Socket and Channel logic into components, so the logic remains separate from the rest of an application.

Write Channels as Components

Components are the heart of React. The type of component that we're most familiar with is a presentation component—this type of component renders the user interface and accepts input events from the user. Components do

---

5. https://reactjs.org/docs/context.html
6. https://reactjs.org/docs/hooks-overview.html

not need to have an interface though. A container component can wire up logic, configure other components, pull data from other sources, or set up a context.

You use container components to separate Phoenix code from the rest of the application. You could get by without this separation, by adding Channels directly into a presentation component, but the lack of separation becomes hard to maintain and grow over time. Use components to create an application that is easy to change and understand.

There's an easy way to tell if your application's components are doing too much. If a component defines the Socket or Channel in the same component that renders the interface, then you may benefit by splitting the Socket or Channel into separate components. In general, it's a best practice to have single purpose components that each perform a single task.

For example, let's imagine an ActivityFeedPage component that renders timeline data in real time. We might implement the component with the following code.

```
class ActivityFeedPage extends React.Component {
  componentDidMount() {
    this.socket = this.setupSocket()
    this.channel = this.setupChannel(this.socket)
    this.channel.on('new_activity', (activity) => {
      const oldActivities = this.state.activities || []
      this.setState({ activities: [activity, ...oldActivities] })
    })
  }
  componentWillUnmount() {
    this.socket.disconnect()
  }
  render() {
    return this.state.activities.map(this.renderActivity)
  }
  renderActivity(activity) {
    // render the activity
  }
}
```

This example is artificial, but illustrates that the Channel is defined in the same component that renders an activity. We could easily include the <ActivityFeedPage /> component in a page somewhere, and it would work as expected. In a single-page app Router, the component might be used like so:

```
<App>
  <Router>
    <Route route="/activities">
      <ActivityFeedPage />
    </Route>
  </Router>
</App>
```

This example seems to work well at a first glance, and it is easy to understand, but it violates our definition of a single-purpose component. Problems would begin to appear once we wanted to use the Socket or Channel in other components, or if we needed to coordinate access to the real-time data across the entire application.

Let's consider an example that separates the Socket and Channel into container components. The Router might look like this if we wanted to use the Socket across multiple routes.

```
<App>
  <AppSocket>
    <ActivityChannel>
      <Header>
        <ActivityAlerts />
      </Header>

      <Router>
        <Route route="/activities">
          <ActivityFeedPage />
        </Route>
      </Router>
    </ActivityChannel>
  </AppSocket>
</App>
```

In this example, the AppSocket and ActivityChannel are defined for the entire application. This allows us to share the logic of new activities across multiple components—ActivityAlerts and ActivityFeedPage. The code is slightly more verbose, but an application built with single-purpose components will be more flexible and easier to work with in the long run.

There's no code for the AppSocket and ActivityChannel components in the previous example, because we're about to implement a very similar example with real code. In the next section, we'll complete an application that implements a component-based approach for Sockets and Channels.

Hands-On with React

Well-factored components can be difficult to grasp without a concrete example to show the way. We'll be working on a Phoenix application with a single-page React front end. You'll see examples of container components, presentation components, and how to wire them together with contexts and React Router. There will be a bit of React-specific patterns that you may not be used to, but don't worry too much if you're not familiar with React.

The application has several different single-purpose components. We'll build a container component that holds a basic Phoenix Socket, and also a presentation component that sends and receives data from a Channel. This example will be based on a mostly complete codebase so you can jump right into the code without worrying about setting up React.

This example has four pages and looks like the following image.

This is a single-page app; the browser will not perform a full-page reload as you navigate around it. Here's an overview of the four pages in the app:

- Home—This page serves only static content, so it doesn't use a Socket or Channel. The Phoenix Socket is disconnected when this page loads.

- Pings—This page receives data from the "ping" topic and displays it in a textarea element. This page has a button that will send data to the Channel when pressed—the response from the Channel is displayed in the textarea element.

- Other Pings—This page is a clone of the Pings page, but is for the "other" topic. When this page is visited, the "ping" Channel is closed and the "other" Channel is joined.

- Counter—This page receives data from the "ping" topic and shows the number of received messages.

The application is basic but will demonstrate how different pages can use different real-time Channels. When you run the application locally, later in the chapter, you'll see that the Socket and Channel are efficiently cleaned up based on the currently loaded page.

Let's code. First, you'll need to download and set up the base project.

Set Up the Project

Make sure that you have a copy of this book's code, using the instructions found in Online Resources, on page xiii. Next, copy the base application into a development location.

```
$ cp -R code/location/react_example_base ~/react_example
$ cd ~/react_example
$ mix deps.get && npm --prefix assets install
```

This application is mostly complete already. There is an Elixir back end that looks very familiar to what you've coded so far in this book. You don't have to worry about the Elixir this time—we'll be working completely in the React code.

The Routes component defines all of the pages in the application. We'll start by looking at how the Router organizes the Socket and PingChannel components.

Inspecting the Router

Our application's Router defines the page hierarchy of the application. React Router[7] is used to implement the routing mechanism. React Router uses a component-based design—all of our routes are implemented using components, just like anything else in React. This allows us to nest routes inside of other components. We'll use this to clean up our Socket and Channel on pages that don't use them.

Let's look at how the Routes component is put together. The first thing that we'll look at is how the Home component is separated from the rest of the application. You don't need to type any of this code, because it was provided in the base that you downloaded.

---

7. https://github.com/ReactTraining/react-router

react_example/assets/js/Routes.js
```
export default function Routes() {
  return (
    <Switch>
      <Route path={['/pings', '/count', '/other']}>
        <WebSocketRoutes />
      </Route>
      <Route path='/'>
        <Home />
      </Route>
    </Switch>
  )
}
```

This separation allows the Home page to clean up the real-time resources we're about to set up. Let's look at the slightly more complex WebSocketRoutes component.

react_example/assets/js/Routes.js
```
function WebSocketRoutes() {
  return (
    <Socket>
      <Route path={['/pings', '/count']}>
        <PingChannel topic='ping'>
          <Route path='/pings'>
            <Pings />
          </Route>
          <Route path='/count'>
            <Count />
          </Route>
        </PingChannel>
      </Route>

      <Route path={['/other']}>
        <PingChannel topic='other'>
          <Route path='/other'>
            <Pings topic='other' />
          </Route>
        </PingChannel>
      </Route>
    </Socket>
  )
}
```

Every route inside of this component uses the same Socket, so the Socket component is mounted higher in the hierarchy than every Route. We'll implement this Socket component shortly. There are two different PingChannel components. The first, for topic 'ping' is mounted only for the /pings and /count pages. The other, for topic 'other', is mounted only for the /other page.

The content of a Route is only mounted when the current URL matches the provided pattern. When the home page / route is visited, for example, the entire WebSocketRoutes component is unmounted. When the /other page becomes active, the <PingChannel topic='ping'> component is unmounted.

Let's see how the Socket component can be built to clean up after itself when it's unmounted.

Build the Socket Component

The Socket component is arguably the heart of our real-time application, along with the associated Channel. However, not much code will go into building this component, because React provides an elegant way to build the component. We'll hook into the component life cycle to define what happens when the Socket component is mounted and unmounted. This is where we'll initialize and disconnect the Socket connection.

Open the context/Socket.js file and add the following code:

```
react_example/assets/js/contexts/Socket.js
import React, { createContext, useEffect, useState } from 'react'
import { Socket as PhxSocket } from 'phoenix'

export const SocketContext = createContext(null)

export default function Socket({ children }) {
  const [socket, setSocket] = useState(null)

  useEffect(() => {
    setupSocket(socket, setSocket)

    return () => teardownSocket(socket, setSocket)
  }, [socket])

  return (
    <SocketContext.Provider value={socket}>
      {children}
    </SocketContext.Provider>
  )
}
```

First, on line 4, we create the React Context. A Context allows us to pass data to child components without directly passing the data via props. We use this Context on line 15 by returning SocketContext.Provider component. Components are the most important concept in React, so it makes sense that we mount the Context with one.

The useEffect function is a React Hook. This function is called when the selected variables change, in this case the socket variable. This is guaranteed to be called when the component mounts and unmounts, but it might be called at other times as well. On line 10, we call a function that sets up the Phoenix Socket. We'll implement that shortly. We also return a function, on line 12, that cleans up the Socket. This will be called when the component unmounts.

We'll write the setupSocket and teardownSocket functions next. Add these functions to the end of the file.

```
react_example/assets/js/contexts/Socket.js
function setupSocket(socket, setSocket) {
  if (!socket) {
    console.debug('WebSocket routes mounted, connect Socket')
    const newSocket = new PhxSocket('/socket')
    newSocket.connect()
    setSocket(newSocket)
  }
}
```

This function could be called even if a Phoenix Socket already exists, due to how hooks work, so we create the Phoenix Socket only if we don't already have one.

The teardownSocket function looks very similar, but it disconnects the Socket.

```
react_example/assets/js/contexts/Socket.js
function teardownSocket(socket, setSocket) {
  if (socket) {
    console.debug('WebSocket routes unmounted disconnect Socket', socket)
    socket.disconnect()
    setSocket(null)
  }
}
```

The combination of these two functions completes the life cycle for the Socket component. The end result is not that much code, and we have a Phoenix Socket that is completely integrated into the React component life cycle.

Let's build a presentational component next. This component displays information from the Channel and sends a message to the Channel when a button is clicked.

Build the Pings Component

The Pings component is a presentational component that reads data from and sends data to the Channel. It does so with the PingChannel, which you can find in contexts/PingChannel.js. The Channel code is very similar to the Socket code, although it exposes a different type of interface with its Context.

Let's look at how the PingChannelContext is mounted. You don't need to type this code, as it was provided in the project base.

```
react_example/assets/js/contexts/PingChannel.js
return (
  <PingChannelContext.Provider value={{
    onPing: onPingSubscription(pingSubscriptions),
    sendPing: sendPing(pingChannel)
  }}>
    {children}
  </PingChannelContext.Provider>
)
```

The Context does not expose the Phoenix Channel itself. Instead, it provides functions that interact with the Channel. This allows downstream components to not worry about what a Channel is—they simply need to use some functions that are in the domain of the application. We'll use this context when we build the Pings component.

Add the following code to the components/Pings.js file. There is a little bit of code already there, but you can clear everything up until the return statement.

```
react_example/assets/js/components/Pings.js
Line 1  import React, { useContext, useEffect, useState } from 'react'
     -  import { PingChannelContext } from '../contexts/PingChannel'
     -
     -  export default function Pings(props) {
     5    const topic = props.topic || 'ping'
     -    const [messages, setMessages] = useState([])
     -    const { onPing, sendPing } = useContext(PingChannelContext)
     -
     -    const appendDataToMessages = (data) =>
    10      setMessages((messages) => [
     -        JSON.stringify(data),
     -        ...messages
     -      ])
     -
    15    useEffect(() => {
     -      const teardown = onPing((data) => {
     -        console.debug('Pings pingReceived', data)
     -        appendDataToMessages(data)
     -      })
    20
     -      return teardown
     -    }, [])
```

This component is doing a bit more than the previous Socket component. The Pings component uses the useState React hook to give itself a place to store the messages from the PingChannel. The useContext hook, on line 7, gets the functions from the PingChannelContext, so that the component can communicate with the Channel.

The onPing function is used, on line 16, to register the component with the PingChannel subscriber list. The onPing function returns a cleanup function, which is returned as the teardown function on line 21.

The last function to note is the appendDataToMessages function. This uses setMessages, on line 10, to update the state of the component when new data is received.

The final part of this component is the interface's JSX. Change the <button> line to match the following code.

```
react_example/assets/js/components/Pings.js
return (
  <div>
    <h2>Pings: {topic}</h2>

    <p>
      This page displays the PING messages received from the
      server, since this page was mounted. The topic
      for this Channel is {topic}.
    </p>

    <button onClick={
      () => sendPing(appendDataToMessages)
    }>Press to send a ping</button>

    <textarea value={messages.join('\n')} readOnly />
  </div>
)
```

The button uses sendPing to send data to the Phoenix Channel. The response is then appended to the message list.

This completes the Pings component. We are going to try out the application to see how the Socket and Channel behave as we navigate through the application.

Try Out the Application

Now that you have these two components implemented, we're going to try out the different features. We'll be keeping a close eye on the Network tab throughout this process so we can see when the Socket connects, disconnects, joins a topic, or leaves a topic.

Start the server with mix phx.server and then open http://localhost:4000. Next, open the "WS" section in Chrome's Network Developer Tools. This section may be labeled differently if you use a different browser. Refresh the page so you get a completely clean set of requests.

Initially, you'll notice that the only WebSocket connection is for the phoenix/live_reload URL, which is provided by Phoenix and is not our application's Socket. Next, click on the "Pings" tab. You will see that a new Phoenix Socket connection is opened in the browser, because we visited a page that requires a Socket connection. Next, click back and forth between "Pings" and "Home". You'll see that the Socket connection is closed when you visit the "Home" page and opens again when you visit the "Pings" page.

Visit the "Pings" page again and open the Socket connection in the Network Developer Tools. You will see the data being sent over the connection. Keep an eye on "phx_join" and "phx_leave" messages. When you navigate to the "Other Pings" page, the 'ping' topic is left and the 'other' topic is joined. If you navigate from the "Pings" page to the "Counter" page, then no change is made to the Channel, because they use the same topic.

This demo shows how you can use React's life cycle management to ensure that Sockets and Channels are joined at the right time. You may, however, want to have a Socket or Channel connected at all times in the application. This is where the component-based approach to our application design shines. You can simply move the <Socket> and <PingChannel> components to a higher position in the application, such as under the main <App>. Nothing else would need to be changed to make the Socket and Channel always on.

Before wrapping up, we're going to talk about React in mobile apps.

React Native Channels

React is a great library for building web applications. However, it has moved into other technologies besides the web. React Native[8] makes it easy to build native mobile applications on iOS and Android. React Native executes Java-Script in a native context, which makes it easy to include web libraries, such as Phoenix Channels, in a mobile app. There may be slight inconsistencies over time, due to the difference between the mobile JavaScript engine and a web JavaScript engine, but issues have been small and easy to work around.

Mobile apps have push notifications available to them, so you may not see the need for Channels on them. However, using the native push service for real-time messages means putting a lot of trust in a system that cannot be easily monitored, and that has certain limitations. You can use Channels to

---

8. https://facebook.github.io/react-native/

provide real-time messages and to keep control of the flow from end-to-end. Native push services should still be used for push notifications when your app is not in the foreground.

When you use Channels in React Native, the advice in this chapter still applies. Focus on creating a clean component-based architecture that puts a layer between the Phoenix Channel library and your application. You can use the latest React features like Hooks and Contexts to help create this clean architecture.

Another benefit of Phoenix Channels in React Native is that you can enable long-polling support if you experience challenges with WebSockets in a mobile environment. Things have largely settled in a way that allows WebSocket-based Channels to be used on mobile, but the location of your users may cause problems. It's nice to have a quick fix, if necessary. No one can tell the future, but it looks like Phoenix Channels will continue to be supported on React Native.

Wrapping Up

Front-end frameworks have become quite popular for web and native applications. All major libraries out there, such as React, Vue.js, or Angular easily support Phoenix Channels, but you'll need to write code to integrate the front end with your back-end Channels. You should strive to create a clean component-based architecture that allows your application to grow and change easily over time.

React comes with many features that make it a breeze to integrate Phoenix Channels. There are several different ways that you can store state in a React app. You can use local component state, Contexts, and Hooks to create a clean interface between your Channels and the components that use them. You can even use third-party libraries like Redux to manage your state. No matter what mechanism you use for state management, you can use Channels.

We built an example of component architecture, with well-factored Socket and PingChannel components. These components were used by a presentational component to send and receive data from the Phoenix Socket. The components we built respected the life cycle of React components, which allowed the Socket and Channel to be cleaned up when they were no longer used. The ease of React came out in this example, and we didn't have to write too much code to tie everything together.

The End of Our Journey

Thanks for allowing me to lead you in your real-time journey. Real-time applications are important, and the toolbox that you're equipped with is going to provide an amazing boost to your development productivity. I am constantly amazed at the libraries provided in the Elixir ecosystem for working with real-time applications, and I sincerely hope you're able to leverage these tools to achieve your goals.

Go forth and build great real-time applications.

Bibliography

[IT19]   James Edward Gray, II and Bruce A. Tate. *Designing Elixir Systems with OTP*. The Pragmatic Bookshelf, Raleigh, NC, 2019.

[Tat18]   Ben Marx, José Valim, Bruce Tate. *Adopting Elixir*. The Pragmatic Bookshelf, Raleigh, NC, 2018.

Index

Thank you!

How did you enjoy this book? Please let us know. Take a moment and email us at support@pragprog.com with your feedback. Tell us your story and you could win free ebooks. Please use the subject line "Book Feedback."

Ready for your next great Pragmatic Bookshelf book? Come on over to https://pragprog.com and use the coupon code BUYANOTHER2020 to save 30% on your next ebook.

Void where prohibited, restricted, or otherwise unwelcome. Do not use ebooks near water. If rash persists, see a doctor. Doesn't apply to *The Pragmatic Programmer* ebook because it's older than the Pragmatic Bookshelf itself. Side effects may include increased knowledge and skill, increased marketability, and deep satisfaction. Increase dosage regularly.

And thank you for your continued support,

Andy Hunt, Publisher

SAVE 30%!
Use coupon code
BUYANOTHER2020

Designing Elixir Systems with OTP

You know how to code in Elixir; now learn to think in it. Learn to design libraries with intelligent layers that shape the right data structures, flow from one function into the next, and present the right APIs. Embrace the same OTP that's kept our telephone systems reliable and fast for over 30 years. Move beyond understanding the OTP functions to knowing what's happening under the hood, and why that matters. Using that knowledge, instinctively know how to design systems that deliver fast and resilient services to your users, all with an Elixir focus.

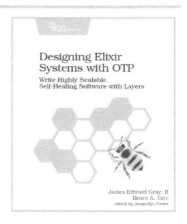

James Edward Gray, II and Bruce A. Tate
(246 pages) ISBN: 9781680506617. $41.95
https://pragprog.com/book/jgotp

Programming Phoenix 1.4

Don't accept the compromise between fast and beautiful: you can have it all. Phoenix creator Chris McCord, Elixir creator José Valim, and award-winning author Bruce Tate walk you through building an application that's fast and reliable. At every step, you'll learn from the Phoenix creators not just what to do, but why. Packed with insider insights and completely updated for Phoenix 1.4, this definitive guide will be your constant companion in your journey from Phoenix novice to expert as you build the next generation of web applications.

Chris McCord, Bruce Tate and José Valim
(356 pages) ISBN: 9781680502268. $45.95
https://pragprog.com/book/phoenix14

Programming Elixir 1.6

This book is *the* introduction to Elixir for experienced programmers, completely updated for Elixir 1.6 and beyond. Explore functional programming without the academic overtones (tell me about monads just one more time). Create concurrent applications, but get them right without all the locking and consistency headaches. Meet Elixir, a modern, functional, concurrent language built on the rock-solid Erlang VM. Elixir's pragmatic syntax and built-in support for metaprogramming will make you productive and keep you interested for the long haul. Maybe the time is right for the Next Big Thing. Maybe it's Elixir.

Dave Thomas
(410 pages) ISBN: 9781680502992. $47.95
https://pragprog.com/book/elixir16

Learn Functional Programming with Elixir

Elixir's straightforward syntax and this guided tour give you a clean, simple path to learn modern functional programming techniques. No previous functional programming experience required! This book walks you through the right concepts at the right pace, as you explore immutable values and explicit data transformation, functions, modules, recursive functions, pattern matching, high-order functions, polymorphism, and failure handling, all while avoiding side effects. Don't board the Elixir train with an imperative mindset! To get the most out of functional languages, you need to think functionally. This book will get you there.

Ulisses Almeida
(198 pages) ISBN: 9781680502459. $42.95
https://pragprog.com/book/cdc-elixir

Functional Web Development with Elixir, OTP, and Phoenix

Elixir and Phoenix are generating tremendous excitement as an unbeatable platform for building modern web applications. For decades OTP has helped developers create incredibly robust, scalable applications with unparalleled uptime. Make the most of them as you build a stateful web app with Elixir, OTP, and Phoenix. Model domain entities without an ORM or a database. Manage server state and keep your code clean with OTP Behaviours. Layer on a Phoenix web interface without coupling it to the business logic. Open doors to powerful new techniques that will get you thinking about web development in fundamentally new ways.

Lance Halvorsen
(218 pages) ISBN: 9781680502435. $45.95
https://pragprog.com/book/lhelph

Competing with Unicorns

Today's tech unicorns develop software differently. They've developed a way of working that lets them scale like an enterprise while working like a startup. These techniques can be learned. This book takes you behind the scenes and shows you how companies like Google, Facebook, and Spotify do it. Leverage their insights, so your teams can work better together, ship higher-quality product faster, innovate more quickly, and compete with the unicorns.

Jonathan Rasmusson
(138 pages) ISBN: 9781680507232. $26.95
https://pragprog.com/book/jragile

Programming Flutter

Develop your next app with Flutter and deliver native look, feel, and performance on both iOS and Android from a single code base. Bring along your favorite libraries and existing code from Java, Kotlin, Objective-C, and Swift, so you don't have to start over from scratch. Write your next app in one language, and build it for both Android and iOS. Deliver the native look, feel, and performance you and your users expect from an app written with each platform's own tools and languages. Deliver apps fast, doing half the work you were doing before and exploiting powerful new features to speed up development. Write once, run anywhere.

Carmine Zaccagnino
(368 pages) ISBN: 9781680506952. $47.95
https://pragprog.com/book/czflutr

Agile Web Development with Rails 6

Learn Rails the way the Rails core team recommends it, along with the tens of thousands of developers who have used this broad, far-reaching tutorial and reference. If you're new to Rails, you'll get step-by-step guidance. If you're an experienced developer, get the comprehensive, insider information you need for the latest version of Ruby on Rails. The new edition of this award-winning classic is completely updated for Rails 6 and Ruby 2.6, with information on processing email with Action Mailbox and managing rich text with Action Text.

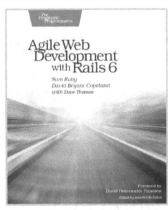

Sam Ruby and David Bryant Copeland
(494 pages) ISBN: 9781680506709. $57.95
https://pragprog.com/book/rails6

The Pragmatic Bookshelf

The Pragmatic Bookshelf features books written by professional developers for professional developers. The titles continue the well-known Pragmatic Programmer style and continue to garner awards and rave reviews. As development gets more and more difficult, the Pragmatic Programmers will be there with more titles and products to help you stay on top of your game.

Visit Us Online

This Book's Home Page
https://pragprog.com/book/sbsockets
Source code from this book, errata, and other resources. Come give us feedback, too!

Keep Up to Date
https://pragprog.com
Join our announcement mailing list (low volume) or follow us on twitter @pragprog for new titles, sales, coupons, hot tips, and more.

New and Noteworthy
https://pragprog.com/news
Check out the latest pragmatic developments, new titles and other offerings.

Save on the ebook

Save on the ebook versions of this title. Owning the paper version of this book entitles you to purchase the electronic versions at a terrific discount.

PDFs are great for carrying around on your laptop—they are hyperlinked, have color, and are fully searchable. Most titles are also available for the iPhone and iPod touch, Amazon Kindle, and other popular e-book readers.

Buy now at *https://pragprog.com/coupon*

Contact Us

Online Orders:	*https://pragprog.com/catalog*
Customer Service:	*support@pragprog.com*
International Rights:	*translations@pragprog.com*
Academic Use:	*academic@pragprog.com*
Write for Us:	*http://write-for-us.pragprog.com*
Or Call:	+1 800-699-7764

Milton Keynes UK
Ingram Content Group UK Ltd.
UKHW012319120824
446858UK00004B/14

9 781680 507195